St. Matthews
The Crossroads
of Beargrass

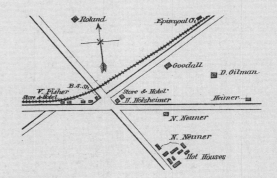

St. Matthews
The Crossroads
of Beargrass

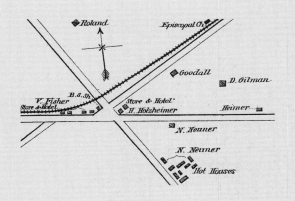

Samuel W. Thomas

Samuel W. Thomas

1999

Dedicated to Iva-Louise Oliver McElwain, who died on 17 April, 1998, at the age of 94. She instilled lasting values while allowing me to work during college at her place (now Locust Hill) on Blankenbaker Lane. The core of her wonderful rambling house had been but a tenant house on a potato farm. Mrs. McElwain first told me about St. Matthews being a produce center. In the spring of 1962 she asked if I also wanted to be a caretaker at nearby Locust Grove, which was to be restored. The rest is history, and I will always be indebted.   *SWT*

ISBN 1-884532-34-9

Book design: William S. Butler and Samuel W. Thomas

Book production: Butler Book Publishing, Louisville, Kentucky

Printed in Canada by Friesen Printers through Four Colour Imports, Louisville

First printing July 1999

EDWIN JOSEPH "EPP" STICH STANDS AT THE CAB OF HIS FATHER'S TRUCK ABOUT 1925. COURTESY OF EARL COMBS STICH.

ENDSHEETS: AERIAL VIEW OF ST. MATTHEWS, 2 AUGUST 1937. JEFFERSON COUNTY HISTORIC PRESERVATION AND ARCHIVES.

This publication by the Beargrass–St. Matthews Historical Society, Inc. was made possible through the generous support of the City of St. Matthews, the James Graham Brown Foundation, Inc., and the Jefferson Banking Company. In addition, PNC Bank, Kentucky and the Wood and Marie C. Hannah Foundation, Inc. made significant contributions.

CONTENTS

FOREWORD

BY
ROGER J. WOLFORD

BAUER BROS. GROCERY, 1928, IS NOW THE SITE OF NATIONAL CITY BANK'S ST. MATTHEWS BRANCH. CAUFIELD AND SHOOK COLLECTION 94444, UNIVERSITY OF LOUISVILLE PHOTOGRAPHIC ARCHIVES.

Communities, like people, strive to be unique, and as they mature often search their history for a separate identity. It is no wonder, then, that in 1985, more than two centuries after the area's settlement and thirty-five years after St. Matthews became incorporated, no less than eighty-one residents subscribed to Mrs. Fred Olympia's timely idea of forming a St. Matthews-based historical society. While our name, Beargrass-St. Matthews Historical Society, does not roll trippingly off the tongue, it does imply our rural roots entwined with Beargrass Creek as well as our urban development grounded in St. Matthews proper. Now headquartered in the old Greathouse School, we are a growing organization of over 250 members that maintains a collection of historical materials and educates the public mainly through lectures and site tours.

For some time it has been the society's desire and intention to publish a book that would encapsulate our historical identity. The project was first given serious thought by George H. Yater, the highly respected author of local history. George begged off, however, to concentrate his efforts on other research. In the beginning of 1996, Samuel W. Thomas agreed to author our book. A prolific historian, Dr. Thomas has confirmed his reputation as a meticulous and resourceful researcher.

His early manuscript drafts were reviewed and critiqued by Evelyn Wolford and Thorp Wolford and board members Carolyn Barth, Mary Jane Benedict, Cynthia Buttorff, Judy Cook, Judy Ochsner Edwards, Georgia Ellinger, Sally Keith, and Mary Jean Kinsman. Board members Dorothy Daub, Kent Groemling, Robert Groemling, Joyce Ruffra, Mike Ruffra, and Wanda Staebler all devoted themselves to ensuring the success and high quality of the book. David Morgan, a board member and former vice president of the society, deserves particular acknowledgement. He has brought order to our archives, and his particular professional knowledge of Jefferson County's records as they relate to this region was absolutely invaluable. We are also grateful to the great number of people in our community who stepped forward with their stories and photographs. Their contributions were essential and are noted throughout the book.

This book would not have been possible without generous financial support from leaders in our community. Early on, Arthur Draut, mayor of the City of St. Matthews, and members of the city council provided significant funding. The James Graham Brown Foundation, Inc., as well as the Jefferson Banking Company, encouraged by its president, James Clay Smith, made substantial contributions. Support from the Wood and Marie C. Hannah Foundation, Inc. and PNC Bank, Kentucky helped initiate the project.

This effort has been a collaborative one. All who participated understand the importance of preserving local history and establishing a community identity based upon its heritage. We hope that this book will provide the historical perspective necessary to reveal this identity.

Two decades before William J. Levitt began in 1947 to impose the country's first mass-produced suburb on some fallow potato fields on Long Island, New York, Henry Holzheimer's old 68-acre potato farm on the west side of Breckenridge Lane in the heart of St. Matthews was being subdivided. There had been other land developments in the area where five roads converged with railroad and interurban lines, but the three sections constituting Breckenridge Villa was the largest. As cultivated land, it was flat and there was no need to curve roads to meet contours as had been done in the Eastleigh subdivision on Lexington Road or in the Indian Hills layout. Every square foot of the farm was worked into a grid network of new roads, creating some 17 blocks that would spur contiguous development. The lots all had 40- or 50-foot frontages and depths generally of 130 feet. No alleys were provided, as had been traditionally. In the age of the family car, a detached one-car garage at the end of a long driveway beside the house would suffice. Water, gas, and electricity were provided, and "made streets" were advertised, along with sidewalks. Little wonder, with the cost of these amenities added to that of the land at $3,000 an acre, that the tract was platted wall-to-wall with lots. Shelbyville insurance and real estate man Joseph Chester Turner had purchased the property from the estate of St. Matthews pioneer, Henry Holzheimer. The sale netted $202,660, which was distributed in varying amounts among ten heirs. Some of the Holzheimer family would move farther out on Westport Road, build new residences, and continue to farm. *The Louisville Times* would later comment that the "sale of the Holzheimer farm, in fact, marked the beginning of the end of the potato-growing era for St. Matthews, because Breckinridge [*The Louisville Times'* spelling] Villa, built on the farm, became one of the first big subdivisions there and erased the rural atmosphere."

While further muddling the spelling waters, Breckenridge Villa also serves as a prototype of the disappearance of the family farm of which much has been written recently. The conversion of a multi-generational family farm to subdivision or commercial development is documented numerous times in this book. The conversion of rural landscape to man-made development is much lamented, but it is a fact of life. It is difficult enough for subsequent generations to maintain family-owned businesses. Why should we expect more of farmers, except that we enjoy the way their undisturbed land looks. The obvious question becomes, can we achieve both? It comes down to how much control is acceptable and fair to place on developers. Commenting on the changes made subsequent to the Holzheimer farm being subdivided, *The Louisville Times* pointed out in 1963: "St. Matthews still bears the marks of its transformation, in a relatively few years, from farm land to suburb. The individual farms have become a collection of individual subdivisions, and the business district clusters around what were intersecting roads beside a railroad grade crossing. Since the change was innocent of any urban

PREFACE

BY

SAMUEL W. THOMAS

We never realize how rapidly a place is changing until we go away for awhile, or someone comes back after a number of years' absence. A gentleman came to our house a few days ago who had not been in St. Matthews for ten years. He said actually he did not know which way to go, all the old buildings were made over and so many new ones, even streets, that he did not recognize the town.

From "St. Matthews," *The Jeffersonian*, 10 November 1921.

8

planning, the area presents a study in the advantages and handicaps of haphazardhood." Much debate and some improvement in the planning process have occurred since 1963, but problems still remain.

St. Matthews emerged because the surrounding farmland was well watered by springs and traversed by the pioneer road from the Falls of the Ohio to the seat of state government and the Bluegrass region. In time, crossroads appeared, and the railroad and interurban. The pioneer road was upgraded to turnpike status and, long after the tollgates disappeared in 1901, two lanes were provided. During the Depression, Shelbyville Road was made into a divided highway—four lanes divided by a median. The 1937 flood prodded many in Louisville's West End to higher ground. The housing market expanded at the end of World War II. Development was enticed, schools and churches were built. St. Matthews, without knowing it, was much like the village concept now being espoused. Then, the Watterson Expressway encircled its outskirts; I-64 transected them. Larger developments with farm-like parking lots began to lure regional customers in cars. Roads were widened to handle the increased traffic. Rain, once a godsend, could not be absorbed through concrete and asphalt and became a major problem. More police and a larger fire department were needed. But, the new tax base brought about by this expansion also made possible Brown Park, a delightful example of public open space.

This book is the story of how and when this transformation took place. Maybe it will serve as a case study for future development. As *The Louisville Times* noted on 8 March 1963: "Traffic is an insoluble problem, but there is a certain charm in the variety of big stores and small shops, parking lots and walkways, and the devious traffic patterns that have grown up out of necessity." Thirty-six years later, positive changes are still taking place, but more can be done to unify the area. If not, the all-important residential base will continue to move farther out.

Due to the limitations of space, this book cannot be a definitive history of St. Matthews and the area encompassed by the meanders of the eastern branches of Beargrass Creek. It does provide most of the tools for further research on particular topics, and many of the institutions not covered here have their own elaborate histories. This is primarily a history of land use. No other section of Louisville's metropolitan area—and few other places in Kentucky at large—can show an evolutionary change from pioneer forts and stations to malls and office complexes. While firsthand recollection is incorporated, the book's basis is grounded in probate and land records and in contemporary newspaper accounts. Documentation is provided, so new-found material can be compared and evaluated. This is not the last word. Incredibly, historical materials regularly come to light from near and far, and surely in time this work will be supplemented by new findings and revelations. Recently, for instance, a set of blow-up photographs used in a court case involving zoning for a new Sears store on Shelbyville Road in 1953 came to light. They had been given to the Louisville Free Public Library and stored out of sight in the main library. Two years ago the 21 prints were given not to the

St. Matthews/Eline Branch, but to the University of Louisville Photographic Archives, where several went on display. They provide a real refresher course on what St. Matthews and Shelbyville Road looked like. I am a relative latecomer to the area, having joined my family here in 1956. Some of my more memorable summer jobs during college were working for the Arctic Ice Company, delivering block and bagged ice to its St. Matthews plant and working the platform there. The 1953 photographs graphically record the St. Matthews I first saw and had occasion to work and shop in. But the ice house has been drastically altered, Vernon's barbershop on St. Matthews Avenue, where for years we went monthly for good talk and a trim, is long gone, and so much has changed, one needs such photographs to recall even the living past.

Articles about St. Matthews have appeared periodically before, but its general history has not been published. The first profile of St. Matthews was prepared by Clarence E. Cason for *The Louisville Herald* series, "Live Towns Around Louisville." It appeared on 30 July 1922. The next was Hewitt Taylor's article in his series, "Salubrious Suburbia," that appeared in the old Louisville *Herald-Post* on 7 October 1936. An illustrated promotional pamphlet, *St. Matthews Makes Its Bow*, was published by James Speed in 1938. An article, "St. Matthews. An Old Area Grown Young," appeared in *The Courier-Journal* on 29 June 1941. The most comprehensive account of St. Matthews' history was prepared by Emil Aun, owner and publisher of *The Voice of St. Matthews*, and published in two parts beginning with the "5th Anniversary Edition" of his weekly newspaper, on 15 July 1954. "The Story of St. Matthews" concluded a week later. "Rush To Suburbia Made St. Matthews," by Ward Sinclair and Harold Browning appeared in *The Louisville Times* on 22 October 1965. Suzanne Darland's "Historic St. Matthews," was published in *The Voice* on 13 May 1981. Gayle Cutler's piece on St. Matthews for *The Courier-Journal*'s series, "A Place In Time," appeared in 25 October 1989 issue.

In 1968, Robert O. Dorsey, Jr., presented to the Sidney Eline Memorial Library a three-ring binder containing 52 pages of retyped, published articles and lists of tidbits he had collected and typed out, as well as copies of photographs. His particular insight stemmed from the fact that his father, Robert O. Dorsey, Sr., had been in the real estate business in St. Matthews beginning before World War I, and Bob Dorsey, Jr., had been a local insurance man and had served on the city council. Later, Dorsey's work was discovered by Marilyn Olympia; and while a student at the University of Louisville, she decided to expand upon it using oral history techniques. Her project had been given impetus in the fall of 1984 by the death of longtime community leader and mayor, Bernard Bowling. Mrs. Olympia had already begun, according to *The Courier-Journal*, "preserving the voices of St. Matthews" when she received a grant from the Kentucky Oral History Commission. A year later, she began to incorporate excerpts from her taped interviews into a slide program funded by the Kentucky Humanities Council. She had gathered photographs and other illustrations, which the University of Louisville Photographic Archives was asked to accession and copy in slide format. In November 1985, she asked me to view her slides and help prepare the program,

If the pioneers were coming west today they'd stop, most likely, at St. Matthews, where five roads come together. They'd think they'd got as far as possible. Anyhow, they'd see no point in going on to Louisville for St. Matthews has everything or nearly so.

From Hewitt Taylor, "St. Matthews," *The Herald-Post*, 7 October 1936.

Local history…exists mainly in the minds of area residents or their descendants. Since 1986, members of the Beargrass—St. Matthews Historical Society have been transferring this fragile, remembered history to the permanent record through taped interviews, old photographs and other research.

The group has also sought to acquire scrapbooks, diaries and other collected materials from notable citizens of the area. That effort has been so successful that the society needed a place to house its collections.

From Tom Stephens, "St. Matthews historical society sets up archives at Trinity," *The New Voice*, 8 November 1989.

which she envisioned to be similar to one I had completed on Crescent Hill two years before. In the process, I got my first comprehensive look at St. Matthews' history. In finished form, "Historic St. Matthews: Potatoes and Progress on the Beargrass" was shown on 19 January 1986. The program's reception was favorable, and as Mrs. Olympia showed it to various organizations, she became convinced that a local organization needed to be formed to preserve and disseminate St. Matthews' history. In March 1986, she assembled area residents interested in forming such a group, and within several months the Beargrass-St. Matthews Historical Society, Inc. was up and running with a full complement of officers and a newsletter. Lynn Olympia was elected the society's first president, and to her belongs credit for its founding and creation.

Among the charter members of the organization was George H. Yater, who has long contributed to our understanding of local history and in particular railroads and railways. His *Two Hundred Years at the Falls of the Ohio: A History of Louisville and Jefferson County* remains the definitive history of this community. When the society became interested in publishing a history of the St. Matthews area, it quite naturally turned to George, who already had considerable knowledge about the transportation system that had allowed St. Matthews to grow and prosper. In addition, he had written a lengthy piece, "The Stations on Beargrass," for *Louisville* magazine in October 1967 that twenty years later was the basis of his script for "Stations Along the Beargrass," a Kentucky Humanities Council sponsored slide/tape program. George agreed to undertake the book project. However, in time, he decided to concentrate his efforts on a book dealing with the railway system for which he had had a lifetime passion. When George begged off the St. Matthews project, the historical society's very persuasive president, Roger J. Wolford, asked me to fill in. That was in February 1996. And what started out to be a modest book has mushroomed into an extensive endeavor. While the Beargrass-St. Matthews Historical Society has a small archival collection, which was initiated by Mrs. Olympia, its contents are contemporary and ongoing and will be extremely helpful to future historians. However, in this project its assistance was limited. For the most part, this book is the result of detailed research and personal interviews undertaken specifically for this project.

Many people were of great help in providing information and material. Each member of the board of directors of the Beargrass-St. Matthews Historical Society provided information, made valuable suggestions, or offered positive critique of the manuscript. In particular, David Morgan, should be singled out for all of his assistance. As vice president and archivist of the historical society, combined with his being in charge of Jefferson County's various archival collections, he was always able to suggest ways and places to look for some fact or illustration. Included are the office's site files arranged by the county prefix JF and designated herein as such. In addition, the staffs of The Filson Club Historical Society, the Louisville Free Public Library, and the University of Louisville Photographic Archives were always helpful. Information or materials were also provided by Ann Sturgess Kostmayer Bradburn, Charles B. Castner, Fred E. Coy, C. R. and Glenda Davis, Helen DePrima,

HESKAMP & BAUER'S BLACKSMITH AND WAGON-MAKING ESTABLISHMENT ON CHENOWETH LANE ABOUT 1900. NOW SITE OF PARKING LOT NORTH OF WHITE CASTLE. COURTESY OF PETER GUETIG.

Philip J. DiBlasi, George Drescher, Lucille Drescher, Sidney W. Eline, Jr., Robert French, Peter Guetig, Neal O. Hammon, Len Hays, Edith and Maury Hite Henchey, William Heyburn, Bonna Holzheimer, Sally Sherwood Keith, John E. Kleber, Mary Maloney, Bettye Lee Mastin, Noel McDonald, Tillie Neuner Oberheim, Kathy McDonald Panther, Jane Durning LaPin, Mary Elizabeth Ratterman Ruckriegel, Dona Schicker, Martin F. Schmidt, Leslie Shively, Earl Combs Stich, Margaret Ann Winter White, George H. Yater, Melchior Zehnder, Sr., and Bruce Zoeller.

The following residents made this narrative more interesting and genuine with their personal recollections. Their words set the tone, and this collective memory is for all of you. Thank you: Carolyn Rudy Barth, Frank L. "Tubby" Barth, Ralph Biernbaum, C. L. Boden, Jr., Henrietta Sara Eline Breeland, Barbara Hewett Brown, George Drescher, Georgia Ellinger, Robert Michael Kirn, Robert Woodrow "Buck" Marshall, Alice O. Monohan, Richard Ochsner, William M. Otter, Jr., Guy Redmon, Jr., Mary Elizabeth Ratterman Ruckriegel, Hope Oldham Rudy, Lucille Manneman Schuler, Richard Leo Schuler, Samuel G. Swope, Earl Combs Stich, Sue Hall Arterburn Stich, Dace Brown Stubbs, Matthew G. "Doc" Stuedle, Cornelia Drescher Stone, Norbourne H. "Skip" Thorpe, and Dominic E. Zehnder, Jr.

This book would never have come to fruition without the persistent encouragement and support of Roger J. Wolford, president of the Beargrass-St. Matthews Historical Society. With his natural ease and finesse, his overall knowledge of the area and the society's holdings, he kept the project moving forward and pushed for a more comprehensive result than first envisioned. He saw to it that the means to publish a book, twice its originally intended length, were there, too.

And finally, I would like to thank Debbie McGuffey Thomas, who provided much editorial support and encouragement–to the point of our having lunch in St. Matthews, South Carolina, after we were married in Charleston. She made the computer function, and the manuscript more readable, and me more productive and very content.

During all of the changes which have come to St. Matthews, the fertility of the soil has been conserved. The early settlers took good care of their land. The gardeners, who followed them with their intensive cultivation of small crops and vegetables, increased this fertility. Today trees, shrubs, flowers and vegetables grow splendidly in the good soil. The land and the culture of the early days are still a part of this most unusual suburb.

From James Speed, *St. Matthews Makes Its Bow* (1938).

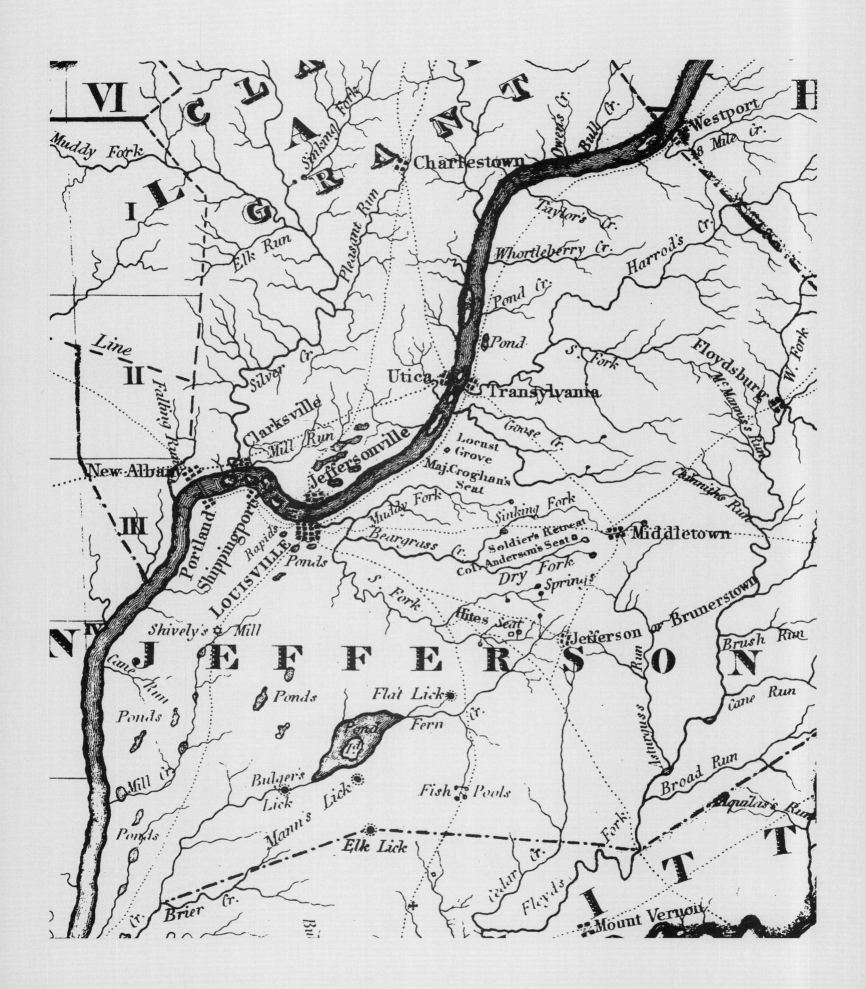

INTRODUCTION

E arly in July 1883, four gentlemen particularly interested in history enjoyed an excursion in the Beargrass region.[1] Their all day carriage ride was arranged because the former governor of Ohio, Charles Anderson, wanted to revisit his childhood home, Soldier's Retreat, on the Shelbyville Road.[2] The younger brother of Robert Anderson, whose defense of Fort Sumter marked the beginning of the Civil War, had for some years resided at Kuttawa in Lyon County, Kentucky. Former newspaper editor and local historian Reuben T. Durrett arranged the outing for Gov. Anderson. To accompany them, Col. Durrett selected Richard H. Collins, whose two-volume *History of Kentucky* published in 1874 remains a standard, and the distinguished lawyer Thomas W. Bullitt, who had grown up nearby at Oxmoor. The group set out along the middle fork of Beargrass Creek to examine the sites of the station settlements as delineated on John Filson's map of Kentucky, published almost a century before the excursion.

It might be noted that less than a year later, this day of reminiscence and camaraderie lead to the founding of The Filson Club.[3] Col. Durrett would serve as the historical society's first president, and Gov. Anderson was among the first members elected to the club; and even though he was residing in western Kentucky, he was present at some meetings. His speech, "Recollections of Pioneer Times," presented spontaneously at a Filson Club dinner commemorating the hundredth anniversary of statehood, "added a new chapter to Kentucky history," Durrett recalled.[4] Gov. Anderson's "Story of Soldier's Retreat" is a valuable document of early life on a Kentucky farm and ranks with Thomas W. Bullitt's *My Life at Oxmoor*.[5]

Bullitt was only 45 years old when this excursion took place—the youngest of the participants. But he, like Charles Anderson, would step into his family's graveyard, where parents and siblings were buried, and confront a rush of personal memories. He would later express his remorse in a paper he was to give at the March 1910 meeting of The Filson Club in Col. Durrett's library. "When 16 years old I left Oxmoor for college. Later I joined the Confederate army. When we boys left for the army my mother and father were on the place alone. When the war ended, Oxmoor was no longer a home. Thus ended the life of the home at Oxmoor...No sadder fact ever came into my life than this." Thomas W. Bullitt died before the March meeting, but his paper was presented by his son in April.[6] Although not reflected in his remarks, it must have been comforting to Thomas W. Bullitt to realize that a year before, his son, William Marshall Bullitt, had reopened Oxmoor. Soon after, Marshall Bullitt had his father's recollections published as *My Life at Oxmoor: Life On A Farm In Kentucky Before The War*.

The group visited five Beargrass stations, including Floyd's and the A'Sturguses' that are within the purview of this book. Near the settlement created by the A'Sturgus brothers, Peter, John, Minard, and James, Jr., and their father in 1780, the group visited the Bullitt family graveyard where Col.

I find letters to my grandfather addressed to "Beargrass," and sometimes to "Kentucky."

From Thomas W. Bullitt, *My Life at Oxmoor* (Louisville, 1911), 18.

I am quite, now absolutely sure, that Floyd's Station was where I have noted it. It belonged in all my day, to Hon. James D. Breckenridge the father of the great heiress Mrs. Shakspeare Caldwell. It is about the best farm on earth....I never heard of a "Sullivan's Station" or have forgotten it if I ever did. The "Low Dutch Station" I have heard of, I faintly believe. But my vague association of it is with our upper central country. We had a large settlement of first class people of that race. Geigers, Hikes, Hites, Hokes, Funks, Doups, Brentlingers, Gooses (Gans), Tracenriders, Yenneweins, Fredericks, Kelleys, Kalfuses, Bruners (Town now Jefferson T.) etc, etc. Some of them were our earliest settlers and well might have had and indeed must have had "Stations" or "Forts."...But, I think I never heard of their having a station of that name. It would be our "nickname" for one of their own, if it ever were in use. They were marvellously "Bell-weather" populace; in all things honoring their "leaders" (as you Democrats do) as Gods....There was another little squad of them North of us on the "divider ridge" between Bear Grass and Goose Creek—the Rudys, Herrs, Geigers (again) &c. But I am sure that they had no "Station" in fact, or by name.

There were several other stations down Beargrass (towards Louisville). ...I did recall the names of several of these "Stations" in our jaunt with Durrett, Collins & Tom Bullitt—six or seven years ago. But I cannot now to save my life.

From letter of Charles Anderson to Lyman C. Draper, 11 March 1891. State Historical Society of Wisconsin, transcribed in *The Kentucky Genealogist* 25 (January/March 1983): 6.

William Christian was buried after being attacked by Indians in 1786. Thomas W. Bullitt was his grandson. Before traveling to Linn's station, the group inspected the site of Soldier's Retreat, where Charles Anderson was born on 1 June 1814. The massive stone house had been struck by lightning, and its shattered remains had been carried away for other uses. Only the ground plan remained evident in the embedded foundation.[7] The site was still easily identified by the existence of stone outbuildings and a handsome springhouse.

"Here beneath the branches of a century-grown walnut, at one of the finest springs that ever poured its cold waters from the living rocks," *The Courier-Journal* said, "the excursionists rested and partook of a lunch prepared for the occasion." Just beyond, was Linn's station, marked only by its gushing spring. "At this, as at all the other forts along Beargrass creek," *The Courier-Journal* observed, "nothing seems to have determined their position as much as the springs. But for the advantages of these splendid springs which now after the lapse of more than one hundred years still pour out generous streams the sites of the forts seem to have been illy chosen. But abundant water was a necessity when so many persons were shut up in the forts, and hence their location was always at ample springs." Before Ohio River water was pumped and piped, all development was predicated upon the existence of water sources. The mere existence of the various branches of Beargrass Creek was an indication of the region's abundant natural water supply.

Departing Linn's station, the group "crossed the country through lanes and by-ways toward the Ohio," stopping at Springfield, Richard Taylor's old property where Zachary Taylor had been raised. A new granite monument had been erected to the twelfth President of the United States. (It was remarked that the marble monument for Colonel Richard Clough Anderson had been designed for President Taylor, but when it did not suit for some

reason, it was purchased by the Andersons and placed at Soldier's Retreat.[8])

Crossing fields, the party came to Locust Grove, William Croghan's country seat, built about 1790. Its famous inhabitant, George Rogers Clark, had been buried in the family cemetery behind the brick house, but his remains were reinterred in Cave Hill Cemetery in 1869. On the way back into town along the river road, the party "passed over the land on the Ohio river, opposite Six-mile Island, where John Cowan in 1773, selected his home and erected his cabin and raised a crop of corn in 1774. Here was the first settlement in Jefferson county, if not the first in the State."

These distinguished gentlemen had witnessed Louisville's earliest development. They did not report on the development in the eastern region brought on by the railroad and the railways. Both Durrett and Bullitt lived to see the automobile, but they never could have imagined what the combustion engine would bring on, and therein lies the fodder for this book.

Even with its environs factored in, St. Matthews had a population of about 3,400 at the time of the 1937 flood, and by post war 1946, it had swelled to 12,500. When incorporated in 1950, the city proper was contained within a three-and-a-half-block area and its population numbered only several hundred. As a fourth-class city in 1954, its residents numbered 6,366.[9] Within several years it was estimated that the city had grown to 10,000, and when the 1960 census count of 8,009 was made known, Mayor Bowling thought it was "preposterous."[10] The figure was later increased to 8,738, and by 1970, the population numbered 13,152.

According to 1990 census data, more than a third of the residents over 25 years of age had undergraduate, graduate or professional degrees. The median household income for the previous year was $40,867. The median year the 8,236 houses were built was 1965, and their median value was $70,600. Two-thirds of the household owners had two or more cars.

When St. Matthews' government, under the leadership of Mayor Arthur Draut and eight-member city council, profiled itself in 1995, its police department had increased to 37 employees, its administrative staff, headed by City Clerk Gretchen Kaiser, numbered eight, its works department had six full-time employees, and a construction department had been created.

The July 1996 estimated population of St. Matthews was 16,562, an increase of 871 since the 1990 census. It ranked as Kentucky's 20th largest city.[11]

Nearly as many patrons used the St. Matthews/Eline Branch Library (36,415) as visited the Louisville Free Public Library's main facility (39,685) in September 1998.

The fire department's budget is presently $1.3 million. Eighteen full time employees are augmented by 40 volunteers, who man six pieces of sophisticated apparatus.

Another important measure of St. Matthews' development is the number of people who work within its limits. A 0.75 percent occupational tax became effective on 1 July 1986. Combined with a property tax rate of 20 cents per $100 of assessed value, the proposed budget for St. Matthews for 1998-1999 is $6.2 million.[12]

Tuesday 21 [October 1812]....We came down to Baregrass Creek. What is called the Baregrass Settlement, is the garden of the state. It is a low, level country, and in wet seasons must be sickly, as it is now. I saw a native of Saxony who had lately arrived, and had joined us: Oh! what a work has been amongst the Germans, and would more abundantly have been, had they had the discipline of the Methodists!

From *The Journal of the Rev. Francis Asbury, Bishop of the Methodist Episcopal Church* (New York, 1821): 3, 336.

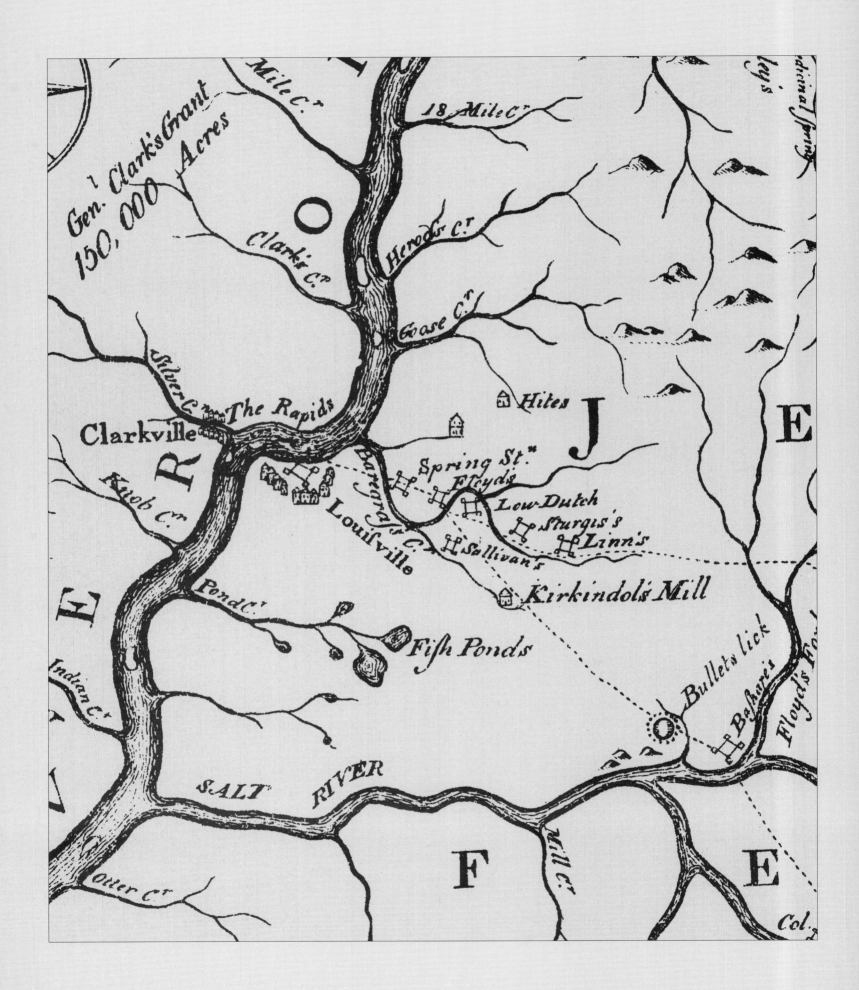

Chapter I

Pioneer Peril

I am in a dangerous situation," John Floyd wrote William Preston on 26 November 1779, "only five men, and the Indians killed or took a man from Bullitt's Lick and wounded another since I came here." He was writing by fire light in a tent that was sheltering his family. He anticipated moving soon into the "fine cabbin" he had raised only that day on the Middle Fork of Beargrass Creek at his station he would call Woodville. "My Company all disappointed me in coming out, but I have no doubt of settlers enough from the falls as many are preparing to join me here."[1] Only a week before at the Falls of the Ohio, the tiny encampment called Louisville, George Rogers Clark, Virginia's military leader in the West, had written a 75-page letter to George Mason of Fairfax, recounting his campaign into the Illinois country. The venerable Mason and Virginia's first governor, Patrick Henry, had abiding interests in the West, and were marshalling efforts to maintain Virginia's influence in the frontier region known as Kentucky. Although Vincennes and other communities in the region had been captured, along with English troops under Governor Henry Hamilton, and Col. Clark had interceded with various Indian nations, the frontier remained far from safe.

Despite the turmoil and constant threat of attack, migration into Kentucky, coupled with land speculation, continued, even flourished. The root cause was passage of the land office act in 1779 by the Virginia legislature. The bill's intended purpose envisioned by Mason and Thomas Jefferson was to provide small parcels of land on the frontier for homesteading. However, the legislation became flawed. "A colossal mistake," was Thomas Perkins Abernethy's evaluation of the act's effect as scrutinized in his seminal study *Western Lands and The American Revolution* (1937). Land companies and enterprising individuals, with no thoughts of moving from their comfortable and safe surroundings along the Atlantic coast, came into possession of huge tracts of land, at little cost, speculating on the frontier's future development.

Interest in Kentucky lands began to manifest when Fincastle, the western-most county in Virginia, was created out of Botetourt in 1772. William Christian was appointed sheriff, while William Preston was put in charge of the militia and given the added duty of county surveyor. One of Preston's deputy surveyors was John Floyd, who also served as a deputy sheriff under Christian.[2] By 1776, a petition to separate West Fincastle was carried to Richmond by George Rogers Clark and John Gabriel Jones. With assistance from Governor Patrick Henry, Clark was able to secure gunpowder for the frontier defense and the House of Delegates created Washington, Montgomery, and Kentucky counties in Fincastle's stead.[3] Population continued to pour onto the western frontier, brought on by "the Western fever, that chronic lust for land beyond the Appalachians."[4] Within four years, there was the necessity to divide Kentucky County, Virginia, into three—Jefferson, Lincoln, and Fayette, as roughly delineated on John Filson's map.

When William Christian, the designated head of Jefferson County's

I arrived here the 8th inst. with all my family and stock, safe and hearty. I have this day got a fine cabbin raised, and hope in a few days to have a shelter something better than a tent which we have laid in almost ten weeks. I should not have been quite so tedious in building, but the first tree Bob cut down on the place lodged and slipped back on the stump and tore off his right foot, or at least all the skin and flesh from his ancle down. I have nothing to dress it, and am persuaded it must rot off what is left.

From John Floyd to William Preston, 26 November 1779. Draper MSS. 17CC186, State Historical Society of Wisconsin.

OPPOSITE: STATIONS ALONG BEARGRASS CREEK DELINEATED ON JOHN FILSON'S 1784 MAP OF KENTUCKY. THE FILSON CLUB.

On the 12th April 1783, Col. Floyd, his brother Charles Floyd, and Alexander Breckinridge were going to Salt River, about 20 miles from Floyd's Station. Floyd wore a scarlet coat. On their return, a party of Indians attacked them, shot Floyd through the arm. The ball entered his body. Floyd reeled on his horse, which his brother observing, dismounted from his, jumped on his brother's, caught him around the body, and rode off in full speed to a house about five miles distant. By this time Col. Floyd was so exhausted from the loss of blood that he appeared to be dying, never the less he lived that night, talked much to his brother, and expressed unmitigated sorrow for his young wife, the unborn infant, and his two little sons. He desired to be buried at his Station on an eminence he had chosen for a grave yard. All this was fulfilled.

From Laetitia Preston Floyd, John Floyd's daughter in law, to her son, Benjamin Rush Floyd, 22 February 1843. Draper MSS. 6J104-105, State Historical Society of Wisconsin.

militia resigned in 1781, George Rogers Clark, Virginia's military leader in the West, wrote Governor Thomas Jefferson: "I would beg leave to recommend to you Colo. Jno. Floyd an Inhabitant of the County, as a Gentlen. that I am convinced will do Honour to the appointment and known to be the most capable in the County, a Soldier, Gentleman, and a scholar whom the Inhabitants, from his actions have the greatest confidence in."[5] Col. Floyd was duly commissioned, survived a massacre attack while burying the dead from a previous encounter, and served with George Rogers Clark on two expeditions.[6] When a new court was established for the three counties comprising the District of Kentucky in 1783, Samuel McDowell and John Floyd were appointed judges by Virginia Governor Benjamin Harrison.[7] However, Floyd only took part in the court's first session, held in the meetinghouse near the Dutch Station, six miles from Harrodsburg, in March 1783.[8] He was killed a month later in an Indian ambush. In the estimation of contemporaries, only George Rogers Clark was held in higher regard, but that consideration would have soon changed. General Clark's brief military career had eclipsed, and he was unable to move effectively into the next phase of development on the frontier that became the realm of lawyers and politicians. John Floyd's death (and that of William Christian several years later) left such a void in civil matters at the Falls that the disadvantage in state affairs was long experienced in Jefferson County.

James John "Jack" Floyd had been born in Amherst County, Virginia, in 1751, the son of William and Abidiah Floyd.[9] As a deputy surveyor for Fincastle County, he had resurveyed many of Thomas Bullitt's plots at the Falls of the Ohio in 1774 for principal surveyor William Preston. In addition, he also resurveyed tracts south of the Falls known for their salt licks for Wil-

liam Christian.[10] When Floyd returned to the Falls in 1779, he had only recently arrived back in America after being captured on a privateer off the coast of Virginia with booty captured in the West Indies, and taken prisoner to England. He was able to make his way to France, and borrow money from Ambassador Benjamin Franklin to make the return voyage. Arriving at the home of William Preston in early 1778, he soon married Jane Buchanan, his host's ward. In October 1779, with their infant son, William Preston Floyd, they ventured through the Cumberland Gap and along the Wilderness Road to the Falls of the Ohio. Their party included two of Floyd's brothers (Robert and Isham) and four of his sisters, two of whom were married—Jemima, wife of Eleazer LeMaster, and Abidiah, wife of James A'Sturgus, Jr.[11] Brother Charles Floyd came out a year later.[12]

A fellow surveyor described Floyd as "one of the first Adventurers in this Country, an old Surveyor, and one as capable of making a judicious Choice of Lands, as any Man."[13] Being well aware of the area's merits, John Floyd had become the assignee of two 1,000-acre parcels that encompass present day St. Matthews.[14] In doing so, he has been credited as Jefferson County's first landowner.[15] "Col. Floyd went to his fine estate on Beargrass Creek, six miles from Louisville," his daughter-in-law, Laetitia Preston Floyd, later wrote, and "he commenced building a fort; got the houses completed in a short time, and a good stockade made." She noted that he once remarked "he felt that he had placed his foot upon the threshold of an Empire."

Floyd wrote frequently to his mentor, William Preston, providing "details of nearly all the striking incidents of the early settlements in Kentucky." In one such letter, dated 21 July 1776, he wrote Preston from Boonesborough an account of the recapture of Daniel Boone's daughter and Calloway nieces from their Indian captors. Floyd had accompanied Boone in the successful pursuit and confrontation, and his report to Preston became a part of the Boone saga. It would be later noted by Otto A. Rothert of The Filson Club that the reprinting of Floyd's letter in the 14 January 1834 issue of the Frankfort *Commonwealth* prompted a suggestion to create a state historical society, which came about two years later.[16] The proposal was actually made in *The Commonwealth* on 20 June 1835 in connection with the reprinting of other letters written by Floyd to Preston. "In printing these letters," the editor wrote, "it has occurred to us that much light could be thrown upon the early history of Kentucky, by the formation of a state historical society. Such an institution would be instrumental in preserving the few written memorials which have yet escaped the destructive hand of time, while it could adopt some place by which those facts could be preserved which must also soon pass away when the last of the Pioneers has been gathered to his fathers. Such a race of men as the Kentucky pioneers will not be seen on this continent."[17] The John Floyd letters were provided to *The Commonwealth* by Nathaniel Hart, Jr., widower of William Preston's daughter.[18]

Orlando Brown, son of Senator John Brown of Liberty Hall in Frankfort, was then editor of the *Commonwealth*, and an additional fourteen letters written by John Floyd to William Preston between 1779 and 1783 came into

On April 22, 1836, in the secretary of state's office in Frankfort, Sen. John Brown presided over the meeting that voted to organize a historical society to collect and preserve items related to Kentucky history.

From Gretchen M. Haney, *The Kentucky Encyclopedia* (Lexington, 1992), 503.

OPPOSITE: FRONTIER SCENE FROM FRONTIS-PIECE OF HUMPHREY MARSHALL'S *HISTORY OF KENTUCKY* (FRANKFORT, 1812).

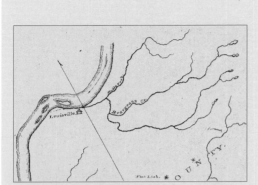

BEARGRASS CREEK AND OTHER WATERSHEDS OF JEFFERSON COUNTY AS DEPICTED ON A *CA.* 1800 SURVEY. WICKLIFFE-PRESTON COLLECTION, UNIVERSITY OF KENTUCKY SPECIAL COLLECTIONS. THE THREE FORKS OF BEARGRASS CREEK CONVERGED NEAR BROWNSBORO ROAD AND STORY AVENUE AND THEN FLOWED WEST, ENTERING THE OHIO RIVER BETWEEN THIRD AND FOURTH STREETS.

Bear Grass, May 31st 1780.

We have very little news in Kentucky but what relates to Indians &c. and they seem determined to make this neighbourhood the seat of war this season....Hardly one week pass without some one being Scalped between this and the Falls and I have almost got too cowardly to travell about the woods without company.

From John Floyd to William Preston, Draper MSS. 17CC12-128, Wisconsin State Historical Society.

his possession, undoubtedly also the result of family ties. Orlando's grandmother, Margaret Preston Brown, was William Preston's sister; and John Floyd, Jr., had married William Preston's daughter, Laetitia. The letters were later copied by Lyman C. Draper of the State Historical Society of Wisconsin, who planned to write a series of biographies of the western pioneer leaders. Excerpts from Draper's transcripts reveal the hardships endured by Floyd and the others residing on Beargrass Creek:[19]

(Falls of Ohio, December 19th 1779): I cant buy a Bushell of corn for 50 Dollars now & every thing else seem nearly in proportion. Jenny and myself often lament the want of our fine crop of corn in the valley of Arcadia, and we both seem to have a fondness yet for that country notwithstanding all the advantages we expect in future....I shall continue to scribble every opportunity. I have several Families settled on my Land where I shall soon have a fine plantation and Fort. The Indians killed 2 men at Bullits Lick last week and took 2 Boys prisoners cold as it is.

(Beargrass, 19 January 1780): Where I attempted to write in Decr. the Ink froze in the pen and it is no better yet, as the Snow has never melted off the south side of the cabbin since the first of last month....Since I wrote you corn has sold at the Falls for 165 dollars p Bushl. and people seem desirous to have every other article in proportion to that. Money is no account here.

(Wilson's Station, 5th May 1780): Our troublesome neighbours have visited us so often this spring that I never got your packet by Mr. Nourse till about the middle of April....I am sorry I made such complaint to you in the winter about Bread as we now have plenty. I think near three hundred large Boats have arrived at the Falls this spring with families, & corn can be bought now for thirty Dollars. We have six stations on B. Grass with not less than 600 men. You wou'd [not] be surprised to see 10 or 15 Waggons at a time going to & from the falls every day with Families & corn. I expect 200 acres will be tended in corn this year on my place but very little of it will come to my share.

(Jefferson 26th April 1781): Our little Settlements here are also in great confusion and distress, owing to the frequent visits we receive from our neighbours from the West side the Ohio. Forty seven of the Inhabitants of this county have been killed and captured by them since the first of January last, and many others badly wounded....I have also had a considerable loss in this way amounting to about fourteen thousand weight of fine Meat Tallow &c. &c. all sunk in the Ohio in a Gale of wind.

(Jeff 30th Sept. 1781): I fear our destruction is inevitable. The attention of near 6000 Savage Warriors is now fixed upon Kentucky. I was defeated the sixteenth Instant by a party of upwards of two hundred. I had only 26 men & they cut us to pieces before I knew of the ambuscade—poor LeMaster fell in this action. [Eleazer LeMaster was the husband of Floyd's sister, Jemima. Their daughter, Abigail LeMaster, married John Speed, later of Farmington, in 1796.]

(Beargrass 1 January 1782): We have had a respite of several weeks from the calamities of war in Jefferson which is almost a miracle. If the savages should kill three more before the 6th of next month they will complete the 100 in twelve months.

(Beargrass 28th March 1783): At present the most of my ambition is to procure a little Furniture some materials for Building, & a few saleable articles which our settlement is in need of.[20] When I parted with you at the foot of the mountain I expected to have seen you again before this day, but now I do not expect that pleasure till the War is ended, if ever I should survive that time.

When one of his wife's relatives died from wounds received in an Indian attack on a nearby salt works, John Floyd wrote William Preston prophetically, dated Beargrass, 28 March 1783: "I have long expected something like this to be my own lot, and if the war is continued much longer I can hardly escape, tho' I am now determined to be more cautious than I have been heretofore, yet every man in this country must be more or less exposed

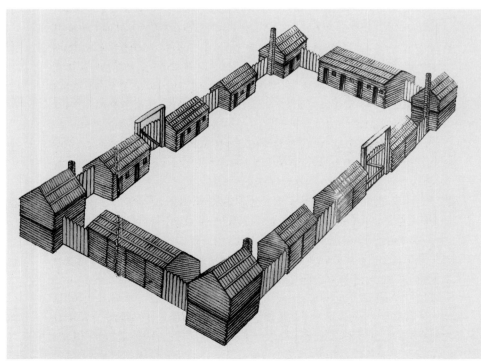

SKETCH OF FLOYD'S STATION, WHICH COL. REUBEN T. DURRETT, A FOUNDER AND FIRST PRESIDENT OF THE FILSON CLUB, NOTED WAS BASED UPON GROUND PLANS FOUND IN THE PAPERS OF GEORGE ROGERS CLARK. OTHER BEARGRASS STATIONS WERE SIMILARLY DEPICTED, BUT NO REFERENCE TO ANY GROUND PLANS HAS BEEN FOUND IN GENERAL CLARK'S PAPERS. WHETHER THE SKETCHES WERE BASED UPON THE ARTIST'S IMAGINATION OR DURRETT'S IS NOT KNOWN. COURTESY OF THE FILSON CLUB.

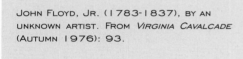

JOHN FLOYD, JR. (1783-1837), BY AN UNKNOWN ARTIST. FROM *VIRGINIA CAVALCADE* (AUTUMN 1976): 93.

to danger."[21] Eleven days later, and probably before his 33rd birthday, John Floyd was mortally wounded in an Indian ambush near the salt licks in present day Bullitt County, while reportedly answering a challenge.[22] His burial established the graveyard at Woodville. Besides his wife, he was survived by a daughter, Mourning, by his first wife; and three sons: William Preston Floyd, George Rogers Clark Floyd, and John Floyd, Jr.[23] The last, born twelve days after his father was killed, began his formal education in 1796 at Dickinson College in Carlisle, Pennsylvania; but financial difficulties forced him to return home, where he did receive some medical training from Dr. Richard Ferguson (who would amputate George Rogers Clark's leg in 1809). Floyd married William Preston's daughter, Laetitia (also spelled Letitia), in 1804, after which he obtained a medical degree from the University of Pennsylvania and settled in Virginia.[24] He was elected to six terms in Congress (1817-1829), and would become the third physician to serve as governor of Virginia (1830-1834). He was a minor candidate for President in 1832, and died in 1837.[25] His son, John Buchanan Floyd, was also elected governor of Virginia in 1850.

In 1784, John Floyd's widow, Jane Buchanan Floyd, married Alexander Breckinridge, who with his brothers, Robert and William, had settled near Woodville.[26] He and his brother Robert had been trained as carpenters, but had come to Kentucky to speculate in land after being released from British prison ships.[27] Alexander and Jane Breckinridge had four sons, the first being James Douglas Breckinridge, although there seems to have been some lingering question whether Alexander's brother Robert was the boy's father. In any case, after attending Washington (now Washington and Lee) College, James Douglas Breckinridge studied law and became a respected attorney in Louisville and was elected to the Seventeenth Congress.[28] His only child, Mary Eliza, received a considerable holding from her great-uncle, Robert Breckinridge, that included the tracts now occupied by Seneca Park and Bowman Field.[29] After Mary Eliza's mother died, her father married Lucy Fry Speed, sister of James and Joshua Speed, all of whom had been raised at Farmington.

When Alexander Breckinridge died in 1801, the entirety of his estate was devised to his wife, except for his land north of the Ohio River allocated for military service that was to be divided among his three sons. When Jane Buchanan Floyd Breckinridge died in 1812 at Woodville, the property was inherited by her son, Henry Brown Breckinridge. His uncle, Robert Breckinridge, had obtained property nearby on which he built "a good house" where he "occasionally lived."[30] When Robert Breckinridge, who had served four terms in the Kentucky House of Representatives and was its first speaker, died in 1833, his funeral was presided over by a Harvard Divinity School graduate who had moved to Louisville to establish a Unitarian Church at Fifth and Walnut streets.[31] On 13 September 1833, the Rev. James Freeman Clarke wrote his friend Margaret Fuller an enlightening account of his experience:[32]

I have just been attending the funeral of one of the first settlers. One General [Robert] Breckenridge, aged 76, came here in 1780, having been in the revolutionary war. At that time the settlers were few—these lived in a fort for fear of Indians. He was never married, but left a large fortune to his nephews. The last part of his life was solitary—he lived with few comforts even of those which wealth can procure—very temperate in his diet—drank no spirit. Master of $100,000, he lived in a room in one of his Louisville houses—avoiding society. I was asked to perform the service which was in the city—but he was to [be] buried on his own place, 6 miles out of town, & they wished me to go out & make a prayer at the grave. So I went with the rest. We passed through an avenue winding through the forest for half a mile until we reached the house—an one story building, poor enough, but very fine for Old Kentucky. The sitting room was decorated with a harp-

One year only had elapsed [after John Floyd's death] when three brothers of the Breckinridge family made suit for the hand of the beautiful, rich relict of Col. Floyd–Alexander, Robert, and Wiliam. The preference was given to Robert; an engagement took place. Robert went to Virginia to settle some business he had there, failed to write, or at least his Letters never reached Mrs. Floyd. Meanwhile Capt. Breckinridge urged his suit; was successful and became the husband of Mrs. Floyd. This union was not a happy one, Capt. Breckinridge had contracted habits of intemperance while in the army. He was a kind tempered man, and always treated his stepsons with the same affection he bestowed on his own children. There were six sons from this marriage. Four lived to manhood. The oldest son, Mr. James D. Breckinridge, is yet living. He was educated at Williamsburg.

From Laetitia Preston Floyd to Benjamin Rush Floyd, 22 February 1843. Draper MSS. 6J105. State Historical Society of Wisconsin.

sichord & two oldfashioned card tables. The family burial place was at a little distance beyond the house. The occasion & scenery worked on my mind & induced me to allude in the prayer to the first settling of the country, & I quoted those striking verses at the commencement of the 44th Psalm....The forest scenery of Kentucky is said to surpass that of any part of Europe. This was chiefly composed of Sycamores of tremendous size and lofty, tapering Beeches with thick clumps at the top....Oak is common also.

Robert Breckinridge's estate was divided among the children of his nephew Henry B. Breckinridge and in trust for the young daughter of James D. Breckinridge. It is not known what became of the homestead house from which he was taken to be buried nearby. Left behind, however, was a fine two-story, stone springhouse to mark the station's site as well as that of a pioneer residence of great historical significance.

When James D. Breckinridge died in 1849, the bulk of his estate, as well as the land held in trust, passed on to his daughter Mary Eliza. She mar-

"To the memory of Genl. Robert Breckinridge Born in the year 1754: He died Sept. 10ᵀᴴ 1833." The Floyd-Breckinridge cemetery on Williamsburg Court, by R. C. Ballard Thruston, 22 March 1922. The Filson Club.

ried William Shakespeare Caldwell and joined the Catholic church.[33] Caldwell made a fortune in real estate and municipal gas works. Two daughters were born to the union before Mary Eliza Breckinridge Caldwell died. Her widower established Saints Mary and Elizabeth Hospital and funded numerous other charities. Daughter Mary Gwendolyn married but had no children. Daughter Mary Elizabeth Breckinridge married Baron Kurt von Zedtwitz and a son was born before the baron died from injuries suffered during a yacht-racing accident. During World War I, some of the local von Zedtwidtz property was temporarily seized. However, in 1928, a part of the old Breckinridge property consisting of 504 acres was acquired by the park commissioners. Part of the land was utilized for Bowman Field, the remainder was named Seneca Park and it was connected to Cherokee Park.[34]

By a court ordered division of Henry Brown Breckinridge's land holdings, his daughter Margaret Preston Breckinridge Drake received the Woodville property, and in 1842, a 50-acre tract that included the family cemetery was sold to William Floyd Parks. The sale agreement specified that Parks double the size of the existing rail-enclosed graveyard and surround it with a plank and post fence. Floyd Parks, who died in 1865, acknowledged this graveyard and the Breckinridge family's access to it in his will; and at the same time, he established his family's own cemetery nearby.[35] A decade later, Floyd Parks's son, Joshua B. Parks, offered for sale "one of the most desirable suburban homesteads in the Southwest," a 27-acre woodland, called The Parks Grove. Included were "a modern style, nearly new" 12-room residence, "a never failing spring," a brick springhouse, large barn and ice house, and "toll free over two of the best pikes leading to the city."[36]

For some years, members of The Filson Club had been interested in

While most of the members were observing the great stone springhouse of Floyd's Station, an airplane circled close overhead, and one of the members made what is regarded as an important historic discovery.
This discovery was of the exact location of the "old Breckinridge graveyard," where many of the early pioneers of Louisville are buried. Records show that the graves of these men are there, but for more than five years members of the club had sought vainly to find the burying ground. Strangely enough, the information came from an old Negro woman living on the farm of Osa Lentz, about a mile from the city limits on the Cherokee Road. One of the members said in her hearing that he thought the graveyard was near. She volunteered to lead him to the spot, only a short distance away.

From "Louisville Pioneers' Graves Discovered By Filson Club," *The Courier-Journal*, 25 April 1921.

FLOYD PARKS' MONUMENT, 1923, BY R.C.
BALLARD THRUSTON. THE FILSON CLUB.
GRAVEYARD IS NEAR 5723 PRINCE WILLIAM
STREET.

The Floyd cemetery and springhouse were on our place. The Osa Lentz cemetery set out more towards Breckenridge Lane. It's in somebody's side yard and the biggest part of the fence around it is down. The Floyd cemetery did not have any fence or anything around it. There are more graves on the outside of that wall they built after we left than on the inside. There are 60, 70, or 80 graves on the outside of that wall. We lived there from 1933 until 1947 and my dad farmed and raised hogs. His name was Matthew I. Stuedle.

From interview of Matthew G. "Doc" Stuedle, 4 March 1997.

the pioneer stations along the Beargrass. Alfred Pirtle presented a paper on the subject in February 1919.[37] This stimulated interest in finding the Floyd and Breckinridge graveyard, which had become overgrown and obscured. In fact, the very name of Breckinridge, once strongly identified with the locality, was being misspelled on maps as Breckenridge, and that misspelling continues on street signs to the present. It was not until The Filson Club's excursion in 1921 that Floyd's Station's location was revealed by an old black woman who lived nearby.[38] Remnants of Woodville's two-story, stone springhouse still remained on the west side of Breckenridge Lane.

The Filson Club appointed a committee to look into renovating the graveyard, and even at that time, only two monuments could be uncovered that were legible. Local historian Hardin H. Herr would simply state in 1930 that the station "was on or near the farm" of the late Osa W. Lentz.[39] His father, Lewis Lentz, had married Floyd Parks's daughter Mary. From 1933 until 1947, the property was farmed by Matthew I. Stuedle. His son, Matthew "Doc" Stuedle, recalls that his father and a neighbor once dug up all the graves. This was at the instigation of Hambleton Tapp, then a history teacher at Louisville Male High School, who in 1934 became quite eager to locate John Floyd's grave. Tapp later told a meeting of The Filson Club that about thirty graves were opened, but the findings were not conclusive.[40] Doc Stuedle confirms that they did not find what they went looking for. Subsequently, his father had a falling out with The Filson Club and became uncooperative, not relishing sightseers coming through his fields to the graveyard. After the Stuedles left, The Filson Club placed large informative memorial slabs in the cemetery and enclosed it with a stone fence at a cost of $5,700.[41] Almost twenty years later, interest was aroused to reconstruct Floyd's log station fortification. However, when various governmental entities failed to support the project, the fort concept lapsed and the site was covered over by apartments.[42] The stone springhouse further deteriorated until purchased by the City of St. Matthews, but unfortunately its restoration was not comparable to the richness of the site's history. It should be noted that Robert and Jemima Suggett Johnson resided at Floyd's Station for a period in 1780, during which their son, Richard Mentor Johnson, was born.[43] Although wounded at the Battle of the Thames, he is reputed to have killed Tecumseh, and later he served as vice president of the United States.

Whenever interest has been expressed about the Breckinridge family, attention has been focused on the proper spelling of Breckenridge Lane. How the street's misspelling came into existence has long been forgotten. Probably by then, no one knew the difference. The first map of the St. Matthews area that provides street names is the New Map of Louisville and Environs, drawn and surveyed by Merritt Drane and published in 1891. It specifies Breckenridge Ave. The 1913 Jefferson County atlas repeats it. The 1892 Sanborn map simply lists it as a private road. Then in its 1905 version, the Sanborn calls it Chenoweth Avenue as a continuation of the street north of the Shelbyville Road. When part of Nanz and Neuner's nursery was platted as Magnolia Subdivision in 1913, a strip of land was provided to widen

Breckinridge Avenue. However, by Sanborn's next series issuance in 1928, it had become Breckenridge Avenue. However, the Caron city directories since 1928 have continued to use Breckinridge Lane as did the United States Geological Survey (USGS) topographical maps of 1930 and 1944. The spelling has continued to be batted around ever since. In 1993, *The Courier-Journal*'s Jim Adams took another whack at the subject. "It is high time somebody did something about the chronic misspelling of Breckinridge Lane," he wrote. "Heaven knows, this is not a new issue," he noted filling in a gap. "Way back

LOJIC-GENERATED MAP OF INCORPORATED ST. MATTHEWS (SHADED AREAS) AND VICINITY WITH OVERLAY OF 1774 SURVEYS AS PLOTTED BY NEAL O. HAMMON AND PUBLISHED IN "THE FINCASTLE SURVEYORS AT THE FALLS OF THE OHIO, 1774," *THE FILSON CLUB HISTORY QUARTERLY* 47 (JANUARY 1973): 14-28.

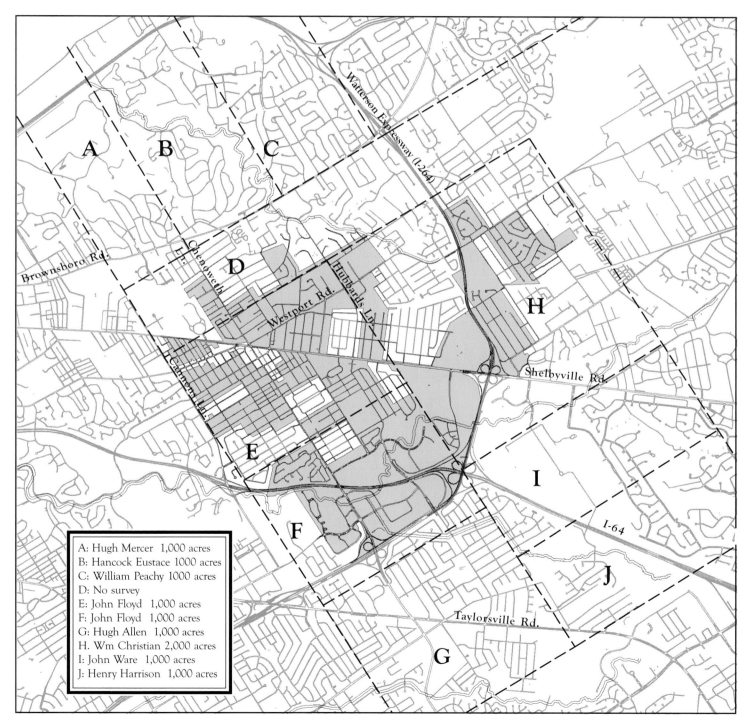

A: Hugh Mercer 1,000 acres
B: Hancock Eustace 1000 acres
C: William Peachy 1000 acres
D: No survey
E: John Floyd 1,000 acres
F: John Floyd 1,000 acres
G: Hugh Allen 1,000 acres
H. Wm Christian 2,000 acres
I: John Ware 1,000 acres
J: Henry Harrison 1,000 acres

in 1960, Floyd Edwards, columnist in *The Louisville Times*, reported that Wendall Wilbar of the old Planning and Zoning Commission had found a plat and a lawsuit 'to prove that the suburban thoroughfare was named for Robert and Newton O. Breckinridge,' spelled with 'en.' Before long, Fiscal Court itself declared the proper name to be Breckenridge, and slowly, one by one, street signs were remade to erase the Breckinridge heritage."[44]

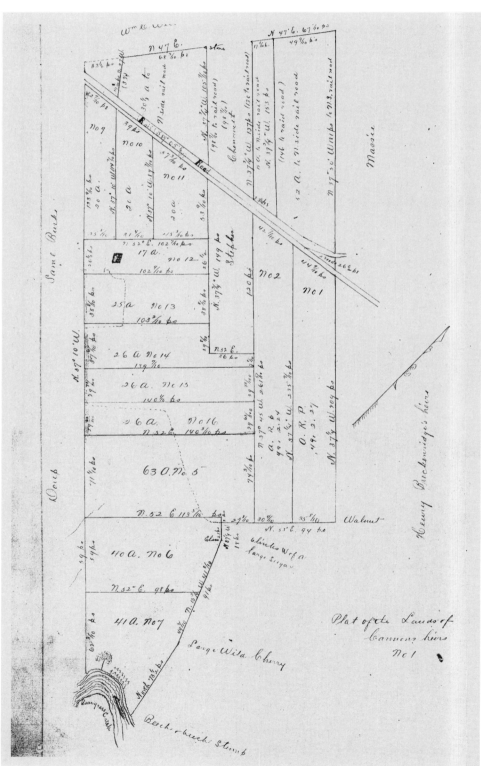

PLAT OF THOMAS CANNON'S PROPERTY, RECORDED IN JEFFERSON COUNTY DIVISION BOOK 1, P. 326. CANNONS LANE NOW RUNS ALONG THE WESTERN BOUNDARY AT LEFT. SHELBYVILLE ROAD IS SHOWN CUTTING DIAGONALLY FROM THE UPPER LEFT TO THE MID RIGHT. THE WESTPORT ROAD BEGINS TO BRANCH OFF AT THE RIGHT. THE CANNON RESIDENCE, LOCATED IN LOT #12, WAS SOUTH OF LEXINGTON ROAD, WHICH WAS PUT DOWN AFTER THIS PLAT WAS MADE.

The Beargrass station nearest the Falls of the Ohio was one of two established on the 6,000-acre tract granted to James Southall and Richard Charlton that was contiguous to Floyd's land. Spring Station was located strategically at a strong spring whose stream became known as Beals Branch in recognition of Norborne Beall who about 1810 built a fine Federal brick residence in the same location that has endured and has even of late been substantially refined. Access to the house, which faces east, was probably along a private drive that marked the division between Southall and Charlton land and Floyd's. Later, this roadway, which intersected the Shelbyville Pike, divided the Spring Station tract from the part of Floyd's property acquired by Thomas Cannon. The road became known as Cannons Lane, and the Cannon homestead was located on the east side. After Thomas Cannon died, a division was made of his property both north and south of the Shelbyville turnpike. In 1852, surveyors marked off the Shelbyville Branch Turnpike Road (later known as the Work House Road, Cherokee Drive, and presently Lexington Road) that split both the Spring Station and Cannon properties, and allowed development to take place along the south side of the branch turnpike road. The Cannon homestead was later acquired by Dominic Zehnder, a dairyman, and he may have lived in the house, which was later torn down when the farm was cleared to create the Lexington Manor subdivision.

Another station was created upstream on Beargrass Creek, on land provided by John Floyd. The families inhabiting this station and providing its

R. C. BALLARD THRUSTON PHOTOGRAPHED THE FILSON CLUB'S EXCURSION TO DUTCH STATION ON 22 MARCH 1922. IN THE BACKGROUND IS THE BROWN/MONOHAN FAMILY HOUSE AND THE BROWN FAMILY CEMETERY. THE FILSON CLUB.

name, New Holland or Low Dutch Station, were of Dutch descent, intermingled with French Huguenots and some Germans. All were members of the Dutch Reform Church, which had established a colony near Gettysburg, Pennsylvania, a century before. Searching for more fertile land, a small group had canvassed the area around Boonsborough in 1779, and were determined to settle nearby at Nathaniel Hart's White Oak Spring Station. Two parties made their way West, one through the Cumberland Gap, the other under Henry Banta, came by way of Redstone Old Fort and the Ohio River. Consisting of at least 75 members, many of which were children, they had familiar surnames like VanArsdale, VanCleve, Cossart, Smock, Westerfield, and Shively.[45] They arrived at the Falls in the spring of 1780, and in need of immediate refuge, they were allowed to create a station above Floyd's on Beargrass Creek, prompting Floyd to tell William Preston: "I expect 200 acres will be tended in corn this year on my place but very little of it will come from my share."[46]

> My father put up his cabin there [Floyd's Station] about as soon as any of the rest. Col. Floyd might have had his. It was all a cane break. A man could be hid at the distance of four feet. All had to cut the cane away to fix to make a living. There were 3 families in each end of Floyd's station, but the sides I don't remember. Not more than 12, I think....
>
> There at Sturgus' station, old David Spangler, a dutchman, went out to git up his oxen, when he was shot. They heard the gun, but couldn't get there in time. The Indians caught and tomahawked and scalped him before any one could come....He died that night.
>
> From a recollection of the daughter of John Thickston, otherwise noted simply as "A woman in Cincinnati," Draper MSS. 13CC9, State Historical Society of Wisconsin.

Squire Boone and his family resided at Low Dutch Station during the winter of 1781-1782, following the back-to-back atrocities known now as the Long Run Massacre and Floyd's Defeat, which occurred on 13 and 14 September 1781. Settlers evacuating Boone's Painted Stone Station (near present day Shelbyville) for safety at Linn Station were savagely attacked by Indians, and as a party went with John Floyd to bury the dead, they were ambushed and slaughtered. Eventually, the Low Dutch Company acquired Squire Boone's old settlement and 7,610 acres and concentrated its efforts there in 1786.[47]

By then, the Low Dutch Station on Beargrass Creek, delineated on Filson's 1784 map of Kentucky, lay in ruins. That part of John Floyd's land, south of Beargrass Creek, was inherited by his son, William Preston Floyd, and at his death by his brother, George Rogers Clark Floyd, who had been named for the western military leader, under whom John Floyd had served as county lieutenant. He leased his "farm, plantation and tract of land called the Dutch Station" to Nathan Marders to farm for six years beginning in 1808. The premises were then described as "very much out of repair," and two years into the lease, Floyd sold the 480-acre tract to James Brown.[48] While the locations of other Beargrass stations remained identified by springhouses, Dutch Station was marked in 1824 by its graveyard.[49] When The Filson Club made a "pilgrimage" to the Beargrass stations in 1921, *The Courier-Journal* reported that the club's secretary, Otto Rothert, announced that "Dutch Station...had been identified as the New Holland Station." "Heretofore," it was noted, "the site and date of the founding of the latter had been unknown."[50]

About two miles east of Floyd's station, the brothers A'Sturgus—Peter, James, Jr., John, and Minard—established another Beargrass settlement in 1780 on land granted to William Christian.[51] They had recently come to Kentucky accompanied by their father from Walnut Bottom, their homestead on the Monongahela River, about 15 miles north of Redstone Old Fort.[52] On 14 September 1781, John Floyd hastily wrote George Rogers Clark: "I have this minute returned from a little Excurcion against the Enemy & my

party of 27 in number are all dispersed & cut to pieces except 9 who came off the field with Capt Asturgus mortally Wounded and one other slightly wounded. I dont yet know who are killed."[53] Floyd would soon learn that his sister Jemima's husband, Eleazer LeMaster, who had been in charge of Dutch Station, had been killed.[54] (In 1784, Jemima LeMaster married James A'Sturgus, Jr. Her daughter, Abigail LeMaster, would marry John Speed, who later built Farmington, in 1796.) Peter A'Sturgus died of his wounds in March 1782. (In early April 1782, an administrator of Peter A'Sturgus's estate was appointed.) His widow was Nancy Ann Tyler, whose father, Edward Tyler, also brought his family to the Falls from above Redstone Old Fort in 1780 and later began the Tyler family settlement known presently as Blackacre.[55]

How long members of the A'Sturgus family resided at the station that continued to bear their name is not clear. When responding to Clark about finding someone who could build an armed row galley in March 1782, Floyd reported: "I have seen no person yet, qualified for the purpose of Boat-

GROUP EXAMINING SPRINGHOUSE AT A'STURGUS STATION IN JUNE 1923. BY ROGERS CLARK BALLARD THRUSTON. THE FILSON CLUB. THE SITE, THEN OWNED BY THE ARTERBURN FAMILY, WAS LATER ACQUIRED BY WILLIAM MARSHALL BULLITT, AND IS NOW PRESERVED, ALONG WITH THE NEARBY CHRISTIAN LOG HOUSE BY THE OXMOOR CEMETERY CORPORATION.

...I don't think that this Country even in its Infant State bore so Gloomy an Aspect as it does at present. The loss of Colonel Christian (whom the Inhabitants had great future hopes in) hath Caused general Uneasyness...

From George Rogers Clark to Patrick Henry, April or May 1786. Yale University Library.

building, except old Mr Asturgus who seems willing and even desirous of Building one, but has no person about him to wait on his Wounded Son, & to do the drudgery about his plantation."[56] His "plantation" was near where Edward Tyler would create his settlement on Chenoweth Run, earlier known as A'Sturgus's Run. Minard A'Sturgus was also killed by Indians near Vincennes in 1786. Brothers John and James A'Sturgus would move on to Missouri after working for Anne Christian at Saltsburg, the salt works at Bullitt's Lick patented to William Christian.[57]

Col. William Christian had intended to move from his Montgomery County residence, called Mahanaim, to Kentucky at least as early as 1780, when he was appointed county lieutenant for Jefferson County. Besides having a large tract on Beargrass Creek, Christian also possessed land about 12 miles south of Beargrass that was made valuable by its salt spring. Used on the frontier as a preservative, salt was a precious commodity, as Robert E. McDowell was quick to point out in his seminal study on saltmaking at Bullitt's Lick delivered in a paper to The Filson Club in 1956.[58] The land on the appropriately named Salt River was surveyed by Thomas Bullitt in 1773 and again the next year by John Floyd's party, by which survey the grant to Christian was made. When Bullitt's Lick was inspected by Christian's brother-in-law, William Fleming, in November 1779, a thriving operation was being carried out in "25 kettles belonging to the commonwealth." By the time Christian first had the opportunity to inspect his saltworks, which McDowell refers to as "the first commercial saltworks in Kentucky," it was being called Saltsburg instead of Bullitt's Lick.[59]

While a teenager, William Christian had served in the latter stages of the French and Indian War, after which he read law with Patrick Henry, whose sister, Anne, he married about 1765. By 1774, he was lieutenant colonel of the Second Virginia Regiment, and then became colonel of the First Virginia Regiment when Henry resigned that position. Leading "an independant expedition" against the Cherokees in 1776, he was able to effect a treaty. Early in 1781, John Floyd wrote Governor Jefferson that he did not

THE WILLIAM CHRISTIAN LOG HOUSE, 6 JUNE 1920. WARREN K. FREDERICK COLLECTION, UNIVERSITY OF LOUISVILLE PHOTOGRAPHIC ARCHIVES. WINGS WERE ADDED TO THE REAR OF THE HOUSE EARLY ON AND TO THE SOUTH SIDE IN THE 1950S.

anticipate Col. Christian's arrival in Louisville for some time to take control of the Jefferson militia, of which Floyd was second in command. When George Rogers Clark learned soon after that Christian had resigned, he quickly recommended John Floyd for the position of county lieutenant. William and Anne Christian finally made preparations in the spring of 1785 to come to A'Sturgus Station, located on the southern edge of a 2,000-acre grant he received for military service.[60] At the compound, located near a strong spring feeding Beargrass Creek, they erected three log structures and settled in, but not without great anxiety. Anne Henry Christian would describe their peril to her sister in late 1785. "We are all well here thank the Lord & we shoud be happy enough only the Indians are very troublesome, having been Continually in our County this fall & killd several people. We cant go out in the least safety, & expect times will be much worse next spring & summer as the Indians have refused the treaty, & as we are very near the fronteer we cant think of staying here much longer. We intend to move off to Danville & continue there until some better prospect here." However, she would conclude, "if we had peace here & a trade I shoud like Beargrass as it is the flower of all Kentuckey."[61]

After William Christian was killed, his widow began referring to their compound at A'Sturgus Station as Fort William.[62] A roadside marker in front of a small, nicely crafted stone house on the northwest corner of Shelbyville Road and Whipps Mill Road notes the existence of Fort William. For many years this structure was known as the Eight-Mile House (not to be confused with a later, well-known night spot by the same name located not far to the west). However, by the time the house had become endangered in early 1967, it was being touted as having been built by William Christian.[63] The Commonwealth of Kentucky and Jefferson County soon purchased the property, but then no preservation group stepped forward to restore or renovate the stone structure. As it sat idle, its history was scrutinized, and after considerable wrangling, the Kentucky Heritage Commission concluded the building

EAST VIEW OF ORIGINAL FRAME PORTION.
FROM _MY LIFE AT OXMOOR_ (1911).

RIGHT: PLAT OF OXMOOR PROPERTY PREPARED
FOR PUBLICATION IN _MY LIFE AT OXMOOR_
(1911).

Oxmoor, as now existing, fronts as to one field, on the Louisville and Shelbyville Turnpike. But this was not its original boundary. My father purchased that field (known as the Evinger field) in order to reach the turnpike. The old road ran farther back, I think along the north or front line of the original or Oxmoor tract. In my boyhood there were manifest traces of a road along that front. Whether it was the original road used by the early settlers I do not know. That I should not have learned or have remembered, shows the carelessness of youth.

From Thomas W. Bullitt, _My Life at Oxmoor_ (Louisville, 1911), 4-5.

Supporting Col. Bullitt's contention is John Filson's map of 1784 that positions the road from Central Kentucky running south of Linn's Station, A'Sturgus Station, and Dutch Station; but the map also delineates the trail from Bullitt's Lick to the Falls of the Ohio as intersecting that road from the east at Floyd's Station, which never happened. And Luke Munsell's more refined map of 1819, places the road from Middletown to Louisville passing north of Soldier's Retreat and therefore north of nearby Oxmoor. The traces of the road Col. Bullitt recalled may very well have been the original drive leading from the Shelbyville turnpike along the grant boundary to the head of the present avenue to the Oxmoor residence.

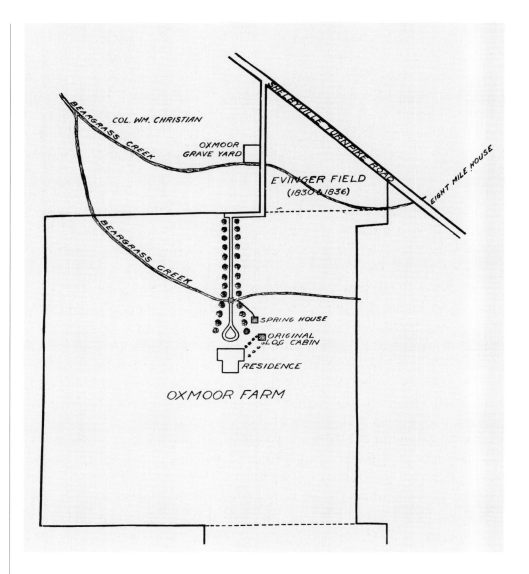

was not "historically significant enough" to warrant further state funding, and recommended its resale.[64] To preserve the obviously old, but as yet undated, stone structure, the county undertook to place restrictive covenants within a new deed, while changing the property's zoning designation from residential to commercial. The structure was converted into a design studio, while the residential character of the corner was also preserved.[65]

Alexander Scott Bullitt (1761/2-1816), the son of Cuthbert Bullitt, a Virginia lawyer and jurist, was probably already living at A'Sturgus Station when the Christians arrived in 1785. He married their youngest daughter Priscilla, and was pursuing marauding Indians north of the Ohio River with a small group of men when William Christian was fired upon and killed.[66] The veteran of various military campaigns, whom Humphrey Marshall referred to in his 1812 _History of Kentucky_ as "a man of activity, intelligence, and enterprise," was buried in front of the log structure, which still exists in its saddlebag form. The burial site was later walled, and continues to serve as the Bullitt family graveyard. Christian County, formed in 1796, honored his presence on the Kentucky frontier.[67]

In 1787, Alexander Scott Bullitt purchased a 1,200-acre tract south of A'Sturgus Station. The land was mentioned in deeds as being "commonly called and known by the name of the Oxmoor."[68] In literary history, Laurence Sterne referred to Oxmoor in *The Life and Opinions of Tristram Shandy, Gentleman* of 1759-1767 as the "fine, large, whinny, undrained, unimproved common, belonging to the Shandy-estate." (The Bullitt family preferred to say the name was derived from published literature rather than from a recorded deed.)

Near a spring on the Oxmoor property, the Bullitts first erected a log house, probably also in a saddlebag configuration, and then set about acquiring the materials for a more refined residence.[69] In the spring of 1791, or thereabouts, they moved into the frame house, clad in clapboard, with four rooms downstairs. The corner fireplaces in each room were rare on the frontier, but on each side they were tied into a single chimney on the gable sides which looked quite common. The frame portion of Oxmoor remains at the rear of a major addition made in 1829 that will be discussed later.

Alexander Scott Bullitt became lieutenant in the county militia, a trustee of the town of Louisville, and helped frame the Kentucky constitution in 1792. He was among the initial state senators elected and was presiding when Bullitt County was formed in 1796. He was elected lieutenant governor in 1800, and after additional legislative service, retired to Oxmoor where he died on 13 April 1816.[70] He was survived by four children by Priscilla Christian Bullitt, who died in 1806, and three children by Mary Churchill Prather Bullitt, whom he had married in 1807.

Jefferson County endured the losses of Floyd, Christian, A'Sturgus, and numerous others, to Indian attacks; and by 1790, the influx of Revolutionary veterans seeking their promised land and fortune had caused the Indians to withdraw, and the region was stabilized enough to allow the pio-

Meanwhile Richard Taylor had gone out to Kentucky to make his uncleared holdings habitable, returning eastward in the spring of 1785 to bring his wife and children to the Dark and Bloody Ground....Their log house was situated on Beargrass Creek, five miles east of the swampy village of Louisville, on a four-hundred-acre place called Springfield which then amounted to little more than wilderness. Zachary was eight months old when he, his brothers, and his parents arrived at the new Kentucky home.

From Holman Hamilton, *Zachary Taylor: Soldier of the Republic* (Indianapolis, 1941), 25.

ORIGINAL TAYLOR FAMILY VAULT AT SPRINGFIELD. BY ROGERS CLARK BALLARD THRUSTON, 14 MARCH 1924, THE FILSON CLUB. THE EGYPTIAN DESIGN OF THE STONE FRONT IS NOW HIDDEN BY A ROUGH COVERING OF STUCCO.

WOOD CUT FROM *THE NEW YORK DAILY GRAPHIC*, 19 JANUARY 1875.

ENGRAVING BY HENRY SARTAIN, PHILADELPHIA, 1848, THE FILSON CLUB.

After General Taylor's death at the White House, his remains were taken to his large farm near Louisville at a place called Gilman's Point for burial.

All of [Floyd] Parks' men were at the funeral, Smith with the number and speaks of it as the grandest funeral he ever saw as there were thousands present.[74] He was buried with great military honors. It was a sad and memorable day all through the United States. His large fine horse, the one he used in Mexico, whose name was Whitey, was dressed in mourning. So many people, to keep in memory this sad event, pulled many hairs out of his tail to make watch chains and different ornaments with, it became quite necessary, in order to keep any hair on him, to lock him up and many offered large sums of money for him. Every day after the funeral he was taken out saddled and exercised accompanied by a large Newfoundland dog owned by the General, but no one was allowed to ride him, being led by his groom.

From Harry Smith, *Fifty Years of Slavery* (Grand Rapids, 1891), 105-106.

neer inhabitants to abandon the station settlements for individual homesteads. Col. Richard Taylor was a part of the post-war wave of migration westward into Kentucky. It has been repeated frequently that in 1785 Col. Taylor erected a temporary log cabin on land near the Ohio River east of Louisville he had received from a military grant. He had already been to the Falls of the Ohio at least twice in 1769, and his brother, Hancock, had been killed by Indians as he returned to Fincastle County to record surveys made at the Falls in 1774, so perhaps the Taylors believed they were entitled to some land.[71]

A flaw in these accounts is that the favored land, south of the Ohio River and above the Falls had already been granted to veterans of the French and Indian War. Col. Taylor did not obtain this land from a military grant, but purchased 360 acres by a deed dated 12 March 1792.[72] He called the property Springfield. Subsequently, the three-bay, side-hall, west portion of a two-story, brick house, was erected. Zachary left home for the military in 1808. He would interrupt that career, but only briefly in 1815-1816, to try his hand at farming.[73] His mother, Sarah Strother Taylor died in 1822, his father Richard in 1829. They were buried in a family graveyard southeast of the homestead where the President was buried in a hillside vault, Egyptian in style, that was erected in haste to hold his sarcophagus.

Zachary Taylor, veteran of the War of 1812, the Black Hawk and Seminole wars, and successful Whig candidate for President in 1848, died in office on 9 July 1850 at the age of 65. In the funeral procession, his horse-drawn hearse was preceded by the pall bearers including General Thomas S. Jesup, who had married Ann Croghan and was frequently at Locust Grove. The hearse was followed by Taylor's fine horse, Old Whitey, with spurs and stirrups reversed. In October, his remains were transported by train to Pitts-

burgh and then brought by packet steamer to Louisville.[75] After a public procession from the wharf to Springfield on November first, his body was placed in a hastily arranged vault with earthen sides and top. Old Whitey was brought to Louisville on mail packet soon after.[76]

A few years later, Congress paid $1,700 for a permanent vault to be constructed, in which a marble bust of Taylor was "in a niche at the end of the aisle and separates the caskets of the dead." Responsibility for maintenance became a burden to the Taylor family. After lengthy discussion about erecting an appropriate monument and concern about the deteriorating condition of the vault and grounds, in 1883, a shaft of Maine granite was placed nearby, designed by the local monument maker Charles W. Pool then of the J. S. Clark & Co. Atop is a marble statue of Taylor, carved in Italy.[77] Consideration was given by the Kentucky Legislature in 1918 to make the homestead into a public park and improve the road from Brownsboro Road to the cemetery, but to no avail.[78] However, on 6 May 1926, the remains of the Taylors were transferred from the 1850 stone vault to a mausoleum of classical design erected by the Federal government in conjunction with the creation of the Zachary Taylor National Cemetery.

In 1990, a Florida novelist theorized that Old Rough and Ready might have been the first American President to be assassinated.[79] She initiated the legal proceedings to have remains tested for arsenic. When the Jefferson County coroner consented to an autopsy, contending he realized "I might have a possible homicide," a media event ensued.[80] On 17 June 1991, the mausoleum was entered and the heavy lid of Taylor's marble sarcophagus was removed exposing a deteriorated walnut casket "with lead lining."[81] The remains were removed for autopsy, and as the tests were being conducted by

Our worthy Magistrate, who is ever on the alert for good in every way, is at present superintending the pike making in Brady Lane, near the Taylor Monument. This pike [Blankenbaker Lane] will connect the Brownsboro road and river road, which will be a wonderful convenience to travelers in automobiles, and also opening beautiful building sites in this neighborhood.

From "St. Matthews," *The Jeffersonian*, 4 May 1911.

TAYLOR FAMILY CEMETERY, 1925. CAUFIELD & SHOOK COLL, 75125, UNIVERSITY OF LOUISVILLE PHOTOGRAPHIC ARCHIVES.

OPPOSITE: ZACHARY TAYLOR NATIONAL CEMETERY, CREATED IN 1925. CAUFIELD & SHOOK COLLECTION. 75123, UNIVERSITY OF LOUISVILLE PHOTOGRAPHIC ARCHIVES.

Dr. George Nichols, Kentucky's chief medical examiner, various contentions about Taylor's demise were floated. But the scientific tests revealed no foul play.[82]

Hancock Taylor purchased Springfield from his sibling heirs to Richard Taylor's estate in 1832 for $13,500. Judging from the trim detailing in the wing added to the east side of the house's main block, it would appear to have been erected after Hancock acquired the property.[83] His widow and son continued to reside there until 1867, when it was sold to George McCurdy. Apparently, McCurdy added wooden verandas and a heavy-bracketed tin roof.[84] He sold it in 1884 to Matthew Brady, who may have painted the exterior for the first time in 1895.[85] Blankenbaker Lane, south of Locust Grove, was known for years as Brady's Lane.[86] A son, Dr. John A. Brady, conveyed the property to Emanuel Levi in 1926.[87] Architect Frederic L. Morgan made substantial improvements to the house at that time, and when the Victorian porches were removed in 1966, he devised a new entrance stoop. The house had undergone restoration by *Courier-Journal* cartoonist Hugh S. Haynie when it was partially destroyed by the 1974 tornado. Structural repairs were made and an appropriate roof was installed. Since 1981, the house has been cared for in a most considerate manner by William Gist, DMD, and his late wife, Betty.[88]

Richard Taylor's land holdings had been considerably larger before he sold the western portion, consisting of 324 acres, to John Veech in 1806.[89] Certified as a surveyor by the College of William and Mary, Veech was about 38 years old when he arrived at Dutch Station in 1785. Reportedly, he erected a log house on his new land; but several years before he died in 1817, he sold the land back to Richard Taylor, after his son, Alexander, had declined to improve it. Born at Dutch Station in 1787, Alexander Veech had married Olivia Winchester and they first purchased her father's place, Vale of Eden, near Lyndon.[90] However, in 1833, they reacquired the Taylor land, and erected a two-story brick house on a rise thought to have been cleared of trees by Indians, which they called Indian Hill. Son Richard Snowden Veech (1833-1918) was born in this house, and when his father died in 1866, he took over the estate.

According to the *History of Ohio Falls Cities* (1882), R. S. Veech "has been peculiarly successful as a farmer, banker, railway official, and as a breeder of trotting stock." After graduating from Centre College in 1853, marrying, and farming for some years, in 1869 he helped form with Bushrod O'Bannon the Farmers and Drovers Bank, serving as its cashier and later briefly as president.[91] In 1879, Veech became involved in the successful reorganization of the Louisville, New Albany & Chicago Railway, becoming president of the railroad that would become known as the Monon. He purchased the New Albany street railway system in 1903.[92]

In 1872, Veech undertook the breeding of trotting horses exclusively.[93] Starting with Princeps, a two-year-old bred by A. J. Alexander, and six brood mares, within ten years his operation was the second largest producer in the state. With the large trotting-stock farm, Glenview, further out Brownsboro

---

Indian Hill Farm is a fine tract of rich, rolling land, with springs of the purest and best water bubbling up in the most convenient places on every part of it. The whole of it is down in grass, which is mostly bluegrass, though orchard grass is deemed worthy of no little attention. Indian Hill received its name in consequence of an event that took place away back in pioneer times. It was when there was only a fort to be seen where Louisville now stands that the savages to the number of three hundred encamped on and around the spot now occupied by Mr. Veech's residence.

From John Duncan, "Indian Hill Stock Farm," *The Courier-Journal,* 14 December 1877.

Road, and those along the Shelbyville Road, including that of J. J. Douglas, the center of trotting-stock breeding was in Jefferson County. While some trotters were bred to race, their useful function was for driving. Later, the old farm at Dutch Station, consisting of almost 800 acres, was also put into a stock operation, run by son Bethel Veech.[94]

By the time I grew up there, the glamorous horse breeding was past. On the hillsides were some cattle and sheep....Our crops were varied—the main one being potatoes, which were sold at the St. Matthews Produce Exchange, one of the largest potato markets at that time.

From Agnes Veech Viser, daughter of James Nichols Veech.

Sometime after taking over his father's Indian Hill farm, Richard Snowden Veech made an elaborate entrance wing, marked by an Italianate tower. The addition, however, was removed in 1924, when the residence was acquired by the Sidney Smiths.[95] Some 200 acres of Indian Hill, inherited by Annie S. Veech, M.D., was purchased by the Louisville Country Club.[96] Dr. Veech had been born at Indian Hill. After traveling extensively, she began the study of medicine at age 34, and graduated from the Women's Medical College of Pennsylvania in 1909. Returning to Louisville, Dr. Veech organized the first maternal- and child-health program in Kentucky.[97] The remaining part (302 acres) of Indian Hill, inherited by her brother, James Nichols Veech, was sold to a syndicate including I. T. Axton, R. S., J. K., and D. R. Reynolds, and Paul F. Semonin and subdivided as Indian Hills—"The Home Community Adjoining The Louisville Country Club," laid out by Olmsted Brothers.[98]

Indian Hill had two good springs and a major source of the Muddy Fork of Beargrass Creek flowed along the eastern edge of the property, providing enough water for the Croghans to operate a mill where the stream crossed Locust Grove. Obviously by its very name, Springfield or Springfields, the Taylor property was also well watered, a prerequisite in homestead site selection. But how did Indian Hill and Springfield, further to the east, con-

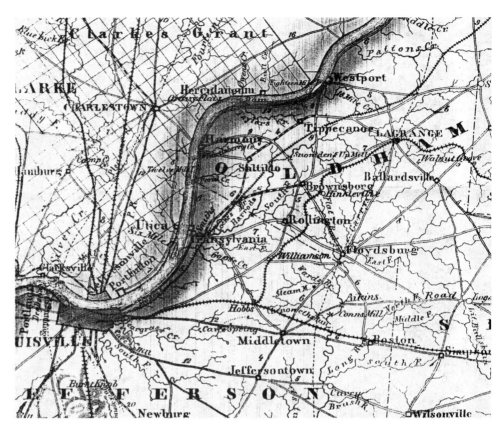

form to the other pioneer-site requirement of accessibility? The properties were not initially on or near a main road. The Brownsboro Road was made later; Brownsboro, the town, was not incorporated until 1830, three years after its post office was established. The primary accesses to Indian Hill and Springfield were probably wagon roads up from the river or along farm boundaries from the Shelbyville Road. Unfortunately, little is known about the early roads in Jefferson County. The first map that shows the road system and property bounds was published by G. T. Bergmann in 1858.

So while Alexander Veech and Richard Taylor might wend their way to and from Louisville via the Shelbyville Road or the River Road, how did their neighbor to the south, Frederic Edwards, travel to town? The two-story brick house he built about 1790 shows on the 1858 map as being south of the Westport Road. By the time the 1879 atlas appeared, the road had been rerouted in front (south) of the house, then owned by Alfred Herr. Certainly some precursor of the Westport Road must have been in place by the 1790s, but no record of a survey being ordered can be found in the early Jefferson County Court minutes. No such road is delineated on Luke Munsell's 1818 map of Kentucky. However, by the time J. H. Colston & Co. published its "New Map of Kentucky" in 1856, there were two routes shown to Westport: the old one along the Ohio River, and a second originating as it does now on the Shelbyville Road and then running through Worthington, Rollington, and Brownsboro before terminating in Westport. However by 1840, Westport's promise as a thriving harbor on the Ohio River, unencumbered by limestone outcropping as Louisville was, had been eclipsed, and it was no longer the seat

My dad Norbourne Oldham Rudy was named for Aunt Kitty Oldham. Grandmother Rudy was a Hubbard. They owned the corner of Hubbards and Rudy lanes, and that is where my daddy and his brother were born. When she passed away, she left the Hubbard house and 10 acres to my daddy. He sold it for $1,000 an acre to Ed Wilder, who was in the landscape business. His son tore the house down and built a new one. You went into a good-size entrance hall and then the stairs went up to two bedrooms. The kitchen had been built away from the house and was connected under roof by a beautiful brick patio. Later they made the dining room into the kitchen, and made another room into the dining room and they also had a bedroom and sitting room downstairs.

Old Dr. Hopson in St. Matthews sent Daddy to Denver for his health, and Mother followed him there when she was pregnant with me. I was born there on April 4, 1904. Daddy bought a little house on Westport Road and then a big, white, frame house, where Target is today, from the Leverones. I used to ride my pony over to Grandmother's, and at three o'clock we would have lemonade and tea cakes. Daddy got into the real estate business with Blakemore Wheeler and he opened up many subdivisions including Lakeside, Norwood and Elmwood. He also fooled in politics. He lived to be 96 and he died in 1977.[101]

From interview of Hope Oldham Rudy Shipley, 4 November 1997.

of Oldham County.

When Frederic Edwards acquired the 500-acre tract from Alexander Scott Bullitt in 1788, he was mainly attracted by the good spring, another of the headwaters of the Muddy Fork, around which he built a stone springhouse. His brick house, a hundred yards from the springhouse, was the subject of a *Courier-Journal* article in 1891.[99] When Edwards died in 1813, the dwelling and property were devised to his widow, Mary Rudy Edwards, and a son. A year later, they sold the homestead to her brother-in-law, John Herr, who had married her sister, Elizabeth Susan Rudy, and it has remained in the family ever since.[100]

The Rudy sisters' father was Jacob Rudy, who after participating in the Revolutionary War, had decided to move to Kentucky from central Pennsylvania. He brought along his family and young John Herr, the son of a neighbor friend killed in the conflict, but on the trip down the Ohio River,

Hubbard house at Hubbards and Rudy lanes. University of Louisville Photographic Archives.

Major Joseph Walker Taylor was very fond of coon hunting. He had two hounds which were trained coon dogs. There was a woods on the farm which Bob Hite now owns and the Major went out one night to hunt coons on this place. A storm came up. At that time there was a Methodist church on the Westport Road on a corner next to Bob Hite's place. It was on Albert Herr's place. It was known as Rudy's Chapel. Like a number of old country churches it had the reputation of being haunted. The Major and his two hounds went inside the Church. He claimed that the hounds went up towards the pulpit and then ran back out of the church. The Major said that he never was afraid of Yankees nor Mexicans but he was afraid of goblins and he and his dogs took to the lane that used to be between the old Albert Herr place and the old Alfred Herr place.

From Hardin H. Herr, "St. Matthews History," *The St. Matthews Booster*, 17 April 1930.

his wife died. Rudy obtained land from William Spangler, and built a log house located near the Rudy family cemetery behind the Christ Church United Methodist on Brownsboro Road, opposite the old entrance (now Blankenbaker Lane) to Springfield. Subsequently he erected a small, stone abode for his son, Daniel, upon his marriage to Mary Shively in 1803. That house, much improved, and called Microphylla, is at the end of Old Stone Lane off Rudy Lane.[102]

Daniel and Mary Shively Rudy's daughter, Lydia, married Thomas Wines Hubbard in 1822. A carpenter, Hubbard is credited with building houses in the area, and Norbourn Arterburn was apprenticed to him before striking out on his own.[103] Little is known about Hubbard, but the *Louisville Daily Courier* on 21 January 1854 claimed that he and J. O. Sawyer were architects of Walnut Street Baptist Church. The Hubbards' house, which he probably built, was on the northeast corner of Hubbards and Rudy lanes. Their daughter, Ella, married Frederick Oldham Rudy, who continued to reside in the frame house. They were the parents of James Hubbard Rudy and Norbourne Oldham Rudy.

As already noted, after Elizabeth Susan Rudy Herr died in 1814, her widower, farmer and blacksmith John Herr, purchased the property and brick home on Westport Road occupied by her widowed sister Mary Rudy Edwards. Within two years, however, John Herr married Elizabeth Wayne Simcoe, the niece of General Anthony Wayne and a widow of reputed wealth. Where they continued to reside is murky, but until hard evidence to the contrary is produced, it can be assumed they lived in the old Edwards place, until John Herr deeded it to his son, Alfred Herr, in 1838. Alfred's son, William Wallace Herr, was born in the house and attended the Buckeye School, which was located at the southeast corner of the property in a grove of Buckeye trees.[104] (After the frame schoolhouse was dismantled and moved to Herr Lane, the small brick church known as Rudy Chapel, which occupied the same lot, was torn down.[105]) Wallace Herr served in the Civil War as a scout for the Confederate Orphan

Brigade after helping to organize Capt. Benson Ormsby's cavalry company in the State Guard. Alfred deeded the property to his daughter Jane Helen "Jennie" Herr, wife of Samuel Sneed Hite. She died of food poisoning after the wedding of Fanny Herr and Albert Snooks at Magnolia Farm, the nearby residence of Albert G. Herr in 1891.[106] When the former deputy sheriff and retired farmer and real estate dealer S. S. Hite died in 1911, the property was inherited by his two sons, Alfred Herr Hite and Robert Warner Hite.[107] Alfred was a graduate of Louisville Male High School and the University of Louisville School of Law. He served as superintendent of Jefferson County schools from 1894 until 1898, and then in the Jefferson Circuit Court Clerk's office. He was a student of history, a collector of Indian artifacts and an accomplished gardener, known as "Farmer Hite." He died on 14 February 1923 at the age of 58 having been struck by an eastbound interurban at Browns Lane.[108] His younger brother R. W. Hite continued to reside on Westport Road until he died there at the age of 92 in 1961. The property was inherited by his two daughters, Anne Hite Corn and Helen Hite Henchey Sallee, and it remains in the family of the latter.

The five-bay, two-story, brick house with a rear wing, now painted white, at 726 Waterford Road in the Wexford Place subdivision was built by John Herr before he deeded the old Edwards place to his son in 1838. His youngest daughter Ann and her husband Norbourn Arterburn lived in this house after being married in 1840. When Herr died in 1852, Ann Arterburn received a half interest in the house. Southwest of that property is a very similar, but obviously older brick house that has been owned by J. Paul and Sally Sherwood Keith, Jr., since 1944. It was the residence of John Herr's son, George, who married his half sister, Sarah Simcoe in 1825. The land on which the house was built was deeded perhaps after the fact from father to son in 1832.[109]

BOTH PHOTOGRAPHS OF THE GEORGE AND SARAH HERR HOUSE IN 1945 AS RENOVATION WAS UNDERTAKEN BY NEW OWNERS, THE J. PAUL KEITH, JRS. COURTESY OF SALLY SHERWOOD KEITH.

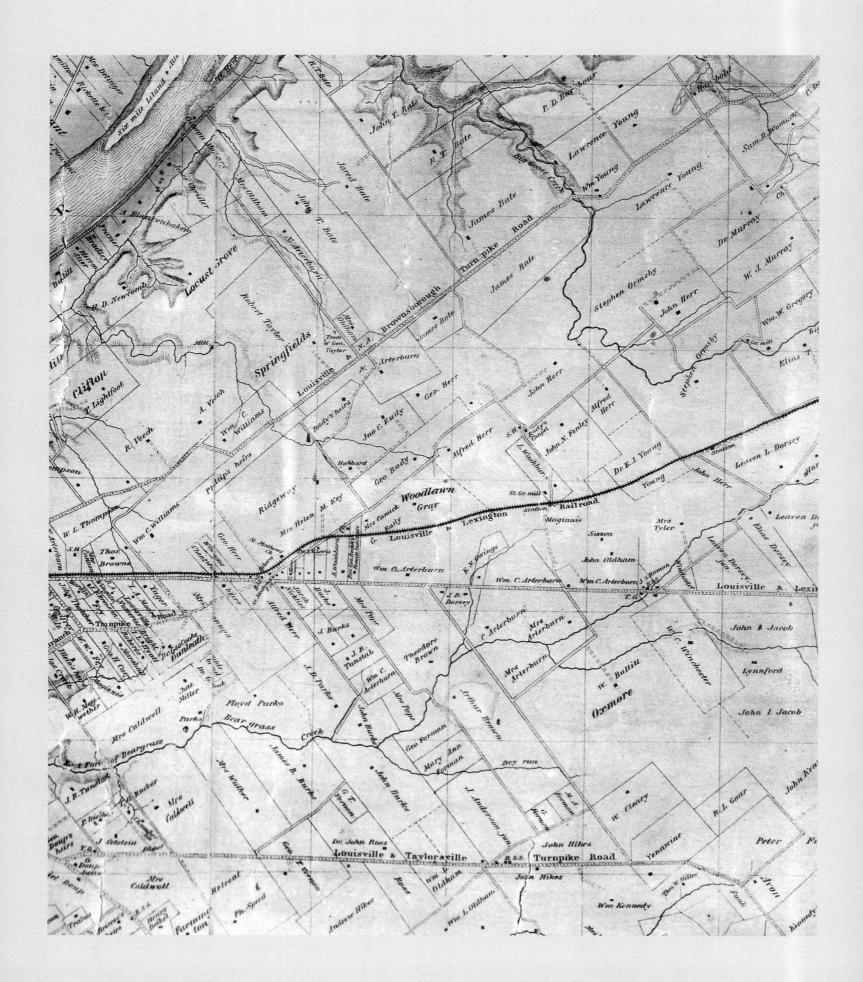

Alexander Scott Bullitt's 18-year-old daughter, Helen Scott Bullitt, married 40-year-old Henry Massie on 9 November 1808. Massie continued to enrich himself by land speculation in Ohio, and the couple acquired a 437-acre tract near Oxmoor in 1811 from Benjamin Sebastian for $4,000, simultaneously mortgaging the property to him for $8,000. The deed was released late in 1816, and it was about that time the Massies built Ridgeway, regarded as one of the finest Federal style houses in Kentucky.[1] Nearby Spring Station, erected a few years earlier, but also in brick, is the only other local example of the linear, five-part massing system. Ridgeway, however, is different from Spring Station and other similar residences in Central Kentucky with five-part floor plans, in that it has a recessed portico entrance.

After Henry Massie's death, "Nelly" Bullitt Massie married John Lewis Martin (1779-1854). He was considered one of Louisville's wealthiest citizens when he died. Major Martin's grandchildren included Catherine Anderson, who married Thomas S. Kennedy and lived in Crescent Hill, and Pattie Anderson, who married Richard Ten Broeck. The Ten Broecks later purchased the John J. Jacob place on the Shelbyville Road and renamed it Hurstbourne after

CHAPTER II

ANTEBELLUM

ADDRESSES

OPPOSITE: SECTION FROM G. T. BERGMANN'S 1858 MAP OF JEFFERSON COUNTY, KENTUCKY. LIBRARY OF CONGRESS.

BELOW: RIDGEWAY AFTER RESTORATION BY CAROLE AND BEN BIRKHEAD, 1996. BY SAMUEL W. THOMAS.

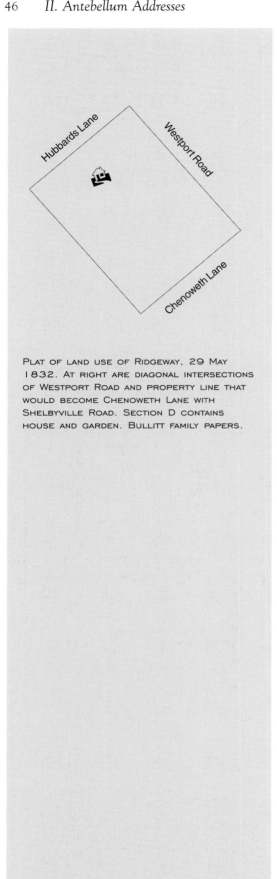

PLAT OF LAND USE OF RIDGEWAY, 29 MAY
1832. AT RIGHT ARE DIAGONAL INTERSECTIONS
OF WESTPORT ROAD AND PROPERTY LINE THAT
WOULD BECOME CHENOWETH LANE WITH
SHELBYVILLE ROAD. SECTION D CONTAINS
HOUSE AND GARDEN. BULLITT FAMILY PAPERS.

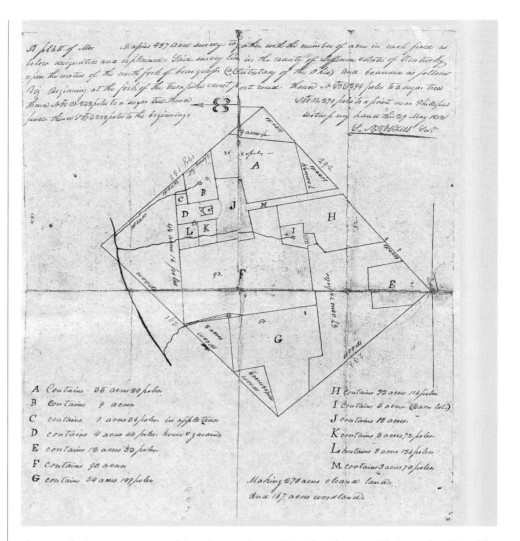

the English estate owned by the Duke of Portland, an old friend of Dick's. Orville Martin Anderson, who had become very rich at his grandfather's death, died suddenly in Rome in 1857, leaving but a single heir, Mary Martin Anderson. She was raised by her aunts, and on 26 April 1871, she eloped with Meriwether Lewis Clark, grandson of the explorer, and grandnephew of George Rogers Clark. Together they would formulate and foster Churchill Downs and the Kentucky Derby.[2] Helen Bullitt Martin's third marriage was in 1857 to Col. Marshall Key (1788-1860), and she was known thereafter as Aunt Key.[3]

Helen Scott Bullitt Massie's brother, William Christian Bullitt (1793-1877), inherited their father's property, Oxmoor, and in 1829, he set out to repair the old frame part and to add three rooms in brick to the front, tied by a transverse hall. Ten years before, Bullitt had married Mildred Ann Fry of Danville, whose sister, Lucy, was the wife of John Speed. During 1815-1816, the Speeds built Farmington on the Bardstown Road based upon drawings by Paul Skidmore.[4] The contract for the carpentry work on Farmington has recently been uncovered in William C. Bullitt's papers on microfilm at The Filson Club by reference specialist Pen Bogert. Interestingly, William C. Bullitt's front addition also had a recessed portico, similar to both Farmington

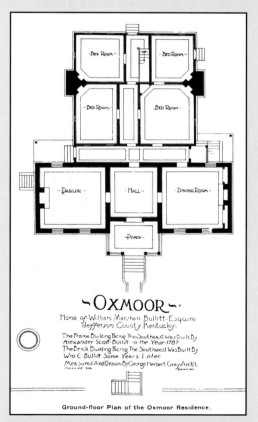

FLOOR PLAN MEASURED AND DRAWN BY GEORGE HERBERT GRAY. FROM *MY LIFE AT OXMOOR* (1911).

and Ridgeway. This Massie-Speed family connection, forged in 1819, could mean that Ridgeway was built after that date, and there are letters in the Bullitt family papers that indicate the Massies were not in residence at Ridgeway until sometime in the 1820s. However, there is a direct link between Ridgeway and Oxmoor. William C. Bullitt's contract for the brick addition specifies "one Portico of which 4 feet to recess under the Rough [roof]...on the Plan of the Porticoe of H. Massie." Remarkably, the contracts, which included one for painting and were executed in 1829 by John Chenoweth, Ejiaphroditus Titus Northam, Nathan Sackett, and Benjamin T. Rue, are preserved in the Bullitt family papers.[5]

William C. Bullitt had studied law, but for health considerations he spent much time at Oxmoor as a gentlemen farmer. He represented Jefferson County with David Meriwether in the third state constitutional convention in 1849 as his father had done in the previous convention fifty years before. He was an advocate of the dueling system and opposed the constitutional provision that became part of the oath of office.[6] During the Civil War, Oxmoor was closed and Bullitt and his wife, Mildred Ann Fry Bullitt, moved into Louisville. Before he died he had W. J. McGonigale survey the Oxmoor property and divide its 1,029 acres into six tracts for his living children. In order to provide access to all the parcels, an avenue was laid off perpendicular to an old road that ran along the west side of the property that connected the Shelbyville Road with the Taylorsville Road. That road is delineated on both the 1858 map and the 1879 atlas of Jefferson County. However, the road was subsequently abandoned, and there was some consideration of remaking it in 1914.[7] W. C. Bullitt was boarding at the Willard Hotel when he died on 28 August 1877. His funeral took place at the residence of his daughter, Mrs. Henry Chenoweth, and his remains were interred in the family graveyard.[8]

The frame house he had enlarged with brick at Oxmoor was on the tract devised to his daughter, Susan Peachy Bullitt, who had married U.S. Senator Archibald Dixon, a widower, in 1853. However, when Dixon retired they went to Paducah where he resumed the practice of law and farmed. She

A section of Division survey by J. W. Henning and Philip Speed, filed 23 December 1853. Louisville Chancery Court case 9146. Old Browns Lane is shown running top to bottom and in an arc over Beargrass Creek and between the James Brown homestead and the family cemetery. The site of Dutch Station, based upon the photograph on page 29, was just south of Beargrass Creek in an area opposite the western edge of present-day Brown Park that unfortunately is covered over by I-64.

would later write a book on Senator Dixon's successful efforts to repeal the Missouri Compromise.

The Bullitt family did not return to Oxmoor until 1906 when William Marshall Bullitt, a grandson of William Christian Bullitt, began to reassemble the estate which had been divided up among the family. Eventually, the son of Thomas Walker Bullitt (1838-1910) who published *My Life at Oxmoor*, had acquired 1,000 acres in fourteen tracts. As for the initial improvements to the frame and brick house, all painted white, they were carried out by the prominent local architect George Herbert Gray. The gardens and grounds were laid out by Marian Cruger Coffin (1876-1957).[9]

James Brown had worked for David L. Ward selling salt, and in 1809 he married Urath Lawrence, the daughter of Samuel Lawrence. He began the acquisition of land immediately west of Oxmoor, at the center of which was the fine spring of the old Low Dutch Station.[10] Brown's holdings by 1824 comprised over a thousand acres between the Shelbyville and Taylorsville roads, and included a fine brick house, later called Wildwood (JF 311), which

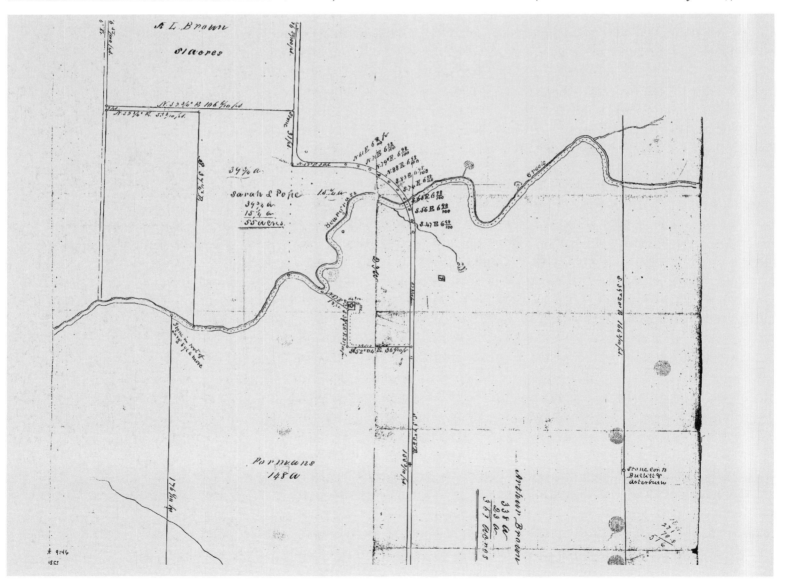

he reportedly erected in 1820.

"Grandpa was a man of intellectual tastes; an ardent Whig, and a great admirer of Henry Clay," a grandchild recalled. "He never voted the Democratic ticket, except once, when his son-in-law, Patrick Pope, was elected to Congress. He read *The Louisville Journal* and took the *Washington Intelligencer*; and was very much interested in the Congressional news. Grandpa loved to read history."[11] When James Brown died in 1853, the Dutch Station Farm was divided among his children, and the various parcels were made accessible along a road that later would be called appropriately Browns Lane. Bergmann's property map of 1858 also delineated the division of land for his two sons, Theodore and Arthur, and his married daughters: Mrs. Patrick Pope, Mrs. James Anderson, Jr., and Mrs. Thomas S. Forman. The latter was the mother of George W. Forman (1844-1901), who was a bookkeeper for wholesale whiskey concerns that became Brown, Forman & Company in 1891. He was the son of a large bagging and rope manufacturer, Thomas Seabrooke Forman.[12]

The land inherited by Sarah L. Pope included the Dutch Station site, as well as the Brown family cemetery. An effort got underway in 1945 by Louisa Anderson Waters to raise money for the cemetery's perpetual care and maintenance by the James and Urath Brown Graveyard Association.[13] The surrounding property was acquired by James V. Prather, who built a fine house on it, which was later the Bethel Veech home called Greyholt.

The part of James Brown's farm that included his residence was inherited by his youngest son, Arthur. In 1882, Edward S. Monohan, Sr., acquired the property, and later he would occupy the house. He had come to Louisville with his uncle who raised him, and after graduating from Notre Dame University in 1876, he went to work for the Bank of Kentucky. Monohan acquired a section of Arthur Brown's land before he obtained the Brown residence site and moved there. Along with his considerable farming interests, he remained deeply involved in banking and was one of the founders of the Bank of St. Matthews as well as the First National Bank. He was a director of various banking institutions. In 1894, he helped start the Gardeners and Farmers' Market Company, which operated the Haymarket on East Jefferson Street, serving later as president for twenty years. When he died in 1930, his son, Edward, was in charge of the family's large farming operation; his other son, John, was president of First National Bank.[14] The property has been subdivided, and the house now serves as the clubhouse for a residential development with an address at 400 Mallard Creek Road.

In 1842, John Norris Fenley began building a two-story, two-room-deep, brick house on the Westport Road where Herr Lane once terminated. His grandfather, Isaac Finley (later Fenley), acquired the property in 1790, erected a two-room log house, and had a license to operate two whiskey stills by 1797. It might be noted that his son, William Carr Fenley, married Frances Marion Williams, the granddaughter of distiller Evan Williams.[15] John Fenley's account book now in The Filson Club records his purchase of building material, and the particular brick cornice confirms the building period, although the form and style of the Georgian survival house were not new. The house

My grandfather Veech's place had a large spring on it which had been the Dutch Station when it existed there. But the spring water had given both my mother and her sister typhoid fever when they were little. So they drank water they brought in from St. Matthews. When I was young, it came in 5-gallon jugs. They also used cistern water from a cistern which had been next to the old house. That was their utility water. My grandfather had a World War I water wagon with a row of faucets along each side. And when that cistern water would get low, they would drive that to the St. Matthews railroad station which had a tank for the steam engines. Beargrass Creek was polluted by then. I think my grandfather ran septic overflow into the creek. When I played in the creek, they would point out the pipe and tell me to stay above it.

From interview of William M. Otter, Jr., 18 November 1996.

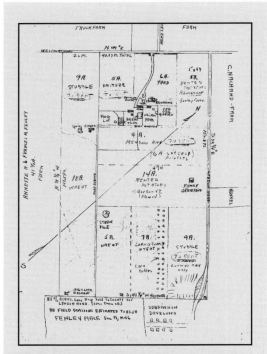

FARM PLAN FOR FENLEY PLACE, DATED 13
DECEMBER 1946. WESTPORT ROAD RUNS
LEFT TO RIGHT AT TOP. FENLEY-WILLIAMS
PAPERS, THE FILSON CLUB.

Uncle Martin was buried at Lexington—taken up on the railroad cars. My father accompanied Aunt Key to the funeral and brought her home with him. It was a glorious fall day; Indian summer I think. Father had never been on a train. We were eating supper in the "celler" when they came back. As they entered the room, Aunt Key in her mourning weeds leaning on his arm, my father, forgetful of all else but the novelty and beauty of the ride, exclaimed to my mother, "Ann, we have had a most delightful excursion!"

From Thomas W. Bullitt, *My Life at Oxmoor* (1911), 40. Helen Bullitt Massie Martin's second husband, former Lexington banker John Lewis Martin, died in 1854.

also had coal-burning grates as opposed to large wood-burning fireplaces. William C. Fenley was born in the house and lived on the property all his life, most of it as a farmer. His brother was Oscar Fenley, president of the National Bank of Kentucky and a stockholder in the Bank of St. Matthews. William's son, John Carr Fenley, remodeled the house in 1918 and added an inside kitchen in 1923. John's son, William Logan Fenley, sold the house and 100 acres to the Kentucky Lumber Company in 1961. The land was developed as Camelot, and the house was razed for the extension of Herr Lane.[16]

On 14 September 1849, *The Louisville Morning Courier* reported on a railroad excursion:

> We had the pleasure yesterday of taking a trip on the Louisville and Frankfort Railroad, and we beg leave to congratulate the citizens of Louisville on the excellence of the structure and general arrangements of the road. The "Iron Horse"—the new locomotive—works to perfection, and is creditable to the mechanical skill and genius of Norris & Brothers. It runs smoothly and with perfect regularity, and is managed by the engineer with great ease and precision.
>
> A large number of the prominent citizens of Louisville were present on this occasion, and enjoyed the trip very much. The cars were run out beyond the farm of the late Leven Lawrence, and made the trip in thirty minutes.[17] The return trip was varied by detaching a portion of the cars from the locomotive, and letting them run about three miles by the power of gravity. The grade of this part of the road is about fifty feet to the mile.

Earlier plans for the Lexington & Ohio Railroad to connect Lexington with the Ohio River at Westport and then Portland had languished in the depression that followed the Panic of 1837, but not before rights-of-way had been obtained such as through the Thomas T. Shreve property that would become the Woodlawn Race Course.[18] The Louisville & Frankfort Railroad was incorporated in 1847, and on 7 May 1849, *The Louisville Morning Courier* noted: "We had the pleasure on Saturday of seeing his Honor, the Mayor drive the first spike in the chain on which the Trail of the Louisville and Frankfort Railroad rests." By April 1850, Beargrass Creek had been bridged just north of the merger of the East (Middle) and South forks, allowing railroad cars access to a temporary depot at the head of Jefferson Street. They left there every morning for LaGrange. "The new arrangement will prove of great accommodation to travelers, and farmers bringing in their produce and taking out goods and groceries."[19] The railroad's superintendent announced in September 1850 that two trips a day would be made between Louisville and LaGrange.[20] Service would not be entirely completed to Frankfort until 1851, which is its accepted opening date, although travel was not yet safe nor pleasant. *The Louisville Daily Courier* remarked on 18 December 1851 that "great complaints are made daily by those who have to risk themselves on our 'model' railroad, of the filth and discomfort of the passenger cars," and "an invention to hold the cars down and keep them on the track, would be hailed with great pleasure." The trains were being "rendered almost entirely useless on account of the cold weather," and the stoves inside were too small—"about as large as a man's head, and supplied with coal that cannot be coaxed to burn."

The first real test of the railroad system came in July 1852, when the remains of Senator Henry Clay were brought to Louisville from Washington by boat, as had Zachary Taylor's, and then transported to Lexington on the railroad. The cortege of some 700 persons made the excursion on two trains pulled by "powerful locomotives." *The Louisville Daily Courier* reported that "as the train passed the various way stations between Louisville and Frankfort, large crowds of spectators were seen assembled, all anxious to manifest, even by their presence, some slight token of feeling regard for him they had long known, and whose memory they still cherished with the fondest affection and love."[21] As Clay had already resigned his seat effective the first of September, the Kentucky Legislature had determined that former Lieutenant Governor Archibald Dixon, who had been narrowly defeated for governor in 1851, would be his successor. Dixon, a widower, served until March 1855, during which time he married Susan Peachy Bullitt, born at Oxmoor, the daughter of William Christian.

The Louisville & Frankfort's rather circuitous route split at Anchorage with the main route running through LaGrange before heading southeast

Louisville and Frankfort Railroad. Quickest and cheapest route. The subscribers have put on a line of Four-Horse Coaches, to run daily to and from Frankfort and the terminus of the Railroad. Passengers will find this the cheapest, speediest, and most pleasant route between Louisville and Frankfort. Leave Frankfort daily at 8 A.M., and the railroad terminus on arrival of the cars. Giltner & Link, Frankfort.

From *The Louisville Daily Journal*, 5 March 1851.

LOOKING EAST TOWARD TRAIN STATION ABOUT 1915. COURTESY OF MARY ELIZABETH RATTERMAN RUCKRIEGEL. NOTE IN BACKGROUND HUGE BRICK STACK FOR BOILER OF THE ST. MATTHEWS PRODUCE EXCHANGE.

A single track of broken stone, with a quagmire on each side, and the whole space frequently submerged for several hundred yards, is the delectable and inviting entrance into the city of Louisville from all the central portions of the State. On this disgraceful and insufficient road an immense commerce passes, and a heavy tax is levied upon that commerce by the corporation which furnishes such facilities of intercommunication.

This was bad enough. But the turnpike company has quietly permitted another corporation utterly to destroy the value of this road as a public highway by the location of the Frankfort railroad within a few feet of the turnpike road for three miles, with a crossing [at Clifton] the most dangerous that can be conceived. No man can now travel or transport his produce upon this road except at the imminent and constant peril of life and property.

From "Louisville and Frankfort Turnpike and Railroad," *The Louisville Daily Journal*, 5 April 1852.

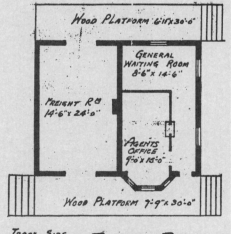

STATION BUILT AT ST. MATTHEWS IN 1879. L&N COLLECTION, UNIVERSITY OF LOUISVILLE ARCHIVES.

to Frankfort. A branch from Anchorage dead-ended at Shelbyville. Passenger service improved and in the spring of 1854, an "Accommodation Train" was added that left Louisville in the afternoon for Bagdad and returned the next morning. "In a year or two, we will expect to see the road from Lagrange to the city dotted with cheerful looking cottages and country seats," *The Louisville Daily Courier* remarked. "Now is the time to purchase a few acres of ground to advantage, and those who wish to escape the dust and heat of the city in the sultry months of summer, and provide a pleasant home for their wives and little ones, where they can take plenty of healthy exercise and breathe pure air, should avail themselves of it."[22] The normal morning and afternoon trains to Frankfort would continue to operate, but the excursion duration would be reduced from three and a half hours to two hours and forty minutes. In 1859, the Louisville & Frankfort and the Lexington & Frankfort agreed that the railroads between Louisville and Lexington would be operated as one line. When regular service commenced after the Civil War, Gilman's was listed as a station between Fair Grounds (Crescent Avenue) and Race Course (Ashland Road), but arrival and departure times were not provided.[23] A small frame station, perhaps the first one at Gilman's, was erected in 1879 south of the railroad tracks and along the Westport Road just east of Chenoweth Lane (see page 51). The 30 foot by 24 foot station had small platforms front and back, a bay window in the agent's office, as well as freight and waiting rooms. It was razed in December 1965.[24]

When the united companies were authorized by the General Assembly in 1867 to build a branch from LaGrange to the Ohio River near Covington or Newport, the Louisville, Cincinnati & Lexington Railroad was created.[25] When put into operation in June 1869, the oak-and-walnut-faced passenger cars, including two designated for smoking, could make the excursion between Louisville and Covington in a record four hours.[26] However, the Short Line, as it became known, was not successful financially, and was acquired by the Louisville & Nashville Railroad in 1881. The L & N laid down its own set of tracks between Louisville and Anchorage to handle the increasing traffic. The railroad was a significant factor in the development of the plateau east of Louisville, particularly St. Matthews where the potato and onion farmers depended on rail transportation to ship their cultivated product to markets. However in time, one set of tracks was removed.

West of St. Matthews proper, the railroad tracks were laid down just north of the Frankfort road, which created a problem even though the roadway was upgraded to turnpike status by the legislature in 1851. The Shelbyville Branch Turnpike Road was devised to avoid the nuisance and danger of the railroad. It also made possible the division of the old Spring Station tract into smaller lots. What is now called Lexington Road to "Gilman's point" was surveyed in June 1852 and contemplated to be open in twelve months.[27] However it would be ten years before permission was purchased to cross Alfred Herr's land and complete the road from Cannons Lane to Breckenridge Lane.[28] Prior to then, as can be seen on the 1858 Bergmann map, Cannons Lane was utilized as part of the turnpike branch.

At Chenoweth Lane, the railroad tracks went along the north side of Westport Road, which followed the southern boundary of the Ridgeway property. Bergmann's 1858 map of properties in Jefferson County shows that land in this point had already been subdivided and oriented perpendicular to the Frankfort road—not diagonally following the old survey lines. The railroad tracks crossed the Westport road in front of Dr. John Nichols Lewis's residence and went toward Anchorage. Dr. Lewis reportedly practiced in Jefferson County for thirty years.[29] When he died in August 1878, his funeral was to be held at "the family residence, near Gilman's Point."[30] His son, H. N. Lewis, was born in this house in 1856, and after graduating from both the Louisville Medical College and the Hospital Medical College, he also practiced in St. Matthews. Their five-bay house is brick on the first level and clapboarded on the second, fronted by a two-story wooden porch with Eastlake detailing, covering three bays. In 1893, Joseph Oechsli (pronounced Exly) purchased the property and farmed the 37 acres before creating a subdivision.[31] The house remains in the family and is the residence of his grand-

daughter, Mary Elizabeth Ratterman Ruckriegel.

The election of 1856 had been preceded by the massive Democratic Barbecue at Gilman's Point on 28 August 1856, when regional anti-Know-Nothing forces gathered in Theodore Brown's woods to hear Ohio Governor Charles Anderson, who had been raised at nearby Soldier's Retreat, and others. "Contributors of live meats" had been requested "to send them to Daniel Gilman's" ahead of time, while "contributors of butchered and prepared meats" could get them to Gilman's Point by the day before the rally.[32] Trains loaded with "as many as three thousand persons" helped transport the reportedly ten thousand people to the barbecue. "Long and deep trenches had been dug, where hot fires were baking and roasting the meats as they turned upon spits," and the *Louisville Daily Courier* also reported that "tables more than a mile in length had been erected."[33] It was a defining moment in an area that was beginning to be populated by German and Swiss immigrants.

It is not precisely known when the area around the wedge of land

In 1855 and 1856 the "Know-Nothing" party became dominant in many parts of the country and in Louisville. It had arisen on the ruins of the old Whig party. Its one principle was hostility to the Catholic and foreign vote. In 1855 terrible mobs had occurred in Louisville—foreigners being driven from the polls, beaten up, and in some instances killed.

The order was known to be secret, but in the "Gilman's Precinct," now "St. Matthews," Doctor Lewis was generally known to be its President. He was a very large and powerful man; ordinarily a good citizen and peaceful man. On the election day in 1856, early in the morning a wagon load of roughs from Louisville landed at the polls at Gilman's Precinct. It became manifest that they intended to take control of the polls and to drive off objectionable voters.

My father and Captain Veech (father of Dick Veech) went directly to Doctor Lewis. They said to him: ... "We will hold you personally responsible for their conduct. If they are allowed to remain here and if they attempt to interfere at the polls, then at the first sign of disturbance we will kill you."

Doubtless it was illegal, perhaps harsh, but it was effective. The bullies returned to the city, and the election passed off peaceably.

From Thomas W. Bullitt, *My Life at Oxmoor* (Louisville, 1911), 107-108.

ABOVE LEFT: JOSEPH AND MARY OECHSLI IN EAST SIDE YARD, ON THE SOUTHWEST CORNER OF RIDGEWAY AVENUE AND WESTPORT ROAD, ABOUT 1895. COURTESY OF MARY ELIZABETH RATTERMAN RUCKRIEGEL.

between the Westport and Frankfort roads was first called Gilman's Point. Earlier, in 1830, the area had been designated Sale's precinct for Edmund P. Sale (1786-1832), who operated a tavern on Frankfort Avenue at Reservoir Park.[34] His son, William Sale, tore down "the common country tavern stand" in 1841.[35] By 1850, the election precinct had been established at the house of J. Trenchant, and it was then removed by an act of the legislature to the home of Daniel Gilman.[36] On the 1879 *Atlas of Jefferson and Oldham Counties Kentucky*, the entire region is known as Gilman's precinct. County magisterial districts were sometimes named for prominent residents or their representatives on county court. In the 1870 federal census, the population total of Gilman's precinct was 1,685: native 1,334; foreign 351; white 1,287; and colored 398. Later the precinct was divided into East Gilman's and West Gilman's, and by 1930, St. Matthews and Hurstbourne had been created.

Daniel M. Gilman's wife, Ann Morgan Gilman, died in 1880. When he died in 1885, *The Courier-Journal* carried the following obituary:[37]

> Daniel Gilman, one of the old native citizens of Jefferson county, died suddenly at Woodlawn yesterday, in the 81st year of his age. For 75 years he lived on the Shelbyville turnpike, five miles from the city, his home being known as Gilman's Point, now St. Matthews. Five years ago Mrs. Gilman died, and he then came to reside with a married daughter, Mrs. J. W. Hamlin, in this city. A few weeks since he went out to Woodlawn to escape the heat of the city. Last Saturday he was partially prostrated, but soon rallied, and within a few hours of his death—which was sudden and seemingly painless—he appeared well and cheerful. In earlier life he was engaged in the cattle trade to

> We called it The Point. We never called it St. Matthews. You always went to The Point.
>
> From interview of Alice O. Monohan, 3 October 1996.

Grave markers of Daniel M. Gilman and Ann Morgan Gilman, Cave Hill Cemetery. By Samuel W. Thomas.

New Orleans, and enjoyed a reputation for unswerving integrity and straightforwardness. He was an Old Line Democrat, a Jackson man, he having voted for Old Hickory and at every Presidential election from that time to that of 1884. He leaves three children, a daughter and two sons, all of whom are grown. His funeral will occur from Woodlawn this afternoon at 3 o'clock.

According to Jefferson County Court records, Daniel Gilman was first issued a license to keep a grocery in his house on the Louisville and Shelbyville Turnpike Road in 1857. Along with it came "the privilege of selling liquor by the quart." It is not known precisely where this house was located. However, in 1859 he purchased from George Herr a small but strategically located piece of land bounded by the Shelbyville Road and the Westport Road, east of Cannon's line, which presently would be Chenoweth Lane. Intriguingly, along the eastern boundary of the property was "an Artificial Island and Circular Pond." A decade later when the Gilmans sold the property to Alfred Herr, the pond with an island was still in the east boundary line.[38] Perhaps the occasional reference to Gilman's Pond should no longer be considered a misprint. For instance, Clarence E. Cason reported in a 1922 article on St. Matthews that "some old settlers affirm that several ponds were situated on the present site of the town, and that the locality, consequently, was known as 'Gilman's Pond.'"[39] However, in the late 1860s, Daniel Gilman was granted a license to keep a tavern in Gilman's Point.[40]

According to Hardin H. Herr, who remembered "Uncle Daniel" as quite a character, Gilman's grocery had entrances on both the Shelbyville Pike and the Westport Road. Herr wrote that Gilman moved to Louisville after his wife died, but that he died in "the historic old house of the Woodland [Woodlawn] Race Course, where he once lived himself."[41]

North of the railroad tracks on Ridgeway property was the St. Matthews Episcopal Church. It was erected on a one-acre lot deeded to its trustees by Helen Bullitt Massie Martin in 1839.[42] That edifice burned, and its appearance is not known. It may have been replaced in 1859 as *The Louisville Daily Journal* on August 13th noted that "St. Matthew's Church, in Jefferson county, will be open for divine service to-morrow...on which occasion the Rev. J. S. Large, Rector of St. John's Church of this city, will officiate." In any case, in 1869, the lot was reconveyed to the trustees as well as an additional ten acres for a rectory.[43] A small, board and batten, Gothic-style church, probably designed by the noted local architect, W. H. Redin, was erected about 1872, and a rectory was added later.[44] Apparently, St. Matthews Episcopal Church was not organized as a parish, but operated as a mission. After St. Mark's Episcopal Church in Crescent Hill was organized in 1895, membership and allegiance shifted. By 1912, steps were being taken on behalf of Helen Bullitt Massie Martin Key's heirs to reclaim the land based on a clause that it would revert back if not used for church purposes in five years.[45] Its fate sealed, the abandoned church was sold at the courthouse door in 1913 to Ida Staebler.[46]

This day [19 March 1877] came R. S. Veech, Lewis Lentz, W. S. Parker, Geo. K. Speed and sundry citizens of Gilman's Point and Edward's Pond in Jefferson County and produced and filed in court their petition praying that this Hon Court will not grant license to any person for the purpose of keeping a Tavern or sell liquors of any kind in said Precincts aforesaid.

From Jefferson County Court Minute-Order Book 35, p. 309.

Last Sunday there were services at the old St. Matthews Episcopal Church. Much interest was manifested by the members and sister churches....This is one of the oldest churches at St. Matthews and it is seldom they have services. The members are hopeful of being able to repair the church building in the near future, when more people move into the neighborhood and it will be possible to reorganize and be self supporting.

From "Up-To-Date," *The Jeffersonian*, 18 April 1912.

FROM DIVISION SURVEY OF RIDGEWAY PROPERTY
BY J. W. HENNING, FILED IN JEFFERSON
COUNTY DEED BOOK 163, PP. 144-145.

"VIEW OF DILAPIDATED EPISCOPAL CHURCH IN
ST. MATTHEWS AND THE REV. R.L. MCCREADY,
WHO IS LEADING THE FIGHT TO PREVENT LOT
REVERTING TO HEIRS OF DONOR." *THE
COURIER-JOURNAL*, 15 APRIL 1912.

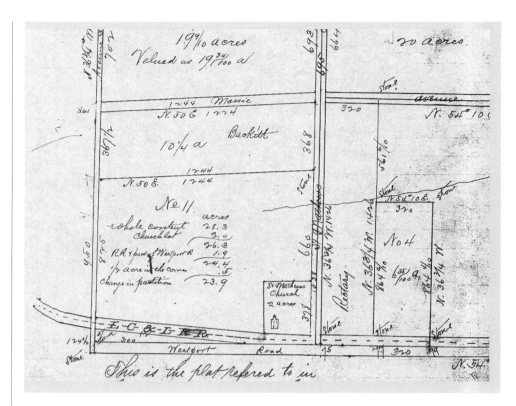

Soon after the Episcopal church was established on Ridgeway land, a small lot was purchased across Westport Road for the Beargrass Baptist Church, which would immediately become "The Church of Christ at Beargrass Road."[47] In February 1842, the old Baptist church had been authorized by the General Assembly to sell two acres of land on Beargrass Creek it possessed containing "an old stone meeting house" and to use the proceeds of the sale to purchase "another more suitable piece of ground, and the erection of another church."[48] According to the *History of the Ohio Falls Cities*, "the first building was a stone structure, erected about the year 1798-99, on the north bank of Bear Grass."[49] The construction date, however, appears to be in error. The trustees of Beargrass Baptist Church did not acquire the land on which the church was erected until 1809. In fact, in the summer of 1803, various gentlemen in the neighborhood belonging to the Baptist and Episcopalian "societies" agreed to erect a stone meetinghouse, which both congregations would share.[50] Evidently, the arrangement for using the facility on alternating Sundays did not suit, and Beargrass Baptist Church struck out on its own. The meetinghouse's present-day location can be pinpointed behind the Bluegrass Manor Shopping Center from deed references placing it on the western edge of William Christian's 2,000-acre grant (later Jule B. Arterburn's property), and extending 40 poles (131 feet) north of Beargrass Creek.[51] On the Westport Road site, a brick meeting house was erected, and it was replaced by a frame church in 1888.[52]

The church was abandoned for a new one erected on Shelbyville Road, and in 1919, George Edinger employed Stich Brothers to renovate the structure into his family residence. Later it was acquired by Dr. Henry Harthill, and then by R. W. Marshall. Remnants of the church were removed in 1967.[53]

Beargrass Christian Church on Westport Road about 1915. Warren K. Frederick Collection, University of Louisville Photographic Archives.

When the post office was renamed on 1 October 1851, it was called St. Matthews in obvious reference to the nearby church. When created two years before, it had been named Lynnford.[54] About that time, John J. Jacob, Jr., built a fine Gothic Revival style residence on the south side of the Shelbyville Pike that he called Lynnford. It was renamed Hurstbourne by subsequent owner Richard Ten Broeck. The famous horse breeder and trainer built an impressive barn out of stone taken from Richard Clough Anderson's Soldier's Retreat, which was once the seat of the property. Jacob's father had purchased a 525-acre portion of the old farm in 1842. Architect Jacob Beaverson designed the brick house, which later was enlarged by architect E. T. Hutchings for the widow of Alvin T. Hert. Lyndon Hall now serves as the clubhouse of the Hurstbourne Country Club.

Beaverson may have designed another prominent residence in the area. When James Brown (1780-1853) died, his son, Theodore Brown (1821-1899), inherited part of his property north of Beargrass Creek. The house (JF 310) that Brown erected on it, called Woodview, later Woodhaven, strongly resembles Jacob's. The foundation stonework for both houses was done by Michael Fillion, so it is probable that architect Beaverson was responsible for both designs. Brown's property was embellished by a grove of indigenous trees, mostly walnut, covering some 18 acres in front of the Gothic-style residence. He prided himself on being a student of landscape architecture, and is known to have assisted Benjamin Bussey Huntoon, who became superintendent of the Kentucky School for the Blind in 1871, in the layout of that institution's grounds along Frankfort Avenue in Clifton with trees native

One of the best-known residents of the St. Matthews district, Mr. Theodore Brown, died yesterday morning at his home, Woodview, after a short illness, succeeding several years of poor health. Mr. Brown was in his seventy-eighth year, and was a son of Mr. James Brown and Urath Lawrence, born on the tract of land, then called Dutch Station, of which his farm is a part. He was well known as a progressive farmer in ante-bellum days, and was active in agricultural and stock meetings. He was an active and devout churchman, one of the foremost promoters of the Sunday-school in Jefferson county, and for many years the main support of the St. Matthew's Episcopal church.

From "Theodore Brown Dead." *The Courier-Journal*, 6 September 1899.

THEODORE BROWN RESIDENCE ABOUT 1890.
THE FILSON CLUB. BELOW: WOODHAVEN IS NOW
A BED AND BREAKFAST OWNED AND OPERATED
BY MARSHA BURTON. THE OCTAGONAL ROSE
COTTAGE AT LEFT HAS RECENTLY BEEN ADDED.
BY SAMUEL W. THOMAS, 1999.

RIGHT: PLAT SHOWING THEODORE BROWN'S
FORMER RESIDENCE. FROM "PRELIMINARY PLAN
FOR EXTENSION OF HUBBARDS LANE BY
STONESTREET & FORD, 12 AUGUST 1940.
JEFFERSON COUNTY HISTORIC PRESERVATION
AND ARCHIVES.

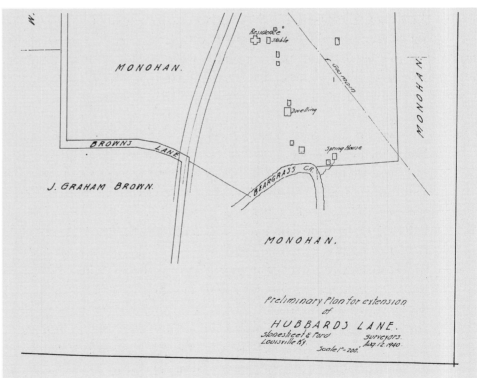

to Kentucky.[55] In 1920, the Monohan family added Theodore Brown's farm to its already considerable holdings. Recently, a new road was placed directly in front of this house and the property was subdivided. Now functioning as a bed and breakfast, its new address is 401 South Hubbards Lane.

On the railroad line just east of Ridgeway was a property called

Woodlawn, its owner simply specified on the 1858 Bergmann map as Gray. In 1848, Henry W. Gray, later the prominent Kentucky representative of an English fire insurance company, purchased the 201-acre tract from Dr. John Esten Cooke for $16,000, indicating there was a dwelling house on the land—perhaps built as a summer residence by T. T. Shreve when he owned the land between 1833 and 1837.[56]

Early in 1843, Orlando T. Alden and his wife established the Woodlawn Institute for Young Ladies in the "delightful summer residence."[57] The proprietors intended "to aid in forming a dignified and genteel address, habits of considerate and independent thought, and a conscientious regard to religious obligations." They listed references in various cities, and clearly intended to attract students from around the country as well as the neighborhood.

Henry Gray advertised the house and property for sale in the spring of 1850, but no sale took place. However, no sooner had Gray satisfied Dr. Cooke and his heirs, and received clear title to the property, than Gray & Co. went bankrupt. He and his brother, George E. H. Gray, turned over all their assets, including Woodlawn, to banker Alfred Harris to cover their debts.[58]

At about the same time Gray & Co. went bankrupt, some sixteen years before Churchill Downs was beginning to take shape in the minds of some Louisvillians, a group of Central Kentucky horsemen were looking for an appropriate site near Louisville along a railroad to establish The National Race Course. When 150 acres of Woodlawn was purchased, the National Race Course name was dropped. Before stock was issued in June 1860 in the name of the Louisville Association for the Improvement of the Breed of Horses, the Woodlawn Course opened, as described in the *Louisville Daily Courier* on 28 May 1860:

> We predicted yesterday that the four mile race over Woodlawn Course would be a great race. The event exceeded our expectation. About five thousand persons were present, and six hundred of these, at least, were ladies. The stand set apart for them was filled, and the members of the Club yielded half of their stand for their accommodation. At no race within twenty years have so many of the fair sex graced the stand of a Kentucky race course. The track was in fine condition, considering the weather for the past week, and the Superintendent, Mr. Carroll, is entitled to the highest praise for surmounting the disadvantages which would have disheartened one less energetic. The track was, however, a little stiff, and would not permit the fastest time, else the first heat would have been still lower in the forties....Large purses brought together the finest race horses in the State. Woodlawn is yet in its infancy, but so long as it is conducted with the propriety that, so far, has been evident in its management...it will rank as it deserves to rank, with the first best race courses in the world.

Beargrass Farm For Sale.

I offer for sale the Farm on which I now reside, situated on the Westport road, about 6 miles from Louisville and one mile from the Shelbyville turnpike. Said Farm contains about 200 acres, the greater portion of which is of the best quality The improvements are of the best sort and built in the modern style. The dwelling is of brick, two stories high, with a cellar under the whole house. It fronts about 50 feet, with eight rooms in the house exclusive of the cellar, four on each floor—the parlors are 21 feet square. There are good stables, cow-houses, corn crib, smoke-house, ice-house filled with ice, and first-rate servants' houses. The grounds possess much natural beauty and are handsomely planted with shrubbery. There are a great quantity and variety of fruit trees, which were selected from the best Eastern nurseries and are now in full bearing. The garden contains an asparagus bed which yields from $300 to $500 a year, varying with the season. The Louisville and Frankfort Railroad passes through the Farm in a very advantageous manner, which renders it susceptible of division into small tracts fronting on the railroad. The first "water station" is on the Farm, about 1/4 of a mile from the house, which insures the regular stoppage of the train. For further particulars, apply to J. W. Breden, Real Estate Agent, near the post-office, or to me on the premises. Henry W. Gray.

From *The Louisville Daily Journal*, 3 April 1850.

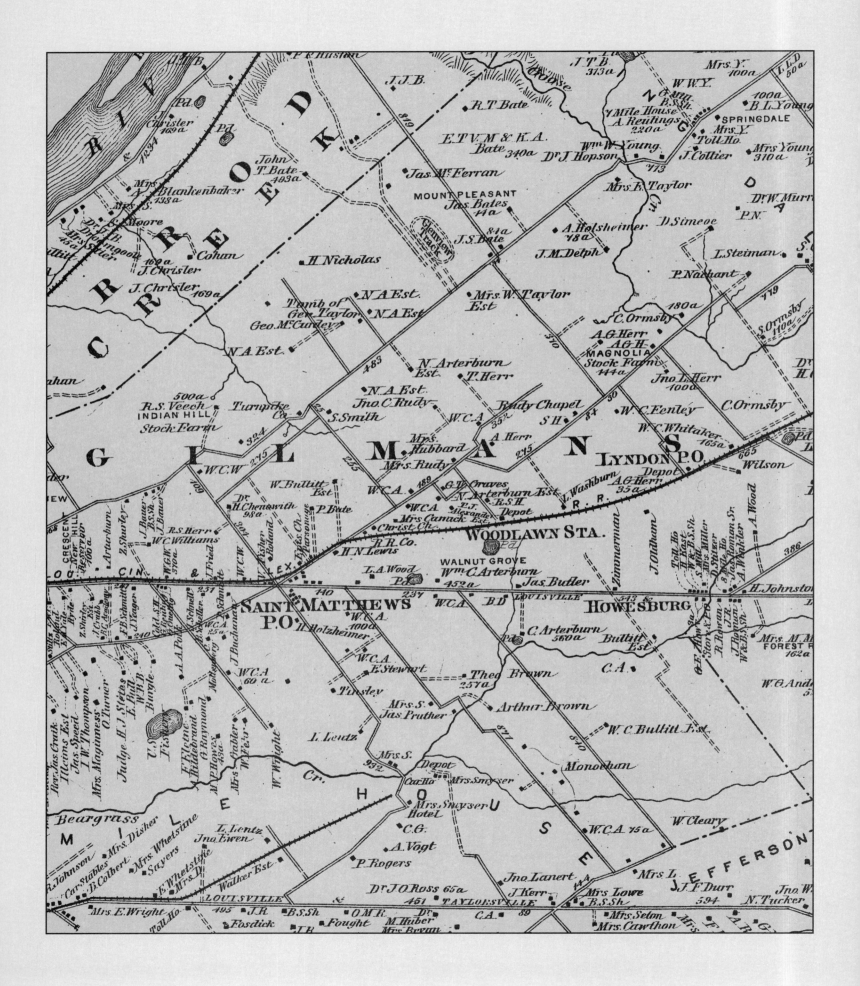

Robert Anderson (1805-1871) was born at Soldier's Retreat, the son of a surveyor who had fought in the Revolutionary War. He entered West Point at fifteen and graduated in 1825 and entered into military service. Major Anderson was in the Charleston harbor in command of Fort Sumter when it was shelled on 12 April 1861.[1] He was evacuated, and came back to Kentucky, assigned to recruit Union volunteers. Then he was headquartered in Cincinnati until the Confederate Army under Leonidas Polk invaded Columbus in far-western Kentucky, whereupon he removed the command of the Department of the Cumberland to Louisville. The state's declaration of neutrality was withdrawn as Southern forces moved on toward its principal city. General Anderson's proclamation of 21 September 1861 was carried in *The Louisville Daily Journal*. "Kentuckians! Called by the Legislature of this, my native state, I hereby assume command of this Department. I came to enforce, not to make your laws, and God willing, to protect your property and your lives."

Although Louisville was reinforced and ultimately protected from invasion, Anderson wilted under the pressure, and on October 8th, citing feeble health, he relinquished his command to William Tecumseh Sherman.[2] Anderson retired to Europe and died in Nice in 1871.[3]

General Anderson's boyhood neighbors, the Bullitts, were of a different persuasion. Henry Massie Bullitt would recall that twice in 1861 on his way home from Louisville to Oxmoor at night, Federal troops "overcrowded my market wagon....They did their robbing at St. Matthews, about one and a half miles above their camp." Soon Henry Massie Bullitt and his brother, Thomas W. Bullitt, joined the Confederate Army. "May 19th, 1862, was beautiful, and Oxmoor the most beautiful of farms, no weeds in fields or fence corners, the front lawn like a carpet, the old spring running clear, cold, water as pure as when grandfather Bullitt took his first drink from it. Meeting father in the stable lot at early dawn, none other present, I told him my intention and bade him farewell."[4]

In September of that year, troops retreated into Jefferson County after the battle of Perryville. Fourteen-year-old Cora Owens, living on the Shelbyville Pike west of Gilman's Point, wrote the following in her diary.[5]

> September 20th, 1862. The retreating soldiers from Richmond, Ky. ran over every body about here, we fed about two hundred of them....September 29th, 1862....We went to school and I did not spend a pleasant day. At 2 o'clock an order came that no living being should pass in or out of town. A guard was stationed at Mr. Beckett's gate...September 30, 1862. Last night at two o'clock the rebels I know not how strong made a dash inside the line. The pickets surely were not at their posts because they were stationed at Mr. Beckett's gate, & the Confed's came this side of that place.

CHAPTER III

THE CIVIL WAR AND ITS AFTERMATH

"Major Robert Anderson, U. S. A., Commanding At Fort Sumter," *Harper's Weekly*, 12 January 1861.

Opposite: Section from plate (p. 39) delineating Gilman's precinct in Beers and Langan's Atlas of Jefferson and Oldham Counties Kentucky, published in Philadelphia, 1879.

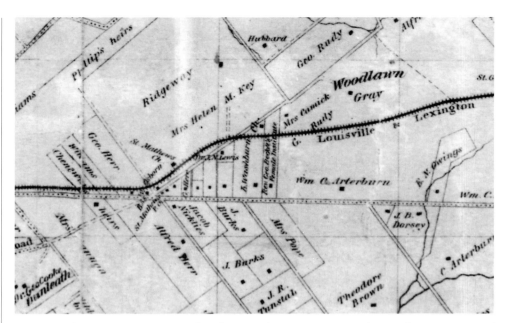

SECTION FROM BERGMANN'S 1858 MAP OF JEFFERSON COUNTY SHOWING PROPERTY ALONG SHELBYVILLE ROAD, EAST OF CHENOWETH LANE.

We have already stated that a party of rebel pickets ventured to Gilman's Point, five miles from the city, on the Frankfort turnpike, on Monday night, a skirmish with Federal pickets ensuing; the Federals sustaining a loss of one killed and another wounded. The same night a party of three or four rebels visited the residence of Mr. John Burks, on the Brunerstown [Taylorsville] road, and wished him to pilot them through to a certain point near the city on the Workhouse [Lexington] road. Mr. Burks refused to act as guide for them, and, when pressed, offered resistance. Very soon, however, his house was surrounded by two hundred rebel cavalrymen, who threatened him with violence if he did not submit. Mr. B. was preparing to act the part of an unwilling guide, when the report of a howitzer was heard in the direction of Gilman's, and the party at Burks's, fearing an attack, left in haste. The rebel who conversed with Mr. Burks was dressed in the Federal uniform, and said he was a deserter from Col. Pope's regiment.

From *The Louisville Daily Journal*, 2 October 1862.

The Rev. George Beckett's Female Institute was located on a strip of property that fronted the Shelbyville Road, east of present day Thierman Lane, and now occupied by the Second Church of Christ Scientist and Circuit City. George and Elizabeth A. Beckett had purchased the 20-acre tract in 1854 for $3,000 after he had served as chaplain and professor of belles-lettres at Shelby College.[6] They sold it in 1865 for $15,000, having purchased a 10-acre lot in the subdivision of the Ridgeway property.[7]

In a retrospective of St. Matthews prepared 79 years later, *The Courier-Journal* would observe: "It seems impossible to believe that near that spot where stands the "triangle" of shining new storefronts was once a lake on the banks of which camped the Confederate Army during the War Between the States."[8] The remark brought on an authoritative correction from Hardin H. Herr, who signed his letter to the editor, simply, Lex.[9] Herr's grandfather owned the triangle formed where Shelbyville Road and Lexington Road merge, as did his great-grandfather and his father, William Wallace Herr, who was married to Kitty Todd, sister of Mary Todd Lincoln, and who served in the Confederate Army. Hardin Herr believed that if the Confederate Army had been on his family's land, that fact would certainly have come to light. Herr contended that because some of Sherman's Union forces were stationed in St. Matthews in the summer and fall of 1865, someone had confused them for Confederates.

On 29 January 1863, Cora Owens (1848-1939) would continue in her diary: "We met 3 companies of calvary & 30 army wagons, on our way to school, & 3 regts. passed after we got there, & all of their wagons. They say that 7,000 men are coming from Danville, & that they are going down to Vicksburg to make another attempt to take it. I was so afraid that they would stop here, & give Ma trouble, but they did not stop here....Some men are camping in Mr. Brown's woods, opposite Mr. Beckett's, & they have been trying to steal his hay this evening."[10]

On 9 October 1861, *The Louisville Daily Journal* printed the general

orders turning Brigadier-General Robert Anderson's Louisville command over to Brigadier-General William T. Sherman. Just below these notices was a reminder: "Our readers should not forget that the great Handicap race comes off to-morrow over the Woodlawn Course....The course should be crowded with visitors, and we advise the ladies particularly to attend." The adjacent column carried a notice that "entries for the challenge vase for the spring meeting, 1862, closed at the Galt House last evening with three subscribers, R. A. Alexander, A. Keene Richards, and T. G. Moore. It will be remembered that Moore has already won the vase twice and if he should succeed in winning it at the spring or any subsequent meeting, it will then be his property." The challenge vase, which is really an elaborate silver trophy, had been made by Tiffany and Company in 1860 and was valued at $1,000. The race was a "dash of four miles," competed for at both the spring and fall meets. Fearing that Moore would retire the trophy, R. A. Alexander acquired it for the Woodlawn Association for $500. He subsequently won it twice, but as he

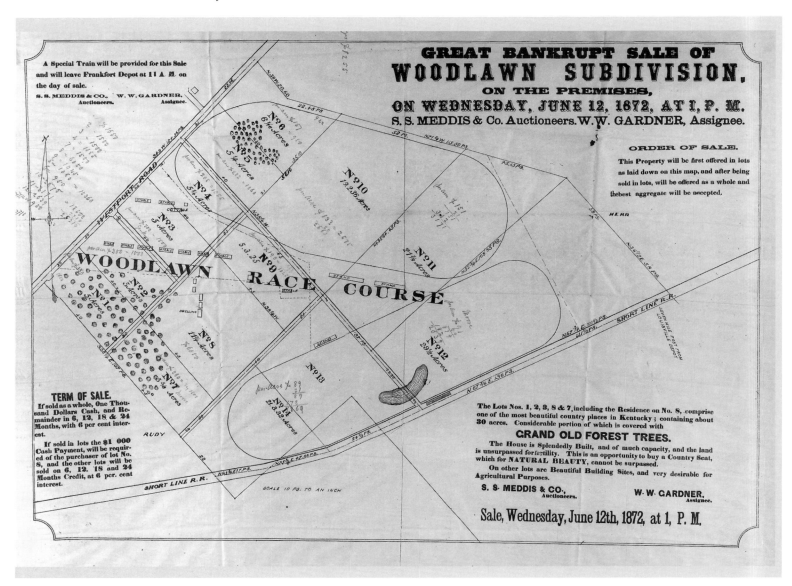

had become Woodlawn's principal stockholder, he kept it. His brother, A. J. Alexander, inherited it, and presented it to the Louisville Jockey Club, which added it to the winnings of its Great American Stallion Stake in the fall of 1878. When the Dwyer Brothers won it, they gave it to the Coney Island Jockey Club. The vase was also raced for at Jerome Park and Morris Park and then presented to the Maryland Jockey Club. Since 1917 it has been awarded to the winner of the Preakness Stakes run on the Pimlico Race Course.[11]

The Civil War had a detrimental effect on every facet of the horse business. Horses killed in the conflict had to be replaced. Many were simply stolen. Racing at Woodlawn continued for the most part, but interest understandably waned.

On 27 October 1866, *The Turf, Field and Farm* wrote about the predicament at Woodlawn:

> The turf is on a decline at Louisville. The people take no interest in racing, and it is thought that the beautiful

Woodlawn will have to be abandoned. Last spring experienced gentlemen became the lessees of the course, and their names alone were a guarantee that racing would be conducted on the highest principles. They expended money with a lavish hand, offered an attractive program, and depended on the citizens of Louisville for their reward. They thought that the old love for turf institutions was strong with the people, and that they felt a pride in Woodlawn. But in this, it seems, they were mistaken. Notwithstanding the number of horses present, and the high principles upon which the fall races have been conducted, the meeting has been poorly attended, and the gate receipts are of the most beggarly character. In the face of such stubborn facts the lessees became disheartened, and on the evening of the 17th of October they surrendered the management of the course to the stockholders.

The stockholders became fewer and fewer as R. A. Alexander, the proprietor of Woodburn farm at Spring Station near Midway, redeemed most of the certificates. He died, however, in 1867. On 16 July 1869, *The Turf, Field and Farm* indignantly announced Woodlawn's demise:

> *The Courier-Journal* informs us that the beautiful race grounds at Louisville, Woodlawn, are to be sold at public auction. Is there not sufficient enterprise at Louisville to keep the grounds intact, or must they be despoiled by the vandal hand of civilization? Woodlawn is one of the very best racecourses in the country, and it should be preserved as a field where the game thoroughbred can write his name on the page of national renown. Surely a State that reaps so much profit from her breeding farms as Kentucky ought to be able to boast of a respectable racing park at her chief city.

Finally, in 1872, the Woodlawn Race Course, consisting of both a running and a trotting track, was sold and a subdivision plat was filed with the county clerk.[12] However for several years thereafter, the trotting track continued to operate.

Sue Hall Arterburn Stich was born in the large, square, brick house, painted white, on the old Woodlawn Race Course property in 1914. Her parents, William Norbourn Arterburn and Ruth Lea Herr Arterburn, had married in 1907. As was Norbourn Arterburn's custom when his five sons married, he gave each a home, including William Norbourn Arterburn. Mrs. Stich's older sister, Elizabeth Adair Arterburn Baker, born in 1908, noted that "the woodwork had been hand carved by a Rudy, who built the place originally, and that people used to come and ask to see it."[13] Sue Stich remembers that the walls of their house were very thick and the plan of the cellar rooms matched that of the first floor. All the rooms had fireplaces.

The famous Woodlawn track, although lately divided up and sold in small lots by the bankrupt court, will still continue to be devoted to turf purposes. Very many noble races have been decided on Woodlawn, and we still hope to see many more. There Asteroid made his grand four-mile trial in 7:23, and there Ericsson made his four-year-old record of 2:32 and trial of 2:26. "Idlewild," "Hertzog," "Enquirer," "Harry of the West," and all the game horses of the past have made it resound to the music of flying feet, and it would be a shame, if, like the world-renowned "Metairie," its name should forever be obliterated from the courses of America. The running track is among the things of the past, but the trotting course, with its stands and stables, is still preserved, and will answer either for thoroughbreds or trotters. During the coming season the wheels of the sulky, rather than the marks of plates, will make their impress on the turf at Woodlawn. Mr. Brown, with his string of trotters, which will include the roan gelding, "Tom Taylor," the Golddust filly "Bettie V.," and several other fast trotters, has already commenced his preparation for the spring and summer campaign.

From "Woodlawn Race Course." *The Courier-Journal*, 12 April 1873.

My grandfather, Alfred Herr, was an engineer for the L & N. When we lived in the old house, there wasn't anything between us and the railroad tracks. He had a certain blow when he was coming by. If it was at night, my mother would turn the light on and raise the shade up and down. That was her signal that she heard him. In the daytime she would wave something white at the window. One day she was getting dressed to go somewhere and she heard his whistle and she ran to the window and waved her corset out the window and she dropped it. Our old Airedale dog got that corset and we kids had a time chasing that Airedale dog trying to get her corset.

From interview of Sue Hall Arterburn Stich, 2 January 1997.

VALENTINE FISCHER (1837-1884) AND SON PHILLIP (1870-1941). GUETIG FAMILY COLLECTION.

The first floor consisted of a large reception hall, living room, music room, dining room, kitchen, and a narrow back hallway. The stairway went up to a large landing with bedrooms and the bathroom around it. The front facade had a large fanlight doorway, covered by a porch, with two windows on either side.

Sue Stich's grandfather, Alfred Herr, was married to Alice Osborn, whose father, William Osborn, was a blacksmith. He and John Bauer, father of the Bauer brothers, were partners in a blacksmith shop where Bauer also turned out wagons. For a time, they also shared a brick duplex cottage next to their frame blacksmith shop.[14] On the other (west) side of the cottage, Valentine Fischer would erect a sizeable establishment.

Valentine Fischer and George Guetig were granted a license to keep a tavern at their house on the Frankfort Road near Gilman's Point, in November 1865.[15] When they acquired the property from George Cunningham's

Looking east on Shelbyville Road at intersection of Chenoweth and Breckenridge lanes, ca. 1910. Fischer's grocery and tavern at left. Bank of St. Matthews on corner with Bauer Brothers' complex beyond. At right is interurban depot. Beargrass-St. Matthews Historical Society.

Fischer's grocery and tavern, ca. 1885. R. G. Potter Collection 1211, University of Louisville Photographic Archives.

heirs the next year, Guetig deeded his half interest in the frame house and stable to his brother-in-law Fischer.[16] Within some years, Fischer replaced the wooden structure with a substantial, two-story, brick edifice for his grocery, tavern, and hotel. (It stood on Frankfort Avenue at the head of Lexington Road until about 1960. The cleared site became a parking area for a new White Castle erected near the old corner at Chenoweth Lane.) Valentine Fischer died in the fall of 1884.

In the meantime, George Guetig purchased a six-acre parcel in the northwest corner of the old Cannon family property, along the Shelbyville and Louisville Turnpike Road in 1866 for $3,000. As he was immediately granted a license to keep a grocery at his house, such a structure must have already existed. He was soon permitted to keep a tavern "with the privilege of

TOP: SOUTHEAST CORNER OF FRANKFORT AVENUE AND CANNONS LANE, FORMERLY KNOWN AS GUETIGS LANE, IN LATE 1921. CAUFIELD AND SHOOK COLLECTION 39883, UNIVERSITY OF LOUISVILLE PHOTOGRAPHIC ARCHIVES. ABOVE: SAME CORNER IN 1946. ZV 234-46 CASE FILE, JEFFERSON COUNTY HISTORIC PRESERVATION AND ARCHIVES. THE BUILDING HAS BEEN RAZED AND THE SITE IS A PARKING LOT.

selling liquors by the small or drink."[17] Guetig evidently substantially improved or erected another structure on the corner, based upon its architectural detailing. The spot was popular, and for many years that section of Cannons Lane from Frankfort Avenue to Lexington Road was known as Guetigs Lane. Peter Guetig inherited the saloon from his father and it came equipped with a baseball field. The story goes that the longest foul ball in history was hit at Guetig's one afternoon when an errant ball landed across Frankfort Avenue on a freight train headed for Cincinnati. In any case, Guetig's saloon marked the end of Crescent Hill and was the gateway to St. Matthews.[18]

Perhaps the first instance of St. Matthews appearing in print was in

1871 on the cover of the sheet music for a song written by J. C. Meininger and published in Louisville by Louis Tripp. "The Fairies of St. Matthew's" was dedicated to "The Young Ladies of St. Matthews," who were students in the Reverend Carter Page's female seminary. Page had purchased George Beckett's property on the Shelbyville Road in 1865, and most likely had taken over his school as well.[19] He may have been related to Susan Page Meade of Charlottesville, who had married Theodore Brown in 1870. Brown had a substantial family by his first wife who had left him widowed in 1866.

Susan Brown brought her young cousin, Thomas Nelson Page, from Virginia to tutor the children in 1872. He had attended Washington and Lee College, and needed resources to study law. According to Harriet R. Holman, Ph.D., in the summer of 1873, after Thomas Nelson Page had completed his tutoring duties for the Brown family, a lawyer "in the neighborhood" asked Page to attend to his office and read law there. Young Page apparently became more infatuated with the young ladies of St. Matthews and was dispatched back to Virginia. He did, however, become a successful lawyer, raconteur, and writer. In 1891, he would return to Louisville rather triumphantly, under the auspices of the local alumni of the University of Virginia.[20] *The Louisville Commercial* of 14 April noted: "Macauley's Theater To-Night, Thomas Nelson Page, A Reading From His Own Writings. Admission, 50c. Reserved Seats, 75c." On the previous day he recorded the following observations in his journal:[21]

> Drove out with Will Thum and Arthur Rutledge to St. Matthews to see the Browns. Trees just budding. Peach blossoms. Found the fine grove which used to cover thirty acres cut and hacked till hardly any of it left. My cousin had come to town to see me. Mr. Brown looked as natural as ever. Says he still keeps up his custom of jumping over a chair every birthday; but perhaps his chair not quite so high as it used to be. He is seventy. Still keeps up his custom of having a child born to him nearly every year. Has eleven by his present wife, who had to get a nurse that day. Dora very pretty and refined—like the Pages—looked like a bit of sunshine in that cold house. On the whole, came away saddened, things so changed, the grove destroyed, the fences patched, the pretty little footbridge over Beargrass gone; Arthur Brown's place abandoned, I older. The pride of revisiting the place as a "lion" not worth the pain.

A few days after Page's talk, he was driving eleven people to Glenview, then the farm of John E. Green, when he flipped the "wagonette." Several in the party were injured, and the *Louisville Commercial* headed its report: "Can Read But Not Drive." Page would continue to write prodigiously and would serve as ambassador to Italy. Unfortunately his papers at Duke University and the University of Virginia do not shed any light on his stay in St. Matthews with the Theodore Browns.[22]

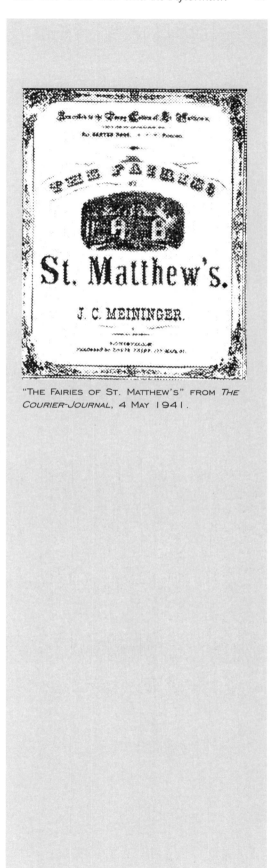

"THE FAIRIES OF ST. MATTHEW'S" FROM *THE COURIER-JOURNAL*, 4 MAY 1941.

The horse-car railway line, running out the Bardstown pike, known as the Beargrass railroad, was sold yesterday by Buchanan, Milton & Co., real estate agents, to L. Smyser and John Burks, the price paid being $20,000. The original cost of the road was $50,000. The sale embraced all the rights, franchises, and privileges of the company. The purchasers intend to put the track in good repair and put on new cars, and make it in every respect a first-class road.

From "Sale of the Beargrass Railroad." *The Louisville Commercial*, 15 May 1874.

A Pleasant Summer Resort.
It will be seen by notice elsewhere that on the 1st of June next the delightful country residence known as "Burks'," five miles distant from the city, will be opened under the auspices of Mrs. Jarvis, with all the appointments of a first-class house.[26] This will afford an opportunity to our better class of citizens whose business interests require their daily presence in Louisville to enjoy the delights of the country during the approaching warm season. Extensive improvements have been recently made on the premises, the house having been enlarged and the grounds beautified. The place is convenient of access, being at the terminus of the Beargrass railroad, over which cars run to and fro every half hour. It is certainly one of the most beautiful, healthy spots near the city.

From *The Courier-Journal*, 14 May 1876.

FROM BEERS & LANGAN, ATLAS OF JEFFERSON & OLDHAM COUNTIES KENTUCKY (PHILADELPHIA, 1879), PLATE 39.

The Beargrass Railway Company, incorporated by an act of the Kentucky General Assembly in 1866, was authorized to run from Beargrass Creek near the city limits of Louisville, out along the Shelbyville and Louisville Turnpike "to Gilman, or near thereto, at the intersection of the said turnpike road and the Westport road." This venture folded and was superseded in 1868 by the Beargrass Transportation Company, which was empowered to venture out from the city limits twelve miles in an undetermined direction. A year later, the Louisville and Beargrass Railway Company was incorporated with authorization to connect Louisville with either Middletown or Brunerstown (Jeffersontown).[23] Evidently, the direction toward Brunerstown was selected when William C. Bullitt complained "To The Voters of Beargrass" that "the promise of building a Railroad from Louisville to Middletown" would virtually confiscate "my estate for five years." His almost incomprehensible broadside diatribe, dated 10 June 1869, must have had the desired effect.[24] Tracks were put down along Bardstown Road and Taylorsville Road from Smith's Garden east of Cave Hill Cemetery terminating on John Burks' property, near where Breckenridge Lane crosses Beargrass Creek. Little is known about the line or the intentions of its owners. Perhaps, before they ran out of money and the financial fortitude to carry on, they planned to extend on to Shelbyville Road. However, on 11 April 1874, the stockholders decided to sell out at the courthouse door. The General Assembly authorized the sale as well as a name change to the Beargrass Railway Company. When Lewis Smyser and John Burks purchased the railway on 14 May 1874, they entered into an elaborate agreement whereby Smyser acquired the Burks property where the tracks terminated.[25]

Lewis Smyser evidently kept the mule cars moving and enlarged the Burks residence, converting it into a resort hotel.[27] It is not known what

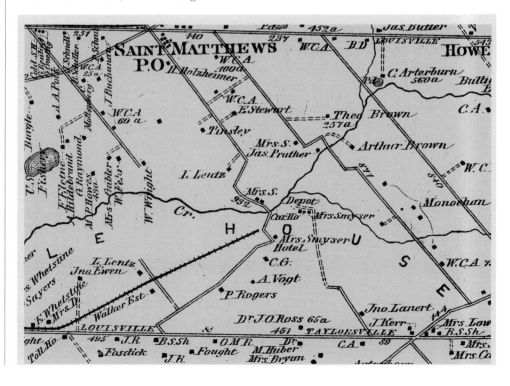

happened to the structures on this site which on the 1879 atlas are shown as a "Car House, Depot and Mrs. Smyser's Hotel." Although late in life Lewis Smyser managed a large farm operation as well as the railway, his principal occupation was that of a flour manufacturer in Louisville. After he died in 1877 at the age of 66, his wife, Frances Ann Smith Smyser, evidently took over operation of the resort hotel.[27] She died in late 1903.

The hotel, pictured about 1920 in the Warren Kellar Frederick collection, was in ruins. The brick section was first the residence of Presley N. Ross, whose widow, Matilda, married James Burks in 1823. University of Louisville Photographic Archives.

The steam-operated railroad through St. Matthews proper not only moved people, but produce as well. Market gardeners began to cultivate rather small plots on the fertile and well-watered Beargrass Creek plateau, and when the produce was harvested, it would be brought to market in Louisville on the railroad. Or it could be sent elsewhere by train as well. Market gardens began to flourish east of the city before the Civil War. The most extensive such operation was Nanz, Neuner & Company's Green-House Establishment. The 30-acre nursery site, located just south of the second station on the Short-line Railroad, was purchased by Henry Nanz from Jacob Nicklies in 1872.[29] Plants, seeds, flowers and vegetables were available on the site that contained 30 greenhouses, or they could be purchased at the company's Central Market store in Louisville.

Henry Nanz learned horticulture in his native Stuttgart before coming to the United States in 1847 and Louisville the following year. He was first listed in the 1851-1852 city directory as a beer maker; however, his obituary states that he was initially employed at Spring Garden, and then became gardener for the Robert Ward family, who lived on the northeast corner of Second and Walnut streets. When those grounds were destroyed in 1854 by a mob after Ward's son killed a respected schoolteacher, Nanz purchased land on the west side of Third Street, between Breckinridge and Kentucky streets.[30] In 1870, Charles F. W. Neuner visited Louisville and met Nanz. He had been born near Stuttgart, where his father was a royal gardener, but he had come to Rochester, New York, in 1868. Nanz and Neuner formed a partnership, and it was made tighter when Neuner married Nanz's daughter, Louise. Another daughter, Sallie, married Henry Kraft. Charles Neuner, however, did

Nanz & Neuner's Floral Offerings. Nanz, Neuner & Co. have published their illustrated and descriptive seed catalogue....This is one of the finest catalogues of seed published anywhere in the country....In addition to the large and varied assortment of flower seeds announced by Messrs. Nanz, Neuner & Co., they advertise a select list of vegetable seeds, which embrace the very best of all the rarities of the vegetables in demand in our market. A number of the descriptions of these seeds are in English and German, by which means German gardeners who do not readily read English may understand the names and qualities of the vegetables he wishes to raise....This enterprising firm, who thus properly appeal to Kentucky for encouragement in their useful and valuable labors, recently purchased thirty acres of the rich land that formerly constituted a part of the farm of Mr. Burks, about five miles from the city.[28] They have already erected three green-houses on this land, and expect to construct thirty.

From *The Courier-Journal*, 15 March 1873

not take an active part role in the company and was successful selling life insurance. He died in 1900 at the age of 52.[31]

When Henry Nanz died in 1891 at the age of 72, his obituary was headed: "Louisville's Pioneer Florist Expires at His Home at Gilman's Point," where it pointed out he had lived for several years.[32] He had been retired for two years, and the business had been transferred to his son-in-law. By the division made of Henry Nanz's property in 1894, Louise Neuner received the smallest lot at the northeast corner of the Shelbyville Pike and "Breckinridge" Avenue. Her sister, Sallie Kraft, got lot 2 fronting further east along the pike, while their brother, Henry Nanz, Jr., obtained lot 3, the 12-acre parcel located further south on "Breckinridge" Avenue where the nursery and greenhouses were situated.

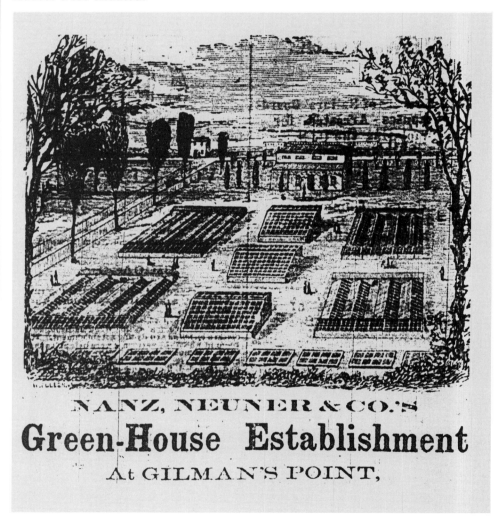

NANZ, NEUNER & CO.'s
Green-House Establishment
At GILMAN'S POINT,

The New Nanz & Neuner Co. applied to the Jefferson County Planning and Zoning Commission for permission to improve the appearance of the property by removing or setting back the existing greenhouses, reducing the size of the business by half, and erecting "a show house along Breckenridge Lane."[33] The name of the business was subsequently changed to Nanz & Kraft Florists to reflect its acquisition by the Kraft family. Further improvements were made to the property before and after a devastating fire in 1976.[34]

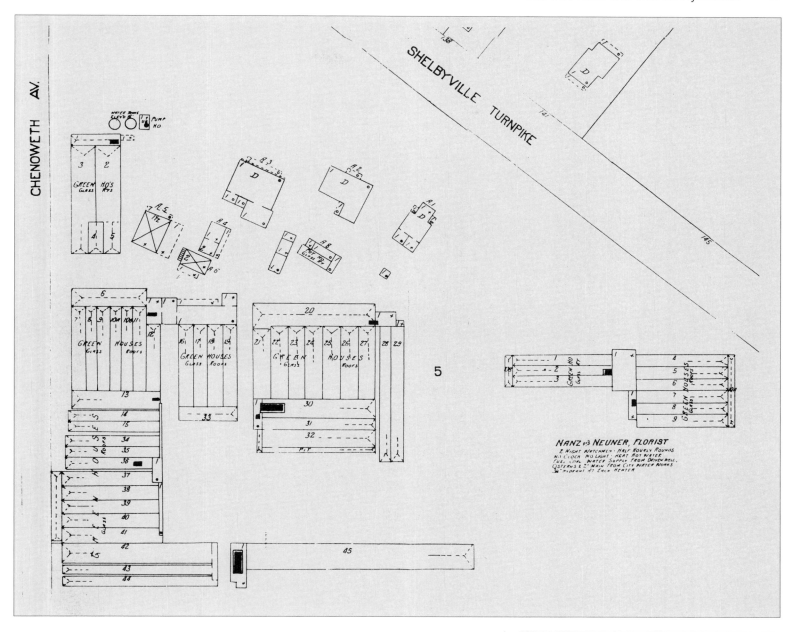

NANZ AND NEUNER, FLORIST

LAYOUT OF GREENHOUSES FROM 1905
SANBORN MAP. BRECKENRIDGE LANE WAS THEN
LISTED AS CHENOWETH LANE.

NEW NANZ & NEUNER CO. GREENHOUSES,
NORTH OF PRESENT SITE OF PEARSON FUNERAL
HOME, IN 1945. ZV 10-45 U FILE,
JEFFERSON COUNTY HISTORIC PRESERVATION
AND ARCHIVES.

Mr. Winchester, who has lived in this community all his life, knows its worth and how much we love him and his family. When we implored him not to leave us he promised to locate near St. Matthews. What would we do without our elder, our shepherd, who so lovingly ministers to our welfare?

From *The Jeffersonian*, 15 July 1915.

Kentwood sketched by Walter H. Kiser, *The Louisville Times*, 27 December 1938.

J. B. Parks subdivision, 15 October 1874, recorded in Jefferson County Deed Book 180, pp. 644-645.

A private lane formed the western boundary of Nanz & Neuner's property. The Floyds and Breckinridges had first carved it out as a means to access the Frankfort road from Woodville. It ran parallel to the pioneer survey lines that are still in evidence today, and would later allow Breckinridge

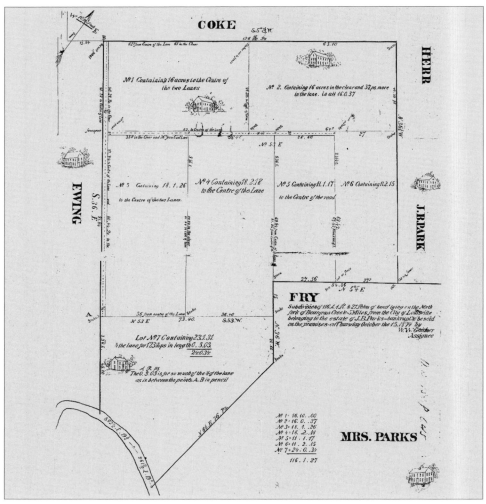

land on the east side of the lane to be developed. In 1854, James B. Burks acquired 42 acres at the head of a spring stream that ran southwest past Woodville and into Beargrass Creek. He erected a two-story, five-bay, brick house in the prevailing Italianate style with a projecting flat roof supported by elaborate brackets. Later the residence, now surrounded by development, was called Kentwood, and owned by the W. C. Winchester family.[35]

Across the lane, Joshua B. Parks had to relinquish much of the land he had inherited from his father, Floyd Parks, several years after he was declared bankrupt in 1871. A 116-acre subdivision was platted and recorded by the assignee, W. W. Gardner, but most of the land forfeited was purchased in a single parcel. William D. and Belle Tinsley purchased 100 acres described as "choice garden lands in a high state of cultivation...well watered by the creek and never-failing springs, and toll is free to the city by turnpike."[36]

We moved to Breckinridge Lane (we spelled it correctly) in 1940, and most of the area back there was still farm land—either horses, cattle or potatoes. The old Tinsley house was where Our Lady of Lourdes is now. It was left to fall apart. It was huge and all brick, and it looked like Hurstbourne in a way. That is how magnificent it was. It had a great staircase inside. W. M. Cissell had a big white house on Breckinridge Lane, between Nanz and Grandview. He had developed the steam iron, and he made a fortune.[37] We thought it was huge because he could get two Cadillacs in the garage.

From interview of Robert Michael Kirn, 15 December 1997.

LEFT: KATHARINA KOEHLER HOLZHEIMER (1835-1926) AND HER HUSBAND HEINRICH (HENRY) HOLZHEIMER (1826-1919), BOTH NATIVES OF GERMANY, WERE MARRIED IN LOUISVILLE ON 5 FEBRUARY 1856. PHOTOGRAPHS *CA.* 1875, COURTESY OF MRS. RUSSELL HOLZHEIMER.

BELOW: GRANDCHILDREN (AVERILL, WILLA, RUSSELL, AND HELEN HOLZHEIMER) OF THE HENRY HOLZHEIMERS PHOTOGRAPHED BY EDWARD C. MARTIN IN 1914 IN THE FRONT YARD ON BRECKENRIDGE LANE. COURTESY OF HELEN DEPRIMA.

Whereas, A. D. Hunt, T. J. Martin, I. Churchill, G. Spratt, and their associates, have formed an association in the city of Louisville, for the purpose of refined social enjoyment and generous hospitality to strangers visiting the city, under the name of the Louisville Club...therefore, be it enacted by the General Assembly of the Commonwealth of Kentucky... Approved March 9, 1868.

Be it enacted by the General Assembly of the Commonwealth of Kentucky: That the Louisville Club, of the city of Louisville, incorporated by an act approved March 9, 1868, be and is hereby authorized and empowered to change its name to Beargrass Club... Approved February 6, 1873.

My sister Helen married Doctor Henry Chenoweth, a physician of ability with an extensive practice, having the confidence and affection of his patients and his neighbors. His health compelled him to live in the country. He was of the best class of country doctors. As a girl she possessed beauty and grace; was an excellent musician, with a remarkably sweet and magnetic voice. As a mother she was quiet, but at once kind, resolute, and tender. To me from the earliest days she was a sister tender and loving. Her death [on 29 March 1896] left a void in my life which can never be filled.[41]

From Thomas W. Bullitt, *My Life at Oxmoor* (Louisville, 1911), 73.

On the west side of the private lane that would be named to honor the Breckinridge family, but now misspelled on street signs, Henry Holzheimer began to assemble a sizeable farm in 1879, in time to be shown on the county atlas published in that year.[38] Prior to that, he had evidently resided over the grocery and tavern he had erected at the head of the lane on a lot he purchased from Daniel Gilman in 1871. By 1892 he had amassed 68 acres, which he farmed. After he died in 1919, the property was sold to realtor J. C. Turner, who inadvertently added to the confusion of the Breckinridge spelling by naming his three-part subdivision Breckenridge Villa. The Holzheimer residence, which sat at the corner of Nanz Avenue and Breckenridge Lane, was also sold and later converted into apartments, and finally razed. From its architectural appearance, the two-story, brick structure was erected by Holzheimer, although Alfred Herr's residence appears in the same location on the 1858 map.

On 9 March 1874, three police commissioners were elected for Beargrass Municipality. Its boundaries encompassed a large area east of the city limits of Louisville and included Gilman's Point.[39] According to a *Courier-Journal* report on 27 May 1874: "The commissioners were invested with the power to appoint patrolmen." The act of the Kentucky legislature further provided for "a capitation [poll] tax, and if that was found by the commissioners to be insufficient, then a tax upon real estate within the municipality was to be levied to supply the deficiency." Before any tax could be levied, a large number of potential payers in the Beargrass Municipality retained the former attorney general of Kentucky, John Marshall Harlan, to make their protest before Jefferson County Court. James Speed represented the police commissioners. Speed had been attorney general of the United States. Harlan would initially support his law partner Benjamin Bristow for the Republican nomination for President, but after he delivered the Kentucky delegation to Hayes, and he won, he was appointed to the Supreme Court. Harlan argued before the county court that the tax imposed was "so unequal and partial as to render it impartial." The law was repealed on 25 January 1876.

The strategic crossroad that connected the Brownsboro Turnpike with the St. Matthews Church and the St. Matthews' post office "was established as a public road forever by County Judge W. B. Hoke on 18 May 1874, over the objections of William C. and Hannah Williams, the contiguous land owners. There was already a private drive that separated the Williams property from Ridgeway and provided access to the property of Richard S. Herr on the west and the residence of John Henry Chenoweth, M.D. (1825-1905) on the east. The through road would be named for John Henry Chenoweth, a descendant of one of Louisville's first families. His grandfather, Absolom Chenoweth, was related to Captain Richard Chenoweth (1734-1802), whose family accompanied George Rogers Clark to the Falls of the Ohio in May 1778, and was responsible for the construction of Fort Nelson before establishing his own station near Middletown. Several of Capt. Chenoweth's children were killed there in an Indian attack in July 1789 and his wife lived to a remarkably old age even though she had been scalped.[40] John Henry

Chenoweth was born at Jeffersontown in 1825, but, soon after, his father moved near St. Matthews on the Shelbyville Road. John Henry attended a local school taught by Robert N. Smith, where he became proficient enough in mathematics, Latin, Greek, and surveying, to enter medical school at age 17. He graduated from the Louisville Medical Institute in 1844. For several years he practiced with Dr. Joseph Knight before moving back to the country to restore his health.

In 1855, Dr. Henry Chenoweth married Helen Martin Bullitt (1835-1896), daughter of the William C. Bullitts, and during the next few years the couple lived at both Oxmoor and Ridgeway. In 1860, Mrs. Chenoweth's aunt,

CHENOWETH/HEYBURN/BROWN RESIDENCE, CHENOWETH LANE, *CA.* 1920. WILLIAM HEYBURN COLLECTION.

Helen Bullitt Massie Martin Key, gave them a 20-acre section of Ridgeway, which they called, appropriately, Ridgeway Corner. On what had been a hemp field, they began building an Italianate residence, which was completed with some Gothic Revival features in 1869. With the gift of an additional 20 acres and the purchase of 58 acres more, the homestead once occupied 98 acres. Dr. Chenoweth's medical practice extended from Clifton to Anchorage, and from the Ohio River to Bardstown Road. House calls were made by carriage or on horseback where there were not roads or they were impassable. His horses were recognized for being quite spirited. In spare moments he tended an extensive garden and raised as many as five hundred game chickens.[42] Subsequently, his son, Dr. James S. Chenoweth, lived at Ridgeway Corner, as well as the young Dr. Chenoweth's daughter's family, the Alexander Heyburns.[43] The property has been the residence of the John Welburn Brown family since 1940.[44]

Henry and Helen Bullitt Chenoweth's daughter, Mildred A. Chenoweth, married John Stites in 1877. He had come from Hopkinsville to study law with his uncle, Court of Appeals Judge Henry J. Stites, who lived in

Drs. Henry and James Chenoweth spent all of yesterday in the neighborhood of St. Matthews, and carefully examined seven of the poisoned persons. Dr. James Chenoweth said: "I am a friend of the Herr family, and intend to investigate this case for my own satisfaction. In all of the seven cases that father and myself examined we found the symptoms the same, and they are not such as to convince me that the root of the trouble is arsenic....The symptoms are those of ptomaine, a product of bacteria. This germ often exists in milk and animal matter generally. I am confident that the seat of poisoning was in the chicken salad."

From "What The Doctors Think," *Louisville Commercial*, 19 April 1891.

the Lexington Road house that was later made quite magnificent and named Whitehall. John Stites had a long career in banking and was president of the National Bank of Kentucky when it was taken over by BancoKentucky and made defunct. The Stiteses built a brick house on the east side of St. Matthews Avenue on land that Dr. Chenoweth had acquired from Bullitt heirs. It was later owned by Albert C. Dick, Jr., who incorporated it into a cluster of townhouses. The Stites's son, James W. Stites, was judge on the old Kentucky

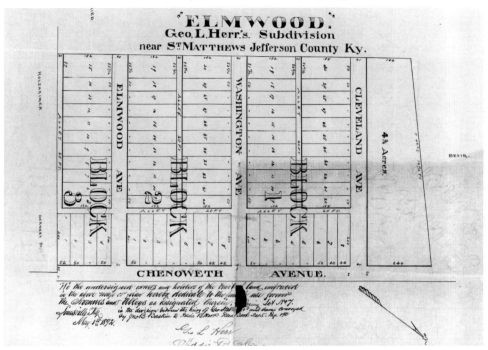

Court of Appeals. John Stites died in 1938 at the age of 88.[45]

The other early house that had access to St. Matthews along Chenoweth Lane belonged to Richard S. Herr. He inherited the property, shown on the 1858 Bergmann map as being owned by his father George Herr, in 1875 and erected a two-story, five-bay brick house in a style that had prevailed for nearly a century. The grounds of Elmwood were subdivided into 75 lots in 1892, with three short streets being made perpendicular to Chenoweth Lane: Cleveland (later changed to Leland), Washington, and Elmwood.[46] When the lots were auctioned off, the newspaper advertisement called Elmwood "the most desirable subdivision between Louisville and Anchorage." St. Matthews, it claimed, was one of the "best improved points in the county, having a post office, three churches, two meat stores, two general merchandise stores, three schools, blacksmith shops, etc."[47]

The Herr house and some surrounding property north of Cleveland Avenue (Leland Road) was kept intact and later was obtained by the Eline Development Company which created 12 lots and built apartments on some. Sara Eline Breeland recalled living in the house and maintaining a large garden in the back. The large portico had been added along with bathrooms, and by the time Dr. Edward Masters purchased the house at 260 Leland Court, it had been duplexed.[48]

In 1882, the first Catholic parish in eastern Jefferson County was

JUDY OCHSNER EDWARDS COLLECTION,
BEARGRASS-ST. MATTHEWS HISTORICAL
SOCIETY.

FRONT OF FIRST HOLY TRINITY CHURCH, 1915.
COURTESY OF MARY ELIZABETH RATTERMAN
RUCKRIEGEL.

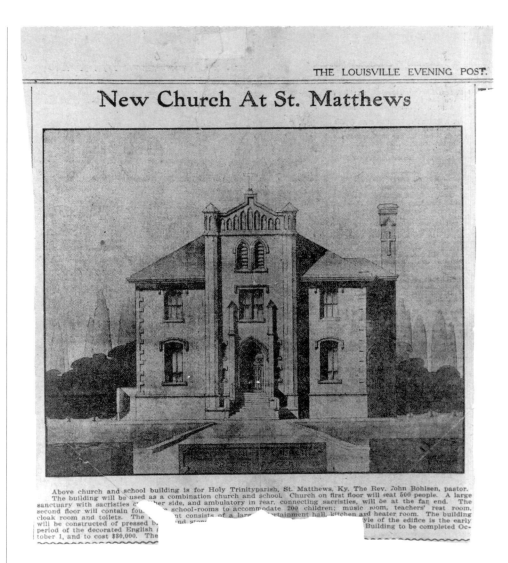

THE LOUISVILLE EVENING POST.

New Church At St. Matthews

Above church and school building is for Holy Trinity parish, St. Matthews, Ky. The Rev. John Bohlsen, pastor. The building will be used as a combination church and school. Church on first floor will seat 500 people. A large sanctuary with sacristies on either side, and ambulatory in rear, connecting sacristies, will be at the far end. The second floor will contain four school-rooms to accommodate 200 children; music room, teachers' rest room, cloak room and toilets. The basement consists of a large entertainment hall, kitchen and heater room. The building will be constructed of pressed brick and stone. The style of the edifice is the early period of the decorated English Gothic. Building to be completed October 1, and to cost $30,000. The . . .

FRONT ELEVATION OF HOLY TRINITY CHURCH AND SCHOOL FROM THE EVENING POST, 15 MAY 1915. COURTESY OF MARY ELIZABETH RATTERMAN RUCKRIEGEL.

Holy Trinity is so full of zeal and good work, they can accomplish any undertaking; having laid the foundation for a new home for Father Bohlsen. The old brick building in which he has been living is being torn down. It was built in 1852 and has been condemned as unsafe. The school building back of the church has been fitted up as a temporary dwelling.

From "St. Matthews," *The Jeffersonian*, 25 January 1923.

created, reflecting the immigration of Swiss and Germans into the farming region east of St. Matthews. On 17 December 1882, a simple, 200-seat, white frame edifice on the north side of the Shelbyville Road was dedicated. The lot had been owned in the 1830s by a house painter, Ben T. Rue. It appears on the 1858 Bergmann map west of the site of Rev. George Beckett's Female Institute, and not far from the former location of the Beargrass Christian Church. Many years later, Charles P. Cammack would tell historian Hardin H. Herr that Professor Anderson's well-known school, attended by Cammack, W. Wallace Herr, Thomas W. Bullitt, and others, had been where Holy Trinity was located.[49] By 1899, the parish included 110 families, and 80 children attended the frame schoolhouse erected west of the church.

In 1915, the school and church were combined in a large, two-story structure, erected where Trinity High School is presently.[50] The church, accommodating 500 people, occupied the first floor, while four rooms for 200 pupils were on the second floor. The edifice, constructed of pressed brick with stone trimming, was designed by Louisville architect Fred Erhart in a style depicting "the early period of the decorated English Gothic."[51]

Souvenir

Dedication and Blessing

OF NEW

Holy Trinity Church

And School

Sunday, November 15, 1936

St. Matthews, Ky.

AFTERMATH OF FIRE ON 21 SEPTEMBER 1937. COURTESY OF EARL COMBS STICH.

Soon after a substantial addition was made in 1936, the entire structure was gutted by fire. Smoke was detected in the air by neighbors for several hours before the blaze from an arsonist's fire could be pinpointed early on 21 September 1937. The son of the St. Matthews Volunteer Fire Department's chief admitted "setting fire to draperies near the altar," which left the school and church in ruins.[52] A fireproof school building was constructed on the foundations.[53] When a complex that included a church, rectory, and school was erected on Cherrywood Road in 1953, the old structure was taken over by newly established Holy Trinity High School.[54] Three years later as preparations were being made to graduate its first class, Holy was dropped from the school's name, while architect Walter C. Wagner made substantial renovations and an addition to accommodate an anticipated enrollment of 600.[55]

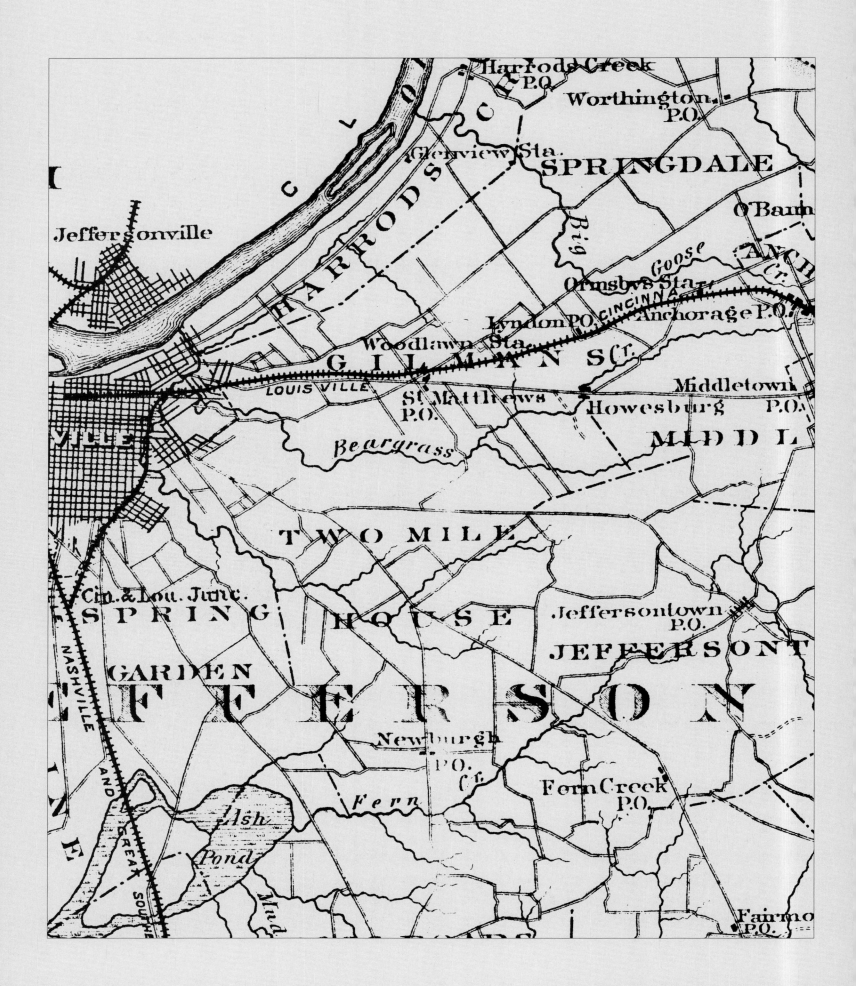

Tucked away in *The Courier-Journal's* "Local Brevities" column in the hog-killing season of 1869 was an observation of related commercial activities in Beargrass Creek. Before privileges to skim grease from the stream's surface could be agreed upon, warfare was reported in the Beargrass valley. But this humorous situation only underlined the more serious issue regarding the future and the very existence of Beargrass Creek. "It is astonishing to see to what means some persons will resort for the purpose of making money," *The Courier-Journal* noted on December 9th. "Beargrass creek, below the pork-houses, is, at every fifty yards, dammed and boarded in such a manner as to catch the grease which floats on top of the water. When this collects about the dams, the man or woman, as the case may be, wades in and skims it off. This they boil down and make soap of. A slow process for making money, but yet it seems a sure one, for it has many devotees, for there were hundreds fishing the grease out yesterday." Fortunately and in time for Christmas, peace was declared and *The Courier-Journal* could announce: "The war among the grease skimmers in the Beargrass Valley, which had its breaking out about two weeks ago, was, it is thought, brought to a close in the court of Justice Doane."[1]

Dams were not new to the Beargrass, as surveyor John May related to Samuel Beall in the spring of 1780: "There is about the Falls of Ohio perhaps 30000 Acres of Ponny rich Land, great Part under Water, but which could with a Little Expense be drained, Nothing more being required than to cut the Beaver Dams, which would leave such Land as in my Opinion, must in a very short Time be far the most valuable in this Country, the Situation being so convenient to the Falls, and the Land itself of a superior Quality to any in the lower Parts of Virginia."[2] (Samuel Beall would acquire the Spring Station tract, on which his son, Norborne Beall, would build a Federal style house that stands on Trinity Road.)

As the grease skimmers' war raged, *The Courier-Journal* addressed the bigger issue of Beargrass Creek's future, and it appeared quite bleak. "The creek, proper, with its eastern, middle and southern forks, or branches, is the subject" *The Courier-Journal* focused upon on 11 December 1869. "These branches are themselves nuisances, because they render unfit for use large tracts of land, which the spread of population now demands as sites for residences, factories and business-houses. They are nuisances because they are so extremely tortuous that private enterprise can do nothing with them. They are nuisances because they block up the progress eastwardly, of our best streets. What to do is the question."

The Courier-Journal's solution lacked any fundamental understanding of the reason for the various runoffs in the first place, but it was an early, if not the first, indication of the way development would try to walk over the environment. For "that which promises the best results in the shortest possible time," Walter N. Haldeman's year-old newspaper proposed "to adopt the channels as routes for main sewers. Let the whole eastern portion of the

Chapter IV

Beargrass Becomes Industrial

Every pond, creek, and river, exhibits some traces of them, but their metropolis appears to have been situated about four miles east of Louisville, where, among a variety of extensive dams, I measured one whose length is fifteen hundred feet, height eight, thickness at the base fourteen...I have been informed by a respectable old gentleman who was among the earlier settlers that, when he first arrived here, the beaver was sometimes seen in the neighbourhood, and that at that time the great dam spoken of, was at least fourteen feet high—a prodigious monument of industry and skill of this social little animal.

From Henry McMurtrie, M.D., *Sketches of Louisville And its Environs* (1819), 59-60.

Opposite: Section of Outline Map of Jefferson and Oldham counties, Ky. from Beers and Lanagan's Atlas (Philadelphia, 1879).

I was told by my father that the volume of water ordinarily in Beargrass Creek had diminished very greatly since his boyhood; that it was then a bold stream. I can fully appreciate it. It has diminished very greatly within my own memory. In my boyhood it never went dry in summer. Now it always does, or nearly so. The clearing of the country has caused the change, I suppose.

From Thomas W. Bullitt, *My Life at Oxmoor* (1911), 17.

city, and the contiguous suburbs be accurately surveyed and mapped out, and a grand sewer-system drawn up and established with these channels as the basis. Let the channels be straightened as far as possible, and then compel the property-holders, beginning at the lower end, to progress, one after another, till the sewers are all built and the valleys filled up." The reclaimed land would pay twice for the work, the newspaper projected. And "it will open the way for extending our principal streets in straight lines, while under present circumstances," it was lamented, "they will most probably terminate at the bank of the creek, and a different set of streets will in time be laid off beyond." Is it any wonder the Ohio River had not yet been bridged at Louisville?

Although *The Courier-Journal* concluded its sewer editorial with "at another time this subject will be continued," the problem with the creek's carry off remained and it would be decades before it was satisfactorily addressed. In "Our Progress," carried on 14 June 1874, it was pointed out that "the Point and the hitherto apparently irredeemable valley of the Beargrass are becoming an attractive spot for real-estate dealers having an eye to a profitable speculation in the purchase of lots now at a low figure on account of their inaccessibility and the uninviting nature of their surroundings....After awhile this fragrant stream will disappear, and the time will come when the memory of its summer smells will linger alone in the recollections of the oldest inhabitant."

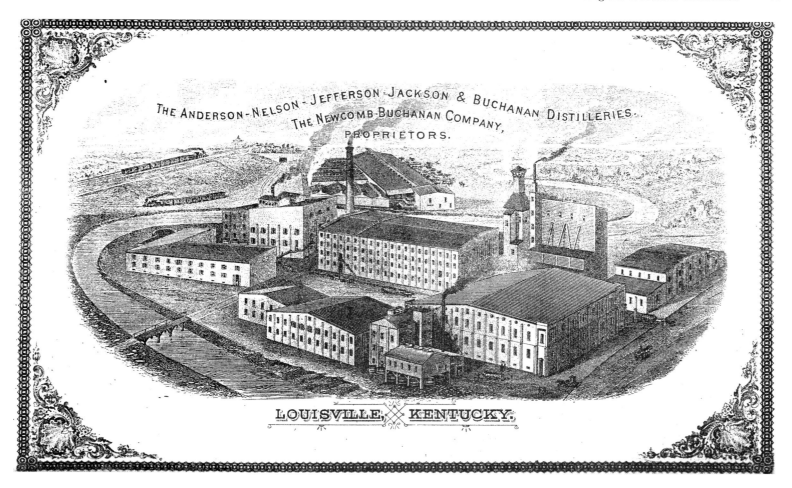

THE ANDERSON-NELSON-JEFFERSON-JACKSON & BUCHANAN DISTILLERIES.
THE NEWCOMB-BUCHANAN COMPANY, PROPRIETORS.

LOUISVILLE, KENTUCKY.

As *The Courier-Journal* cried foul, the largest polluter on the Middle Fork, or on any of the forks for that matter, was emerging just south of the Louisville, Cincinnati & Lexington yards and roundhouse on Spring Street, east of Mellwood Avenue. The huge complex of distilleries operated by Newcomb-Buchanan & Co. was created in 1866 when the Newcombs and the Buchanans, proprietors of two large wholesale groceries, merged resources and turned their collective attentions to distilling and distributing whiskey. By 1874, the firm was reputed to be the largest distiller of Bourbon and rye whiskies in Kentucky.[3] New distillery buildings, designed by architect Henry Whitestone, were in use by 1876.[4] Five years later, "the largest fine whisky-producing concern on the planet," spread over 35 acres, consumed 3,756 bushels of grain a day in its sour mash process.[5]

On 21 September 1884, Andrew and George C. Buchanan absconded to Windsor, Canada, where they sought support from Hiram Walker. They were deep in debt, and soon lost everything.[6] Their whisky production was soon revived as the Anderson & Nelson Distilleries Co. Although press reports stated that "the famous pure and sweet limestone waters of this region are the source of the marked excellence of these whiskies," apparently, the water was supplied by 8-inch pipe from the new Crescent Hill Reservoir.[7] Its source was the mighty Ohio River. The distillery complex on the north side of the old Workhouse Road, later called Hamilton Avenue and still later

SCENE NORTH OF LEXINGTON ROAD, WEST OF PAYNE STREET. FROM 1881 LOUISVILLE CITY DIRECTORY.

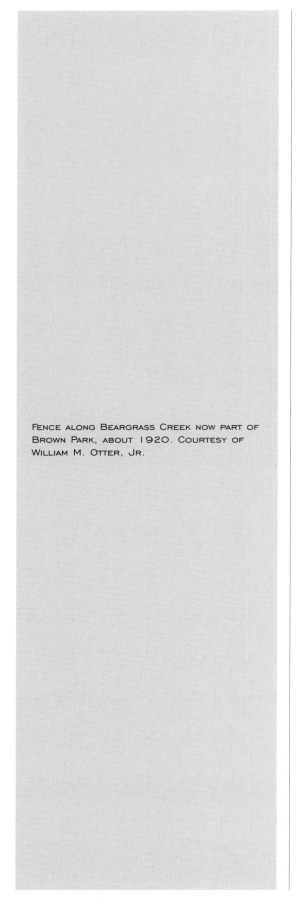

Lexington Road, has been leveled and is now used for waste-metal salvage storage. It was part of a later operation of the National Distillers & Chemical Corporation whose brick structures make up Distillery Commons at Payne Street and Lexington Road.

Beargrass Creek supported several other distilleries and was needed primarily to carry off the industrial waste, which wound up in the Ohio, just below the River Road pumping station. The low ebb, perhaps, was in 1907 when turpentine from sewer runoff into the creek caught fire and various buildings and bridges along its course were threatened.[8] Studies ensued, reports were made, and part of the creek channel was embedded in concrete during the period 1910-1913 as government took on various improvements both social and physical. Beargrass Creek had become historic enough to warrant newfound interest.

Until Beargrass Creek was cut off and diverted, it entered the Ohio River between the foots of Third and Fourth Streets. On early maps, of the three branches of Beargrass Creek delineated, the middle one was generally designated as the creek; the upper branch being called the Muddy Fork and the lower one, the South Fork. (Marking the middle fork as Beargrass Creek may have been for the printer's convenience.) In time, the branches became designated as the North, the East, and the South forks. However, they are now generally designated on maps as the Muddy Fork, the Middle Fork, and the South Fork. The purview of this book is the Middle Fork.

In her significant, but all-too-short booklet, *Old Homes of the Beargrass*, Mrs. Reginald Thompson, pointed out in 1911 that "the Anderson home, Soldier's Retreat, stands at the head of Beargrass Creek, from which stream this section of the county takes its name, including Crescent Hill." Fellow surveyor Luke Munsell on his 1819 Map of Kentucky, located Richard Clough Anderson's Soldier's Retreat on the "Dry Fork" of Beargrass Creek, south of the Shelbyville Road. The headwaters that crossed Shelbyville Road at Eight-Mile House and merged with the Dry Fork on the Arterburn property near Oxmoor, he marked as the Sinking Fork. On Bergmann's 1858 atlas of Jefferson County, neither of these headwaters is named; however, "Dry run" is shown emanating on the western edge of Oxmoor (Dry Run Plantation is noted as early as 1816 in *My Life at Oxmoor*) and entering Beargrass Creek on John Burks' land west of present day Breckenridge Lane. That water source is now called Weicher Creek. Waters from spring sources north of Westport Road flow in McClentick's spring branch through Taylor and Croghan property to the Muddy Fork. It is not known why the spring branch carried the McClentick name, which is variously spelled. John McClentick was appointed constable on Beargrass in 1785, but there is no record of McClentick's owning any land in Jefferson County.[9]

In the evening of 3 February 1919, The Filson Club met in regular session in the assembly room of the Louisville Free Public Library. *The Courier-Journal* reported that "Capt. Alfred Pirtle, president of the club, read the paper of the evening on 'Some Stations on Beargrass Creek,' in the course of which he gave his own, and the most generally accepted, version of the origin of the stream's name." The Filson Club's secretary, Otto A. Rothert, noted in his minutes: "Capt. Pirtle had done much original research work in preparing his MS....The origin of the word Bear Grass was one of the features of the paper. 'Barre Grasse' in French means Big Reef. The creek just above the big reef was given the name 'Barre Grasse' by the French, which was soon changed to Bear Grass by later arrivals." Interestingly, when Otto Rothert offered his own paper to The Filson Club on 3 October 1927, regarding the origin of the name of Beargrass Creek, he referred to Pirtle's version in passing as "a more romantic tale."[10] For Rothert and others who have followed, the name was grounded in nature. "In pioneer times," he read, "this stream was bordered abundantly by yucca, scientifically the *yucca flamentosa* or *glauca*, which was plentiful in the Virginia colonies. It is a succulent plant upon which bears fed to vary their food of roots, fruits, flesh, and fish. The yucca was commonly called beargrass for that reason. Hence, 'Beargrass Creek.'"

The origin of Beargrass Creek may have been the Powell River, which flows parallel to the Kentucky border in southwestern Virginia. Just before Dr. Thomas Walker made the first recorded exploration into Kentucky in 1750 through the Cumberland Gap, he noted in his journal that his party was on "a Branch of Bear-Grass."[11] Walker's subsequent settlement near present day Barbourville, Kentucky, and Bear Grass Creek were delineated

Bear-Grass, which gives its name to the fertile and wealthy settlement through which it passes, is a considerable mill stream, affording a plentiful supply of water, eight or ten months in the year. It rises by eight different springs, 10 miles east of Louisville, that unite and form the main body of the creek within two miles of that place.

From Henry McMurtrie, *Sketches of Louisville And its Environs* (Louisville, 1819), 10.

on Dr. John Mitchell's map published in 1855 in London.[12] Later maps show that Beargrass Creek was renamed Powell River for a member of Walker's party. (Dr. Thomas Walker's daughter married Joshua Fry, the great-great grandfather of the late Thomas Walker Bullitt who helped form the Beargrass-St. Matthews Historical Society.) When Harry Gordon and his party descended the Ohio River and prepared the first map of the Falls in 1766, Beargrass Creek was simply noted as "Creek 15 yards wide." No name was given to it in Gordon's journal. Nor did Isaac Hite make mention in his journal of Beargrass Creek when he accompanied Thomas Bullitt's surveying group to the Falls in the spring of 1773. (Alexander Scott Bullitt of Oxmoor was a nephew of Thomas Bullitt.) However, when the area was resurveyed in 1774, the plat of John Connolly's 2,000-acres that included much of Louisville, specifically noted the mouth of Bear Grass Creek.[13]

It should be noted that yucca was not included in Dr. Henry McMurtrie's very extensive "Florula Louisvillensis," published as part of his *Sketches of Louisville And Its Environs* in 1819. One would think that McMurtrie would certainly have listed the plant if it had been as prevalent as Rothert reported, or he would have made note of its not being abundant but still the source of the creek's name. (Interestingly, the list of most common plants of the Beargrass Creek basin, published in 1975 by the U. S. Army Corps of Engineers as part of the environmental impact study, did not include yucca.)

While the springs that fed the various branches of Beargrass Creek were the main suppliers of drinking water, wells were also dug. However, in at least one section, between the headwaters of the Muddy Fork and the Middle Fork, the well water had a noticeable trace of sulfur. William A. Harris is remembered as operating a works that bottled mineral water on Arterburn property east of where Zimmerman Lane (now LaGrange Road) commenced at Shelbyville Road, near a nightspot known as Norwood Gardens.[14] In January 1923, Norbourn and Sallie Arterburn had filed a plat for Norwood Place,

VIEW UP BEARGRASS CREEK BORDERED BY ANCIENT LIMESTONE OUTCROPPINGS AND THE BACKS OF NEW HOMES ON BALMORAL DRIVE IN THE SPRINGS SUBDIVISION. NEARBY IS AN HISTORICAL MARKER COMMEMORATING JOHN FLOYD, ERECTED BY THE BEARGRASS-ST. MATTHEWS HISTORICAL SOCIETY. BY SAMUEL W. THOMAS, 1999.

prepared by Olmsted Brothers of Brookline, Mass.[15] At the center of the subdivision remains a commons called Norwood Park. The Indian Mineral Wells, a corporation created to bottle and distribute mineral water and carbonated beverages, was formed in 1930; and it acquired a prominent lot overlooking the west end of Norwood Park (now the site of two structures of black glass called the Norwood Office Park).[16] Presumably, this was Harris's operation as he owned the property across the road, which was designated on the Olmsted plat as Boone Highway. Eventually, the Indian Wells bottling works was acquired by the Epping family.

With the proliferation of septic tanks that accompanied development east of Louisville after the 1937 flood, wells became contaminated. Waste seepage found its way into the reaches of Beargrass Creek. "Nothing is more constant than the creek with its infernal stench and tragic beauty," Janet McWilliams pointed out in her August 1979 *Louisville* magazine article, "Stream of History." Ira Simmons would note in his 28 April 1990 *Courier-Journal Scene* piece, "Stream of Conflict," that "it repels at one moment, fascinates the next. Slimy, stinking despair clashes with sun-sparkles of possibility." A task force was appointed in 1992 to develop ways to improve Beargrass Creek's water quality.[17] When a car dealership near the stone Eight-Mile House requested permission to pave over a section of the Middle Fork, various groups weighed in.[18] At least Beargrass Creek is now generating the environmental concern that has been lacking since it provided a means of pioneer transportation.[19]

BEARGRASS CREEK WAS REROUTED AROUND THE SITE OF HQ HOME QUARTERS WAREHOUSE (NOT SEEN AT LEFT), AND PROVIDES A SCENIC FRONTAGE FOR THE SPRINGS OFFICE BUILDING. BY SAMUEL W. THOMAS, 1999.

Construction of the long-awaited sewers of St. Matthews will start this morning. The $2,225,000 project is expected to be completed in 400 days, or by August of next year....

Originally the outfall sewer was to have led to a plant which would have dumped treated sewage into the Beargrass—a plan which brought protests from Louisville officials....

Instead of the treatment plant, the St. Matthews Sanitation District will build a pumping station on the Beargrass site. It is necessary to pump sewage uphill to a tie-in with the City's Beals Branch sewer main at Wilmington and Cannons Lane.

From "St. Matthews Sewer Work Starts Today," *The Courier-Journal*, 27 July 1948.

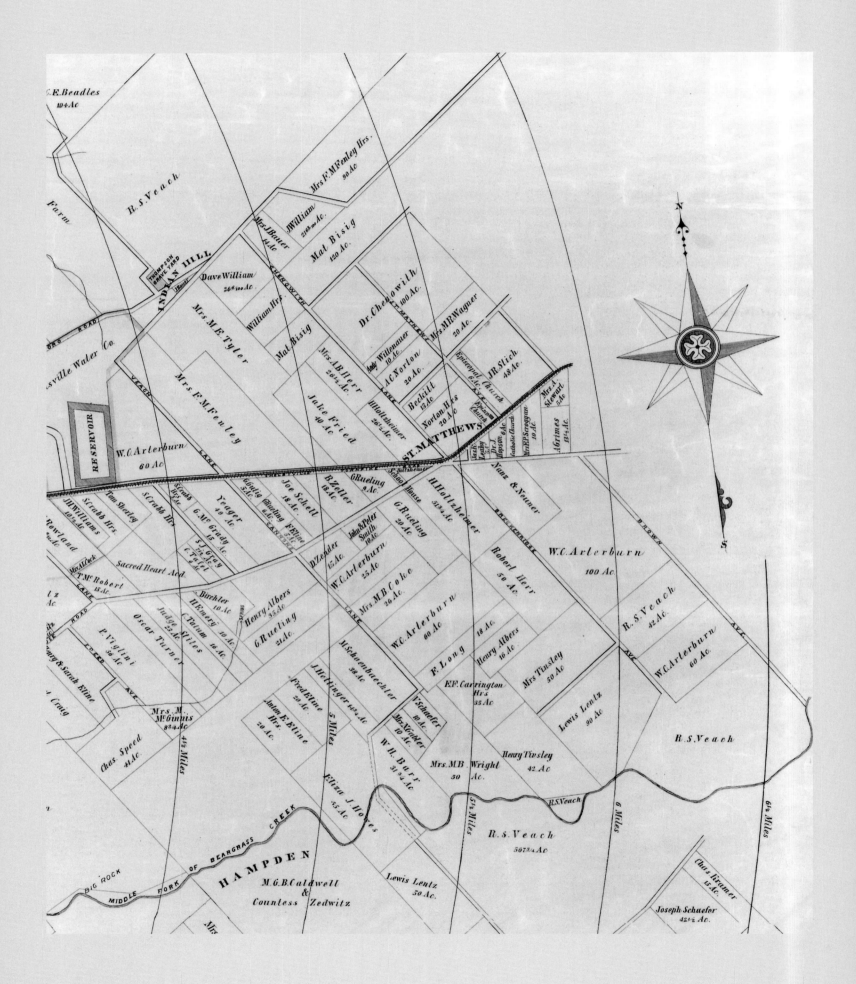

The prominent, working inhabitants of most rural communities appeared in the sporadic issues of the *Kentucky State Gazetteer and Business Directory* published by R. L. Polk & Co. In 1896, the list for St. Matthews was quite select and worthy of inclusion (by last name first). Arterburn Norben [Norbourn], farmer; Arterburn Wm. C., farmer; Bauer Edward, painter; Bauer L & Bros (Louis, Henry and John), general store; Brown Theodore, farmer; Bullitt Henry M., farmer; Butler James, farmer; Chenoweth Henry, physician; Crowder Charles W. barber; Eline Frederick, gardener; Eline Henry, gardener; Fisher [Fischer] Mrs. Teresa, grocer; Gehring Theodore, blacksmith; Guetig Peter, grocer; Hettinger Jacob, gardener; Holtzheimer [Holzheimer] Henry, farmer; Hopson Joseph H., physician; McCarthy Robert, farmer; Monahan [Monohan] Edward S., farmer; Naschand [Nachand] Peter, gardener; Pattie Wm. R., station agent; Stich John L., farmer; Veech Richard S., stock breeder; and Zehender Dominick [Zehnder, Dominic], dairy.

Early in 1887, brothers Louis H. and John E. Bauer had purchased the two-story, brick grocery and tavern at the crossroads that Henry Holzheimer had erected and operated after he purchased the site from Daniel Gilman in 1871.[1] They were joined in the venture by their younger brother, Henry. Their father, John Bauer, had purchased a small triangle of land on

CHAPTER V

TURN OF THE CENTURY

OPPOSITE: SECTION OF "NEW MAP OF LOUISVILLE AND ENVIRONS," 1891, BY MERRITT DRANE.

A DELIVERY FROM THE G. G. EHRMANN CANDY COMPANY BEING MADE ABOUT 1895. STRUCTURE SAT ON THE NORTHEAST CORNER OF CHENOWETH LANE AND SHELBYVILLE ROAD. ICE HOUSE IS AT RIGHT. BEARGRASS-ST. MATTHEWS HISTORICAL SOCIETY.

The Bauers also had a restaurant at Devil's Kitchen—Hikes Point. There were only about five houses over there, but our blacksmith's shop was at Devil's Kitchen, too.

From interview of Alice O. Monohan, 3 October 1996.

the Brownsboro Road from Richard S. Veech in 1868. He had been a blacksmith for Ainslie, Cochran & Co., before setting up his own shop near his residence, where he died in 1880. Bauer's other sons, Charles C. and Albert W. Bauer, expanded the business into wagon manufacturing. When Charles, "a former Deputy Sheriff and wagon manufacturer at Indian Hill, near St. Matthews," died in 1909, he was president of Bauer Bros.[2] His brother, Albert W. Bauer, took over and with his sons modernized the shop. According to Angeline Young Bauer, they served lunch to the men who worked in the shop. When she married Albert W. Bauer, Jr., she started making sandwiches for others. "There was a place to tie their horses out front. They sold soft drinks and we started serving sandwiches for 10 cents and 15 cents. People used to drive out here at night when automobiles first started." From such

VIEW OF A. W. BAUER & SONS' NEW ESTABLISHMENT AS IT APPEARED ON 1917 CALENDAR. IT WAS REPLACED BY A MODERN STANDARD OIL COMPANY STATION, WHICH HAS ALSO BEEN RAZED. SITE IS NOW A PARKING LOT FOR AZALEA RESTAURANT. COURTESY BAUER'S SINCE 1870 COLLECTION.

meager beginnings came Bauer's since 1870 restaurant. As the art of wagon making disappeared, a filling station emerged in its place run by Edward L. Schwartz, who had worked for the Bauers. That has been torn down to create additional parking for Azalea.

John Bauer's daughter, Catherine M. Bauer, married Jacob W. Heskamp, who had moved to St. Matthews from a German-speaking community in Adair County about 1899. He established a blacksmith shop across Chenoweth Lane from L. Bauer & Bro's grocery and tavern. At some point Louis Bauer added a wagon making aspect to the business and the firm became Heskamp & Bauer. The structure was "unroofed and is now decorated with tarpaulin covering" following a violent storm in 1912. Another report on the "Doings of the Saints" in *The Jeffersonian* of 16 May 1912 noted: "Our new blacksmith has arrived and the shop opened this morning. See how quickly one can obtain their desires, if advertised in The Jeffersonian? This gentleman is a Middletown product, but I can't spell his name until I meet him and find the proper number of consonants to give it the German accent."

Albert & Louis Bauer and some more of St. Matthews men had a chicken fight today, and Albert lost 2 fights. They were about 12 men from St. Matthews. They had a fine time.

From Katie Ochsner's letter to husband Martin Ochsner, 19 February 1901. Ochsner family collection, Beargrass-St. Matthews Historical Society.

The 1892 Sanborn map delineated several nondescript structures on the northeast corner of Henry Holzheimer's property facing Shelbyville Road west of Breckenridge Lane. In 1899, he deeded the corner to his son-in-law, Frederick J. Edinger, who erected a substantial brick structure to house his tavern and grocery, as well as his household.[3] A little to the west, Edinger

also built a feed store which had a hall on the second floor that he in effect sold to the trustees of Matamora Tribe No. 25 of the Improved Order of Red Men of St. Matthews.[4] Little is known about the tribe's activities or how long they continued to powwow over the feed store. However, Edinger died at the age of 52 in 1903, and Alfred P. Grieshaber took over the tavern and grocery before relinquishing them to William A. Fehr.

HESKAMP & BAUER WAGON MANUFACTURERS ON THE WEST SIDE OF CHENOWETH LANE AT INTERSECTION OF WESTPORT ROAD, ABOUT 1910. BEARGRASS-ST. MATTHEWS HISTORICAL SOCIETY.

HESKAMP & BAUER
ST. MATTHEWS, KY.
Blacksmiths & Wagon Makers
Rubber Tires a Specialty.

Manufacturers of All Styles of
BUGGIES,
Spring, Platform, Farm and Light Family Wagons and Road Carts.
Also Horse Shoeing and Repairing done in the best manner.

ADVERTISEMENT FROM *THE JEFFERSONIAN*, 17 FEBRUARY 1910.

MEETING OF MATAMORA TRIBE NO. 25 ABOUT 1905. BEARGRASS-ST. MATTHEWS HISTORICAL SOCIETY.

There were some Red Men there. I had an uncle who belonged to the Red Men. I remember attending a Red Men's picnic back on Breckenridge Lane on the Lentz place. I think we ate soup out of a tin cup. It wasn't fancy.

From interview of Cornelia Drescher Stone, 16 December 1996.

When a beautiful suburban, 9-room, brick home with bath, closets, and large attic, complete with all necessary outbuildings, servants' quarters, ice house, and large barn on four and three-quarters acres, "beautifully shaded with grand old forest trees," near St. Matthews, was advertised in the *Louisville Commercial* in May 1898, the main selling point was the "prospect in short time of Electric Cars running to St. Matthews."[5] Almost three years later, a report surfaced in *The Courier-Journal* that a "Trolley Line Will Probably Be Built To LaGrange."[6] The increased speculation that "Louisville is likely to have a suburban electric railway" must have been eagerly anticipated by commuters in the east end who were tired of mule car service or no railway service at all—and the latter included St. Matthews. Reportedly, the greater part of the right of way had been secured, and the project's backers from Cleveland were scrutinizing their investment. Their representative, A. L. Smartt, was optimistic, noting that "Louisville was the only large city in the country that did not have a suburban road." Apparently, the Cleveland backing fizzled out, and the project was taken on by locals with financial backing from Cincinnati interests. According to the noted railway historian, George Yater, Percy Moore of Anchorage is "always given credit for initiating and carrying out the scheme."[7] The Louisville, Anchorage & Pewee Valley Electric Railway was chartered on January 14th. By the spring of 1901, it was not a question of one suburban line but how many? When a major backer was asked about the interurban's prospects, he was quick to point out its convenience. "The train service furnished by the Louisville and Nashville is all right as far as it goes, but the railroad company cannot afford to run a train every time somebody wants to come out from town. We don't propose to do that, but we will run them often enough to satisfy everybody." He pointed out that the route would "present an inviting field to those seeking homes in the country." And "what man can be found who will not take his family on a fifty or sixty-mile ride through the open country on a summer night when he can have that ride at a moderate cost?" Besides allowing people to travel when the roads were bad in the winter, noted the stockholder, the interurban "will be of material benefit to the farmers and truck gardeners, enabling them to get their goods on the market bright and early without having to leave home at an unreasonable hour of the morning."[8]

On 13 November 1901, the first car ventured from Anchorage to Liberty Street and back again to test the operations that would soon begin in earnest. At the same time, an electric car replaced the mule car line to Crescent Hill.[9] The transportation company's name was changed in 1903 to the Louisville & Eastern Railroad. When it extended service to Middletown and Shelbyville in 1910, the operation went under and was purchased at a receiver's sale in 1911 by a subsidiary of the Louisville Railway Company, the Louisville & Interurban.[10] Before old railroad cars became popular as diners, Granville Hooper of St. Matthews made use of obsolete mule cars to create "the streetcar bungalow." A 1910 *Courier-Journal* pictured Hooper building a room to connect two mule cars for farmhand quarters.[11]

In 1911 an improvement club was established in St. Matthews "for

Interurban tracks in front of Plehn's Bakery, October 1933. Caufield and Shook Collection 129340, University of Louisville Photographic Archives.

the betterment of the community at large and beautifying of all avenues and vacant lots....Among their efforts will be urging (in more ways than one) the L. & E. to build a station at St. Matthews worthy of the place, instead of a shed too small for half a dozen persons to stand on and an impossibility to accommodate a few ladies' hats, much less baggage. In this day of progress such neglect is shameful."[12] According to Irvin A. Young, "nearly every one of the places along the road had a station agent and he would take their orders and he would call into the main office and they would ship it out on the car from Belknap's or wherever it might come. They run two baggages in the morning and two in the evening. You could get in or off at any square. It was just like a regular streetcar. In the evening when they would come out, there were only two or three minutes between cars."[13] But later it became Young's job to dismantle various interurban lines that fanned out from Louisville. When the Louisville Railway Company announced service would cease in 1935, it reasoned that mounting losses were caused by "returning prosperity to farmers and truck gardeners who are able to buy automobiles."[14] The tracks were soon torn up and Shelbyville Road was widened.

Simultaneous with the coming of the interurban was the passing of the toll road. In 1901, Jefferson County's turnpikes were purchased by Fiscal Court.[15] There had been agitation for years to make the main roads free of tolls. The first tollgate on the Shelbyville Pike was located at the three-mile mark (Clifton); the next was at the eight-mile post. "Here has been established one of the most modern of tollhouses, with a new frame house, an

There were two interurbans. The yellow cars went on out to the Beechwood Junction and went on over to LaGrange. The other, the L & I, the Louisville & Interurban, they were the big cars. They were four-motor cars. The yellow cars were two-motor cars. They had two trucks with a motor in each one. But the big cars were over-the-road runners. They had a baggage compartment in the front end and they picked up milk and whatever have you, in competition to the L & N.

From interview of Henry W. Metzner, 6 January 1972.

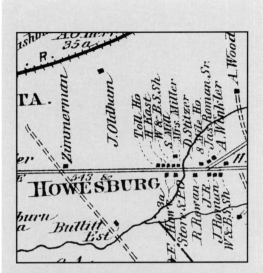

DETAIL OF HOWESBURG SETTLEMENT ALONG
SHELBYVILLE ROAD WEST OF WHIPPS MILL
ROAD. FROM BEERS & LANAGAN'S ATLAS OF
JEFFERSON & OLDHAM COUNTIES, KENTUCKY,
1879.

THE JOHN ORRS AT EIGHT-MILE TOLLHOUSE,
FEBRUARY 1886. REPRINTED IN *THE COURIER-
JOURNAL*, 30 JUNE 1939.

iron swing bar gate that is closed at night and a long-distance telephone," *The Courier-Journal* reported in 1901. "It is not picturesque, it is too civilized and too progressive." An accompanying photograph shows a single story frame building on the north side of the road. A photograph was later published taken from the east side in February 1886, when it was first operated by John Orr and his wife.[16] The tolls were a cent a mile for a person on horseback, 2 cents for a horse and buggy, and 4 cents for two horses and a vehicle. Orr collected less than $40 a week in good months. When asked in 1939 about the idea of collecting tolls for the new Pennsylvania Turnpike, he replied: "What are they going back to them for? Do they want to make everybody mad? Nothing like a toll to put people out of sorts."[17] Orr could recall times of traffic congestion during his 15-year stint on Shelbyville Road when "horse-drawn carriages and wagons would be lined up way down the road." When the tolls ceased being collected in May 1901, the house was sold to George Shadburne. In 1906, Frank Ochsner purchased the property and in 1965 it was razed for a Convenient Food Market.[18]

There has been some confusion over the years as to what the Eight-Mile House was and where it was located. On the 1879 atlas, the Eight-Mile House is depicted as owned by David Stitzer and located on the north side of the Louisville & Lexington Turnpike just west of the intersection with the Dorseys' lane (now called Whipps Mill Road) that led northeastward to Ormsby Station on the railroad. The tollhouse was located east of there across a branch of Beargrass Creek. That area was referred to as Howesburg, as G. F. Howe operated a store and the post office across the turnpike, where the tollgate had been earlier. Little is known about the early history of the small, story and a half, stone house where Stitzer ran a stopping off place for turnpike

travelers. It had been once owned by a stage coach company prior to that.[19] Compounding the confusion was a 1934 newspaper piece by James Speed about this structure, in which the noted Louisville architect, E. T. Hutchings, was quoted: "Why, of course, I know this little old stone house, it's immediately beyond the old Eight-Mile House on the Shelbyville Road, isn't it?"[20] The Eight-Mile House that Hutchings was referring to was the roadhouse dance hall, located east of the old toll house, that had burned to the ground on 4 March 1930. The sprawling complex had been erected 48 years before by Martin Ochsner and operated by him for fifteen years before changing ownership several times.[21]

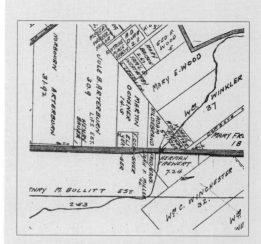

DETAIL OF HOWESBURG, THEN KNOWN AS EIGHT-MILE HOUSE FROM THE LOUISVILLE TITLE COMPANY'S NEW MAP OF LOUISVILLE AND JEFFERSON COUNTY, KENTUCKY, 1913.

FRAME EIGHT-MILE HOUSE, 1948. DANCE HALL AND PAVILION THAT BURNED WERE IN REAR. ZV 10-48U, JEFFERSON COUNTY PRESERVATION AND ARCHIVES.

The interurban was a boon to the early development of St. Matthews, and the Bauers, particularly Louis, capitalized on their strategic location at the intersection of five roads, a railroad and a railway. Louis Bauer also served as postmaster. The post office was located for a time in the rear of the tavern and grocery, and a large icehouse was located just east on Shelbyville Road. However, by 1905 that had been replaced by a large, frame feed and storage (presumably of potatoes and onions) that was attached to the Bauers' brick building. A dance hall was on the second floor.

Then with Louis' lead, the Bank of St. Matthews was incorporated in late 1905, and a classically styled, single story, brick edifice was erected on Bauer-owned land to the west of their tavern and grocery.[22] Forty-eight persons, a who's who of turn-of-the-century St. Matthews, subscribed for the 300 shares ($50 per share) of stock.[23] The principals, holding 20 shares each, were G. T. Dick, Oscar Fenley, Aleck Staebler, W. N. Arterburn, John M. Monohan, and E S. Monohan, Jr. Louis Bauer had only 8 shares, but he became president. He remained in that capacity until he died in 1943.[24] But during that entire period, cashier Gilbert T. Dick was responsible for making the bank work, and he was named chairman of the board in 1940. He also

My dad and his two brothers started the garage business about 1920 across from the Eight-Mile House, which was a night club and beer joint that was right next to where Oxmoor Liquors is now. That is where my aunt and uncle, the Andrew J. Schmitts, lived. She was my dad's sister. My dad, Herman Ochsner, was born back on the Oxmoor farm, where his father worked. Dad used to work on county trucks and for Heskamp before he got into the garage. One of his brothers died and in 1937 he split up with the other, and moved down Shelbyville Road where we are still. My uncle sold the old Ochsner garage to Epp Stich & Sons in the mid-1940s. I was born in 1928 and I started working in the garage after the war. My brothers, Henry and Robert, also worked there.

From interview of Richard Ochsner, 26 November 1996.

HERMAN OCHSNER AND HIS FATHER, FRANK,
INSIDE GARAGE, 1920. FROM RICHARD
OCHSNER COLLECTION.

OCHSNER'S GARAGE, LATER EPP STICH & SONS
GARAGE, 1920. STANDING ALONG THE
INTERURBAN TRACKS WERE, FROM LEFT TO
RIGHT: FRANK AND HERMAN OCHSNER, JOHN
BEIERLE AND ALVIN HAEBERLIN. FROM RICHARD
OCHSNER COLLECTION.

St. Matthews Bank on the northeast corner of Chenoweth Lane and Shelbyville Road, 1924. Given by Sara Eline Breeland to the Beargrass-St. Matthews Historical Society.

operated an insurance agency and found time to be active in almost every facet of community life.[25]

Cornelia Drescher Stone was born on 9 August 1901, but she vividly recalled in 1996 the New Year's day in 1908 when her family came to St. Matthews in a top wagon pulled by a horse, with the family cow tied to the back. They were coming from Farmington, the beautiful, old Speed family place on the Bardstown Road, where she was born. Her grandfather, Henry Drescher, had purchased Farmington in 1865 for $16,000. Only four years earlier, President Lincoln had presented Lucy Speed with a photographic portrait of himself, marking his extended stay at Farmington 20 years before in 1841. When Henry Drescher died in 1907, his will specified that the homestead be sold, and thus George and Philippine Drescher found their way to a four-room cottage on Chenoweth Lane, where his sister, Barbara, and her husband, Will Eigelbach, lived nearby.

As Cornelia Drescher Stone begins to describe the heart of St. Matthews when the Drescher family arrived in 1908, she notes that "the bank on the corner was already there." She continues: "There was a lot of

Entrance of St. Matthews Bank, 1912. Courtesy of Mary Elizabeth Ratterman Ruckriegel

Public scales are visible at base of utility pole in Triangle intersection of Shelbyville Road, Chenoweth Lane, and Westport Road. *Ca.* 1910 view also shows public water trough next to west side of St. Matthews Bank. Bauer bothers building (with one-story brick ell extending back to Westport Road) is behind (east of) it. Westport Road leading east is at left. Beargrass-St. Matthews Historical Society.

open space in the middle of St. Matthews. Right in there was a scale where they weighed produce or whatever they had on the wagon. That was out in the middle of everything—where all the roads came together. That was a public scale, I guess. They used to pull the team up there. The scales were in the ground—flat, you drove onto them. I remember seeing wagons being weighed there."[26] The scales were not indicated on the 1892 Sanborn map, but were delineated on the subsequent version published in 1905.

"When St. Matthews got a new post office," Mrs. Stone remembers, "they moved the old one out of the Bauer building to the new one right across the street. There was a little plot of ground between the railroad depot and Chenoweth Lane, and the new post office was built over there. Mr. Crowder took what used to be the post office in the back corner of the Bauer building and had his barbershop there." When Louis Bauer retired after 24 years as postmaster in 1915, a separate post office was erected, and William Farris took over as postmaster. *The Jeffersonian* reported that Farris would "continue his service at the L & N depot, and his son will take charge of the mail and parcel post."[27]

Cornelia Drescher Stone also observed that "there was no gate or anything at the railroad tracks at Chenoweth. There were a number of people killed around there by the trains. There was one little girl killed there that I remember. She was driving a pony cart, and she was a cousin of one of the people living on Chenoweth Lane. Mabel Kimble was her name. They lived on Cannons Lane."

During the first decade of the twentieth century, farmers in the vicinity of St. Matthews began to concentrate on raising potatoes and onions as cash crops. Tobacco growing had been relegated since before the Civil War to the poor-soil barrens of Hart, Barren, and Metcalfe counties. The "bright wrapper" tobacco produced there had to be fire dried. In the 1870s, Burley tobacco became popular because it could be dried without fire, and considerable criticism was raised when Bluegrass farmers began "skimming their lands." *The Courier-Journal* conceded in 1893 that "they are making money, but they are impoverishing the finest soil on the Western hemisphere."[28] Perhaps that

---

BELOW: ST. MATTHEWS POST OFFICE ON THE EAST SIDE OF CHENOWETH LANE BETWEEN WESTPORT ROAD AND THE RAILROAD TRACKS, *CA.* 1920. THE 12 FT. BY 16 FT. FRAME STRUCTURE HAS FOR MANY YEARS BEEN BEHIND THE MARTIN RUCKRIEGELS' GARAGE AT THE CORNER OF WESTPORT ROAD AND RIDGEWAY AVENUE. AN ADDITION HAD BEEN MADE TO THE BRICK BLACKSMITH'S SHOP ACROSS CHENOWETH LANE. COURTESY OF MARY ELIZABETH RATTERMAN RUCKRIEGEL.

Mabel Kimble, the nine-year-old daughter of George Kimble, a carpenter, was struck by a north-bound L & N train at St. Matthews yesterday afternoon at 5:30 o'clock and instantly killed. The little girl was hurled a distance of sixty feet and almost every bone in her body was broken.

The little girl had been visiting the home of Alex. Staebler, a relative, and was returning to her home when struck by the train. According to the story of J. W. Ragland, the station agent, the girl was walking up the tracks and became confused when she saw the train approaching. There are three sets of tracks at this point, and the child, instead of stepping clear of the tracks, moved to the center track and was struck by the fast train and hurled many feet ahead.

The remains were removed to the home of the father on Guetig's [Cannons] Lane, who when he heard of the tragic death of his daughter collapsed. The physician who worked with him for several hours fears the man's mind will be affected by the tragedy.

From "Child Hurled To Instant Death," *The Louisville Times*, 29 July 1908.

was the reason little Burley tobacco was grown locally, although Louisville had become the leading leaf market. Also rooted in the conservative thinking of the German and Swiss farmers who labored around St. Matthews was the consideration that potatoes were a staple as well as a source of income.

For decades, the area farmers' cash crop had been hemp, but it had required considerable processing before being made into a useful fiber. As Thomas W. Bullitt noted in his memoir about Oxmoor, subtitled *Life On A Farm In Kentucky Before The War*, "the 'crops' raised were hemp, corn, and wheat. Hemp was the money crop, though corn and wheat were also sold. A considerable amount of both, however, were consumed on the place." Recalling that "cutting hemp in the summer and breaking hemp in the winter was the hardest work done on a Kentucky farm," Bullitt pointed out when writing his recollections in 1906 that "little hemp is raised anywhere in Kentucky." Unfortunately the machinery to cut hemp's gummy fiber had only recently been manufactured, and while the demand for hemp seed improved during World War I, it would never approach the production achieved when ropewalks were a prevalent part of commercial activity.[29] Bullitt did mention that in one of Oxmoor's two gardens, "there was always a large space devoted

Isn't it dreadful our post office is robbed so often? Again, the safe was blown open. All money, about $16, and many stamps were taken. Although blood hounds were put on the trail, so far it has been impossible to find the guilty parties. We are sorry for the financial loss, but more troubled that Mr. Farris should be put to this embarrassment when he so recently took charge of the work and is so faithful and honest in his duties.

From A. B. C., "St. Matthews News Letter," *The Jeffersonian*, 26 August 1915.

to sweet potatoes and Irish potatoes." Evidently, with the immigration of Irish and others who depended on the potato as a staple, the market for such produce in Louisville and other towns connected by the railroad grew steadily, and area farmers began to put more land into potato cultivation to satisfy the increasing demand.

In the old days, when the farmer brought his potatoes in to St. Matthews he was met by a phalanx of buyers and commission merchants who had previously decided what price he should receive for his commodity. If he did not accept the price offered he was "out of luck" as there was no other place to sell. Eastern and Northern markets wanted potatoes, of course, but they wanted them only in carload lots, whereas the farmer perhaps had only twenty barrels to dispose of.

From "The Gospel of St. Matthews," *The Courier-Journal*, 30 January 1921.

About 1910, an interurban spur line was constructed over the Shelbyville Road, west of St. Matthews Avenue. Terminating at Westport Road, its function was to service the St. Matthews Ice and Cold Storage and St. Matthews Produce Exchange that had been built on St. Matthews Avenue and were separated by an alley. The ice and cold storage facility, incorporated in 1908 and in operation a year later, was a precursor of the produce exchange.[30] Its business included "the manufacturing and sale of ice, the storing and refrigeration of potatoes, vegetables, fruits, meats and other perishable articles, the buying and selling of coal and other fuels, the buying and selling, either directly or on commission, of various farm and garden products."[31] The days of cutting ice off ponds and storing it in icehouses and using

100-LB. SACKS OF KENTUCKY WINNER POTATOES FROM ST. MATTHEWS BEING UNLOADED AT LOUISVILLE HAYMARKET IN 1943. THOMAS, *LOUISVILLE SINCE THE TWENTIES*, 135.

spring water houses for refrigeration were passing. Farmers and gardeners could ship their perishables by interurban for cold storage prior to sale. What they could not control was the price they would receive when the produce was sold.

To rectify the situation, a cooperative was established, incorporated as the St. Matthews Produce Exchange in 1910.[32] John Carr Fenley became president the following year, and Robert Warner Hite was manager. They were not only officers of the company for years but were near neighbors on the Westport Road where their families had resided and farmed for generations. Fenley died in 1946 at the age of 77. Hite retired in 1945, and the exchange was dissolved seven years before he died in 1961 at 92.[33]

When a wagon or truck arrived at the exchange, it was weighed before the potatoes were unloaded at the warehouse and graded. Culls were put back on the vehicle and the crop was graded as to the percent of first and second class. The driver would return to the exchange office across St. Matthews Avenue from the warehouse, have the culls weighed, and receive a receipt for the difference. He could pick up a check the next day. It was R. W. Hite's responsibility to seek active markets around the country by telegraph when orders here were not brisk. Reportedly, during the initial year of business, the exchange disposed of 250 carloads of potatoes, netting the farmer 60 cents a hundred pounds. By 1920, 13-million pounds were being sold. About 20 percent were trucked to Louisville, the remainder went elsewhere by rail.[34] Not only did the cooperative sell potatoes and other produce, but it also purchased material like fertilizer, "Paris green," and twine in bulk quantities for the farmers.

In 1925, St Matthews was recognized by the *Christian Science Monitor* as "one of the greatest potato shipping centers in the country." " For years," the newspaper pointed out, "Jefferson County was noted as the leader in second-crop potatoes. Its climate and soil permitted two crops of tubers on the same land in the same year. Two-thirds of this crop, and of all the other vegetables crops grown on the rich farms hereabouts, are shipped from this town....St. Matthews is the home of a co-operative produce exchange with 400 members which normally ships 1,200 cars of potatoes and onions annually."[35]

Eventually, the exchange operation was moved across Westport Road and north of the railroad tracks. In late 1952, the property, then owned by Mark Denunzio, was purchased by R. W. Marshall, who wanted to move his planing mill, lumberyard, and warehouse from Breckenridge Lane to larger quarters.[36]

Baseball was first played in St. Matthews in an organized fashion on "Staebler Commons" beginning in 1911.[37] The ball park's grandstand, which faced southwest, was located just west of St. Matthews Avenue, midway between the railroad tracks and Massie Avenue.[38] After World War I, the Stich family provided the grounds and manicured the field. Stichs' Park was a short throw further out Westport Road, west of Ridgeway Avenue. John Lawrence Stich had come to America from Bavaria, Germany, and he acquired almost

St. Matthews, besides being the place where the hand of the constable has cooled the ardor of many a motorist speeding into Louisville, is the second largest onion and potato shipping point in the United States....

Last year, during the months of July and August, the St. Matthews Produce Exchange sold more than 200,000 barrels of onions and potatoes. The price obtained for the lot was about $1,000,000. During these two months of its greatest activity the St. Matthews house is the biggest potato shipping point in the United States. A point in the state of Maine, where winter potatoes are shipped, goes a little ahead of St. Matthews on its total yearly shipments.

From Clarence E. Cason, "Live Towns Around Louisville, *The Louisville Herald*, 30 July 1922.

EDWIN J. "EPP" STICH, CA. 1935, SURROUNDED BY FAMILY, IN WHICH ONE WAS NEVER TOO YOUNG TO START PLAYING BASEBALL. COURTESY OF EARL COMBS STICH.

PLAN OF ST. MATTHEWS AVENUE NORTH OF WESTPORT ROAD SHOWING BALL PARK AND GRANDSTAND, DATED JUNE 1916. JEFFERSON COUNTY PRESERVATION AND ARCHIVES.

48 acres in the division of the Ridgeway property, which he farmed. When he died in 1899 at the age of 67, his obituary said he was "an extensive gardener and a man of considerable means...and no man in that section of the country had more friends."[39] His son, Jacob, continued to farm the land before moving to Browns Lane and he had a fleet of hauling trucks. Jacob's son, Edwin Joseph "Epp" Stich was infatuated with baseball, and they carved a baseball field out of the homestead complete with stands and a concession

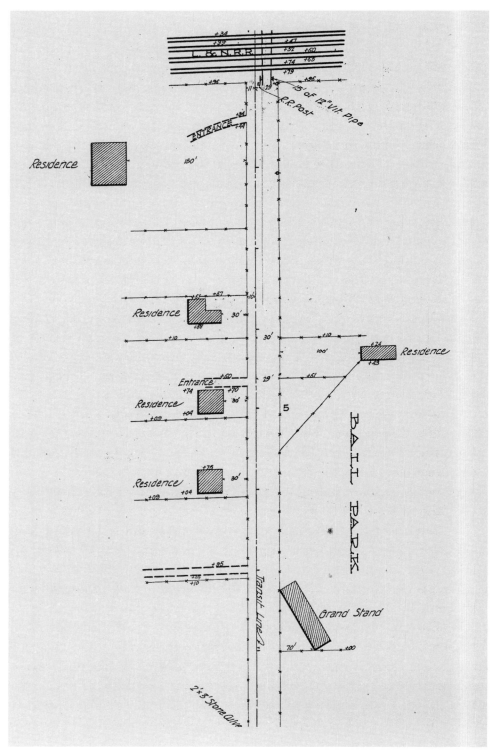

booth. Epp continued to play baseball well beyond his youth, going so far as to name his three sons after New York Yankee stars. Eventually, the Stichs relinquished the operation of their ball field, and a field was established on Holy Trinity property across Westport Road. The St. Matthews Produce Exchange built a new facility where Stichs' Park had once been, and later it was taken over by the Marshall Planing Mill and its lumberyard. Epp Stich worked for A. J. Eline and others as an automobile mechanic, and in 1944 he purchased the old Ochsner Garage on Shelbyville Road across from the frame Eight-Mile House.[40]

In April of 1912, *The Jeffersonian* welcomed Edward Martin and his family who "have moved to their new home in Castleman Avenue."[41] For the most part, the street was known as Massie Avenue, but because Sam Castleman had a 20-acre tract on the north side of the road that honored the first family, it was sometimes termed for him. In any case, Cornelia Drescher Stone, whose family moved to Chenoweth Lane in 1908, knew the Martins and the area well. Edward C. Martin died in 1950 at the age of 75.[42]

Across from our house, looking east, was nothing but pasture land. That belonged to Mr. Gehring. They subdivided that and that is where the Martin family came in. They sold off some lots on Massie Avenue middle ways toward St. Matthews Avenue. Mr. Edward Martin built his house there. P. R. Feigel, who was the dentist, built the house next door. We got acquainted with the Martins through the Dorsey family who lived next door to us. I spent a lot of time over there. We played baseball right in their yard. It was fun. I was good friends with Mary Martin, who was the oldest. Her father worked for W. D. Gatchel at Fifth and Walnut. Most of his work was developing pictures that were brought into the store. He made the trip to town every day to bring home a bundle and work on them for the next day. He did my photograph maybe as a favor. He had a little building out in the back yard, not far from the house, and it was his darkroom. I have been in there a few times. I knew a little bit about developing the film and I knew it had to hang up to dry. I remember seeing that.

"Our little township is still going forward, city people being attracted by its many advantages, combining all of the conveniences of the metropolis with country products and fresh air," Mrs. John Simcoe wrote in her column on St. Matthews for *The Jeffersonian* of 19 September 1912. "The Misses Eline have purchased a lot in Hopson Addition from Mr. Dudley Gregory and will erect an up-to-date department store within the next two months. These ladies are first class milliners and will make a specialty at that department, which appeals to us women folks." The St. Matthews Addition had been platted in 1907 as a subdivision of Dr. Joseph Hopson's property that ran between the Shelbyville Road and Westport Road. It was divided into 28 lots,

EDWARD C. MARTIN'S DARK ROOM ON MASSIE AVENUE, CA. 1915. MARTIN FAMILY COLLECTION.

Roller skating has reached St. Matthews. This craze (for craze it is) has put all on wheels that can possibly stand for five minutes. Pedestrians must be on the lookout more than ever, even then, we are jostled and bumped, but we take it kindly and "butt some" in our frantic efforts to get out of the way.

From *The Jeffersonian*, 17 April 1913.

Northeast corner of St. Matthews Avenue and Shelbyville Road about 1913. Given by Henrietta Sara Eline Breeland to the Beargrass-St. Matthews Historical Society.

separated down the middle by a new 40-foot-wide street designated as St. Matthews Avenue.[43] Dr. Hopson, a native of Trigg County, received his medical education in Louisville and practiced in St. Matthews for many years. He died in 1923 at the age of 77.[44]

The Elines had purchased the three lots comprising the northeast corner of St. Matthews Avenue and Shelbyville Road.[45] Anthony J. Eline erected the first of his many houses in St. Matthews for his mother, Rosa, sisters Rose and Carrie, as well as for his wife and two children. Tony Eline had been born and raised on a small, 20-acre farm near Seneca Park. His father, Anton E. Eline, died when he was an infant, and his mother supported the family by leasing the farmland. He received only a fourth grade education from Miss Tommie Greathouse before setting out to work. He married Elizabeth Hartman in 1911, and two of their children were born on the farm property he would later develop as Homestead Drive and Circle Hill Road. Behind the frame, four square residence on Shelbyville Road that housed on the first floor, as the sign read, "Mrs. R. Eline, Gents Furnishings," Tony built a garage to sell and repair automobiles—at first Overlands and then Fords.

Then on 25 March 1915, *The Jeffersonian* asked its readers to "take

ELINE'S FIRST GARAGE ON THE EAST SIDE OF
ST. MATTHEWS AVENUE BEHIND FAMILY RESI-
DENCE THAT FRONTED SHELBYVILLE ROAD,
1946. ZV 35-46U, JEFFERSON COUNTY
HISTORIC PRESERVATION AND ARCHIVES.

notice of A. J. Eline's new garage, built of concrete blocks. It certainly gives us a city feeling to have it show off our town. Their purified gasoline is on tap in a blazing red tank at the parting of the ways. Aren't we moving along?" By 1917, Eline was advertising Ford cars and touting himself as "Agent for the Whole County." Eline's Garage was located along the south side of Shelbyville Road east of Manemann's drugstore at the corner of Breckenridge Lane on land obtained from a division of the Nanz and Neuner nursery property. Soon the garage would be doubled in size by an addition to the east. Eline handled Ford cars until selling out just before the Depression. Then he sold Buicks and Pontiacs before forming the Eline Chevrolet Company in 1935. That business was sold in 1954, but the Eline Realty Company retained the building.[46] Several businesses occupied the first floor along with the realty

ELIZABETH HARTMAN AND ANTHONY J. ELINE ON
THEIR WEDDING DAY, 8 JUNE 1911. COURTESY
OF HENRIETTA SARA ELINE BREELAND.

INTERIOR OF ELINE'S GARAGE, *CA.* 1920, BY
HOWARD V. WITHERS. COURTESY OF SIDNEY W.
ELINE, JR.

DISPLAY ROOM OF THE ELINE MOTOR COMPANY, LOCATED ADJACENT TO THE GARAGE, *CA.* 1920, BY HOWARD V. WITHERS. PHOTO COURTESY OF SIDNEY W. ELINE, JR.

Now, you will realize we are coming to the front, when in the near future electric lights will be in the residences of many at St. Matthews. The water pipes are being laid, which will make the folks here feel like city people.

From *The Jeffersonian*, 23 November 1911.[47]

GAS PUMPS WERE ON AN ISLAND IN SHELBYVILLE ROAD, JUST EAST OF THE INTERURBAN STATION, SEPARATED FROM THE GARAGE BY THE INTERURBAN TRACKS. COURTESY OF SIDNEY W. ELINE, JR.

company, and the Fraternal Order of Eagles had the second floor when the structure was damaged by fire and water in 1958.[48] Ironically, Eline's Garage had also housed the fledgling fire department from its inception in 1919 until 1924.

At the same time Tony Eline was selling Ford cars and tractors, he was developing property and acquiring land. According to a 1954 retrospective in *The Voice of St. Matthews*, in 1912 Eline "set up St. Matthews' first real estate office" in part of the dwelling house and store on St. Matthews Avenue. Actually he formed competition for Norbourne Oldham Rudy and Robert O. Dorsey's St. Matthews Realty Co. that was already in existence.[49] However, Eline immediately developed Maplewood, Mary Nanz's subdivision, bounded by Grandview, Nanz, Fairfax and Breckenridge, and then an adjacent piece for the Neuner family called Magnolia.[50] In 1915, the A. J. Eline Company (available by the Cumberland Phone, 18-J) was advertising lots in Sallie C. Thompson's subdivision on Browns Lane.

By 1920, Tony Eline could well afford to move his growing family into a new, story-and-a-half bungalow across Shelbyville Road on Fairfax. A fish pond in the front yard was covered by an elaborate arbor trellis, and a garage

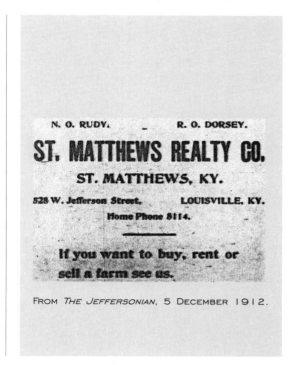

N. O. RUDY.   R. O. DORSEY.

ST. MATTHEWS REALTY CO.
ST. MATTHEWS, KY.
528 W. Jefferson Street,   LOUISVILLE, KY.
Home Phone 8114.

If you want to buy, rent or sell a farm see us.

FROM *THE JEFFERSONIAN*, 5 DECEMBER 1912.

sat in the side yard. *The Jeffersonian* commented that the house was "beautifully arranged and being on the corner of Fairfax Avenue, improves the entrance wonderfully."[51] According to Henrietta Sara Eline Breeland, who was born in the St. Matthews Avenue house on 22 December 1915, the bungalow was designed and built by carpenter Frank Stich, who lived on Browns Lane where the Harvey Browne Memorial Presbyterian Church is presently.[52] Although the site on Shelbyville Road was convenient for business, as traffic increased it became less desirable, except on Derby Day when the family

ELINE RESIDENCE ON SHELBYVILLE ROAD AT FAIRFAX AVENUE, *CA.* 1925. POOL IN FRONT WAS COVERED BY A PERGOLA. COURTESY OF SIDNEY W. ELINE, JR.

The Thompson sub-division lots, with all city conveniences, concrete sidewalks, made streets, free tap to city water, are being sold as low as $12.00 per foot, about 6 1/2 cents per square foot. This property is high, well drained, and is being bought by shrewd investors and home seekers. Buy your lot now in the beginning and get the choice as the price will soon advance.

We also have several nice bungalows, cottages and two-story houses for sale or for rent. Farms and acreage property as well.

From *The Jeffersonian*, 15 April 1915.

Despite the fact that some localities feel the "hardtimes" due to the European war, St. Matthews...is in a flourishing condition; handsome new buildings are being erected and everybody is happy and contented....The new drug store of C. R. Manemann is up-to-date in every respect.

From "A Fine Place," *The Jeffersonian*, 15 April 1915.

There has been an indescribable something lacking in St. Matthews for a long, long while. We realize now it was Mr. Manemann we needed. Never again can we do without him and his interesting family.

"From St. Matthews," *The Jeffersonian*, 3 June 1915.

would sit and wait on the front porch, and as Sara Breeland remembered, "watch the governor and all that mess from Frankfort to come whizzing through with motorcycles and everything." After the family moved to a more secluded residence, the front yard became the site of the Fairfax Building in 1956. The old bungalow behind it was replaced in 1970. The Fairfax Building was replaced in 1987 by a KFC restaurant.[53]

Rosa Eline would continue the dry goods business with her daughters for a time. They then sold the store and the house and built a house on Meridian that is presently a cafe. The Butler sisters continued the dry goods concern until about 1926 when their brother, J. J. Butler, Jr., took over the building for his plumbing and heating enterprise. Doubled in size along the way, it became the St. Matthews Gas and Electric Shop.

Tony Eline would develop a host of properties including English Village, Elmwood, Brownsboro Estates, and Westport Heights. His civic interests and concerns were extensive and far-reaching. He died in 1967 at his home, 707 Circle Hill Road, in a subdivision he had developed on the farm where he had been born 82 years before.[54]

In 1915, Clement R. Manemann built St. Matthews' first pharmacy on the southeast corner of Breckenridge Lane and Shelbyville Road on lot 39 of the Magnolia Subdivision that had been part of Nanz and Neuner's nursery.[55] He had graduated from St. Xavier High School and the University of Louisville, where one of his classmates was architect Tom Nolan, who designed the structure that would house the Manemanns and their nine children, as well as the pharmacy on the ground floor that also provided space for Dr. Zaring's office with an entrance off Breckenridge. Lucille Manemann Schuler, who was born on 26 August 1904, recalled visiting her aunt and uncle Grieshaber, who lived over their grocery and saloon across the street from where the Manemanns would build. After Prohibition began, Alfred P. Grieshaber, his wife and son moved away.[56] Will Fehr took over the grocery.

Abraham M. Zaring, M.D., a native of Oldham County and 1898 graduate of the Louisville College of Medicine, came to St. Matthews and established his office in Manemann's pharmacy in 1915. "With up-to-date fixtures and most obliging manners he can attend to repairs of the human frame, both external and internal, while you wait," *The Jeffersonian* confided on 25 March, soon after he established his office. "If you are unable to come to him, he will come to you." He would continue to practice in St. Matthews for 31 years, and died in 1944 at the age of 74.[57] After Clem Manemann moved into Louisville in the mid-1920s, Buschemeyer-Ogden took over. W. Jesse Ogden, who would become active in the local fire department and St. Matthews National Bank, had married Marie Buschemeyer.[58] After his death in 1945 at the age of 60, the corner housed the Whitehead Drug Store and then the Ashbury-Berman Drug Company. The structure was eventually torn down, and the site is now being used for outdoor cafe seating.

The announcement in September 1912 that a lot had been purchased "in" Browns Lane for a new schoolhouse that would be built by the first of 1913 was a bit premature.[59] Instead, a new room was added to the existing two to relieve the congestion of "three in a seat." "Those children are too young to grip the end of benches all day," *The Jeffersonian* lamented. By the end of 1913, a lot on the north side of the Shelbyville Road at the head of Browns Lane had been obtained.[60] However, dedication of the Greathouse School did not occur until 4 March 1915. The structure appears to have been

THE TIMES, LOUISVILLE, SATURDAY EVENING, FEB

ST. MATTHEWS OPENS NEW SCHOOL NEXT MONDAY

In view of the great schools and school systems of to-day, it may be interesting to know that we had no public school system. This is of a later growth—barely begun a few years before the war. The education given was not broad nor very high; but the essentials of a fairly good education might be obtained in these country schools. Reading aloud, spelling, handwriting, and geography were carefully attended to. The children were well drilled in arithmetic, Latin, grammar, and in reading Caesar, Virgil, etc. They were even carried through Greek grammar and into a few of the easier Greek books.

From Thomas W. Bullitt, *My Life at Oxmoor* (Louisville, 1911), 65.

THE NEW GREATHOUSE SCHOOL IS AT TOP. TEACHERS, MRS. L. H. HARDESTY AND MISS GUSSIE MANSKY, FLANK MISS TOMMIE GREATHOUSE IN MIDDLE PANEL. BELOW IS THE OLD SCHOOL "NOW ABANDONED AFTER TWENTY-FIVE YEARS." FROM *THE LOUISVILLE TIMES*, 27 FEBRUARY 1915. COURTESY OF MARY ELIZABETH RATTERMAN RUCKRIEGEL.

The lunches furnished at Greathouse school by Mrs. George Weaver are superior to any of the kind in the county. She is a wonderful woman to accomplish this task, always on time, always a good nourishing soup, often side dishes of vegetables and a meat sandwich, something sweet, a plentiful supply of milk and a happy smile greets you. There is not her equal any where.

From "St. Matthews, *The Jeffersonian*, 10 November 1921.

PRINCIPAL TOMMIE GREATHOUSE AND PUPILS, *CA.* 1910. BEARGRASS-ST. MATTHEWS HISTORICAL SOCIETY.

a frame version of architect Brinton B. Davis's brick elementary school in Jeffersontown that had opened the previous fall.[61]

"We marched from the old school to the new school right through St. Matthews," Cornelia Drescher Stone would recall. "We marched and sang. The new, four-room schoolhouse had a basement underneath it with a furnace, and we thought we were in heaven. The old school had pot-bellied stoves."[62] The old school was twenty-five years old. The sliver of ground it sat on between the Workhouse Road (Lexington Road) and Shelbyville Road had been purchased by Charles Neuner, S. W. Lewis, and Fred Edinger, trustees of School District Number 60 from Henry Holzheimer in 1890 for $400.[63] There had been several schools in district 60, previously. Beginning in 1877, a school begun by Emma Russell was located on Browns Lane, then on Breckenridge Lane, and then in one room behind the old St. Matthews Episcopal Church near the L & N depot. After teacher Ella Prentice married the depot agent James Allen in late 1884, her duties were assumed by Fannie Tommie Greathouse, a native of Fulton, Missouri, who had moved with her parents to Shelbyville.[64] Miss Tommie retired as principal of the Greathouse School after the 1918 school year.[65] A year later, when she sold her home on Elmwood Avenue and moved back to Shelbyville, *The Jeffersonian* remarked in tribute: "We will miss Miss Tommie, who made St. Matthews her home for

thirty-five years. Her influence in manners and morals, her excellent teaching, the curriculum of the school room, has given to the world great numbers of men and women who fill the most important positions of our city and state. She will make her home in the future in Shelbyville, Ky., but her life work will be in our memory forever. Only eternity can measure and reward her faithfulness."[66] Miss Tommie Greathouse died on 17 July 1935 at the age of 93.[67]

It should also be noted that when the schoolhouse was practically new and just two rooms, it housed Sunday school classes for the outreach ministry of the Crescent Hill Presbyterian Church—itself newly formed. When funds were given to the Louisville presbytery to honor Dr. Harvey Browne, property was purchased on the west side of Bauer Avenue and a church was erected that bore the honoree's name. The church would move to its present location on Browns Lane in 1952.[68]

HARVEY BROWNE MEMORIAL PRESBYTERIAN CHURCH ON BAUER AVENUE. SPEED, *ST. MATTHEWS MAKES ITS BOW* (1938).

The abandoned three-room, frame schoolhouse remained in place west of the triangle development that included the Vogue Theater. It became the residence of Charles Crowder, a neighborhood barber, until R. W. Marshall began to assemble land for the Koster-Swope Buick Company. Lloyd T. Ray purchased the frame house for his residence and moved it to 109 Lyndon Lane.[69] Frank L. "Tubby" Barth recalls Ray telling him about the move. "Lloyd Ray was Carl Ray's brother. He was known as Tubby. Tubby Ray told me that they were bringing the house up Shelbyville Road, and at the busy intersection with Lexington Road, it bogged down. He simply went into the Sada San and got a cup of coffee while they worked it out."[70]

The Greathouse School on Shelbyville Road was twenty-five years old when it was abandoned for a more modern structure on Grandview Avenue.

GREATHOUSE SCHOOL, 1916. COURTESY OF
MARY ELIZABETH RATTERMAN RUCKRIEGEL.

LOUIS BAUER (1859-1943) AND HIS WIFE,
EVA FISCHER BAUER (1882-1941), ABOUT
1905. THEY RESIDED AT 3931 FRANKFORT
AVENUE. JUDY OCHSNER EDWARDS COLLEC-
TION, BEARGRASS-ST. MATTHEWS HISTORICAL
SOCIETY.

The Eline Realty Company converted the structure into apartments, but the complex was razed in 1960 in contemplation of commercial development.[71]

After 24 years as postmaster (along with numerous other offices and duties), Louis Bauer retired as of 1 June 1915. He had "given perfect satisfaction, but time changes everything."[72] The main reason perhaps was the fact that a new post office had been built on the little triangle of land east of Chenoweth Lane and between Westport Road and the railroad tracks. The old one had been in the Bauer Bros. building for years. William Farris took over as postmaster, while retaining his position at the adjacent L & N depot. The Bauer Bros. opened a shoe store where the post office had been, but "Uncle Louie" Bauer was thinking of giving up their old building and expanding his banking interests.[73]

The frame Christian church on the south side of Westport Road and east of where it crossed over the railroad tracks was not yet twenty-five years old when concern began to mount about the location's inconvenience. According to a report in the 14 November 1912 *Jeffersonian*: "There is a movement on foot at present to move Beargrass church to the Shelby pike, so all its members can then take advantage of the electric car lines to attend church. The church is situated in an out of the way place for many of its members who have not conveyances, yet the lot would make ideal residence sites. As times and people change, churches must change their locations, also, to keep in touch with the people." By June 1916, prominent Louisville architect Brinton B. Davis had almost completed his drawings for the new edifice, which was

first planned for the southeast corner of Fairfax Avenue and Shelbyville Road.[74] By November 1916, however, a lot on the east side of Browns Lane had been acquired and Henry Frank of Middletown had been awarded the building contract for $13,275.[75]

After World War II, a mirror image addition to the church was drawn up, but it did not allow for adequate parking. A mundane enlargement was made, but later a new sanctuary was erected to the east, parallel to Shelbyville Road and the original colossal portico was removed.[76]

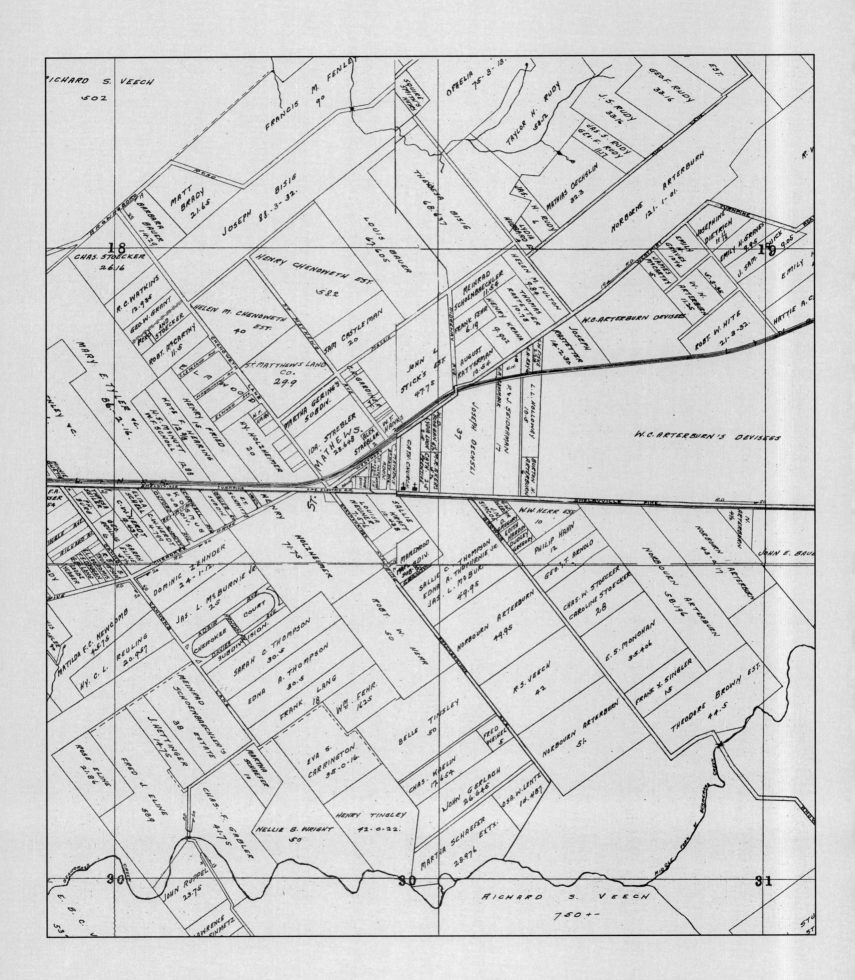

The growing support of the prohibition movement was enhanced as the nation focused attention and resources in the war against Germany. The Volstead Act was passed over Woodrow Wilson's veto, and the 18th Amendment to the Constitution was ratified on 29 January 1919. The manufacture, transportation, and sale of alcoholic liquors was prohibited, effective 16 January 1920. Prohibition dramatically altered the character of the crossroads of St. Matthews. In human memory there had always been taverns or saloons on three corners. That suddenly ended; and for Bauer Bros., it was reason enough to make improvements.

In November 1920, *The Jeffersonian* noted that the Bank of St. Matthews, of which brother Louis Bauer was president, had bought the grocery, saloon, and feed store, and would expand and create "an up-to-date city building."[1] It appears that only a new front was added to the old Bauer Bros. building, but a large new vault, safety deposit boxes, and fixtures of walnut, marble, and bronze were included to the tune of $25,000.[2] The bank was dedicated on 7 September 1921 at what was termed "Booster Day," an all-day gala to show off "how much we have grown in the fifteen years since the bank was built in 1906."[3] The old Bank of St. Matthews was converted into the post office, and the old post office along the railroad tracks was taken over by Charles W. Crowder, the barber.[4]

The grocery part of Bauer Bros. did not give up the ghost. Henry, Albert, Irvin and Martin Bauer erected a fine, brick grocery east of the new bank, where the feed store had been.[5] They handled "fancy groceries, vegetables, fruits and meats while soft drinks are carried at all seasons." The second floor housed a public hall, where monthly dances of the Penrose Club, "composed of the boys of the younger set," were held.[6] Bauer Bros. grocery was sold by Louis Bauer's son, Irvin Bauer, in 1943.[7] The brick structure, fronted by a pilastered parapet wall that terminated in a multi-curved Dutch

Despite the fact that some localities feel the "hard times" due to the European war, St. Matthews, situated a few miles from the city of Louisville on the Shelbyville road, is in a flourishing condition; handsome new buildings are being erected and everybody is happy and contented.

From "A Fine Place," *The Jeffersonian*, 15 April 1915.

There was a poor old man, Crowder, who had a barbershop going out Westport Road—just a little, one-room place. And every Halloween the mean boys in St. Matthews would fix him up. They would bring corn stalks and everything imaginable and pile it up in front of his door so he could never get in. It seems to me, one time they even brought in a cow and had it up on his roof. How they did it, I don't know.

From interview of Henrietta Sara Eline Breeland, 20 November 1996.

LEFT: VIEW AT CROSSROADS LOOKING EAST ON SHELBYVILLE ROAD, PROBABLY TAKEN IN CONNECTION WITH BOOSTER DAY 1921.

OPPOSITE: FOUR SECTIONS OF NEW MAP OF LOUISVILLE AND JEFFERSON COUNTY, KENTUCKY, PREPARED BY WILLIAM B. HUNTER, 1913, HAVE BEEN COMBINED TO COVER THE ST. MATTHEWS AREA.

gable, is no more.

East of Bauer Bros., George John Wurster built St. Matthews' first hardware store, which he operated for twenty years while maintaining his family residence over top. He died in 1941 at the age of 51.[8] The business, however, continued to flourish in the capable hands of Wurster's bookkeeper, George Hammer. His son, Pete Hammer, purchased the business in 1980, and while changes and improvements have been made to the store, its traditional character has remained.[9]

Next to the hardware store, the Zehnders put in a milk depot and creamery. Dominic Zehnder, who was born on 22 August 1911, was the third generation to have that name. His father and grandfather lived on the south-

MILK TRUCK DECORATED FOR 1925 PARADE. COURTESY OF MELCHIOR ZEHNDER, SR.

east quadrant of Cannons Lane and Lexington Road, where they had a dairy. Before his father and uncles, Joe and Albert, started the creamery in St. Matthews, they would bottle their father's milk by hand in a small building on the farm and then deliver it by horse and wagon. After they built the creamery, milk was brought to them from various farms in cans by horse and wagon or on the interurban, which had a small platform right in front of the creamery where the cans were deposited. The milk was heated to about 145 degrees for about 15 minutes to pasteurize it, then it was cooled over coils of city water and chilled by other coils of ammonia. After bottling and being put in cases, it was ready for home delivery. Few people came to the creamery for milk, and little was sold at the grocery stores. Zehnder Bros. had four or five horse and wagons for delivery and the horses were stabled in the rear. The wagons were built, and repaired when necessary, by Heskamp, and the horses were shod there, too.

Zehnder Bros. Creamery, which would operate for many years, is now Maier's, The St. Matthews Tavern.

Just east of Zehnder Bros., Bert Nally remodeled his house and modernized his barbershop in 1923. The native of New Haven, Kentucky, established his tonsorial shop in 1913 and for a while he shared the community's hair-cutting duties with Charles Crowder. Nally even had "a ladies' attendant," who was "prepared to do marcelling in the private apartment away from the men's shop."[10] He died in 1946 at the age of 54.[11]

ZEHNDER BROS. AND B.A. SCHOENBAECHLER MILK BOTTLES FROM THE COLLECTION OF PETER GUETIG. BENJAMIN ALPHONSE SCHOENBAECHLER LEASED LAND AT THE SOUTHEAST CORNER OF CHENOWETH LANE AND BROWNSBORO ROAD FOR HIS DAIRY ABOUT 1920.

As a boy, I worked in the creamery and I helped deliver, too. I was a jumper. The horses knew exactly where they were going. As soon as you jumped back in, they would go off to the next customer. The horse and wagon would come home sometimes, after they were finished delivering the milk, and the driver would be sound asleep. The horse would bring them home. Dad would be madder than the devil.

From interview of Dominic E. Zehnder, Jr., 12 November 1996.

BERT NALLY'S BARBERSHOP, 3925 FRANKFORT AVENUE, 1939. SG 82.40.08, UNIVERSITY OF LOUISVILLE PHOTOGRAPHIC ARCHIVES.

Professor Hamilton B. Moore, principal of Louisville Girls' High School and former head of the English department at Male High School, lived on Massie Avenue. In the early evening of 27 March 1923, he drove his wife to the interurban line so she could attend a church meeting in Louisville, and as

It was dark, around six o'clock. I guess Mother and I had gone to pick up Daddy. I was a tiny child. I can still hear those animals crying when I pass there. The train had killed Professor Moore and it had turned over on all these animals.

From interview of Carolyn Rudy Barth, 20 January 1998.

We moved to Massie Avenue in St. Matthews in 1926. The house was where Professor Moore lived. We lived there a good while. He had two sons, Martin and Bobby. Martin was older and he wrote the Looking Back column.

From interview of Frank L. "Tubby" Barth, Jr., 20 January 1998.

RIGHT: OPENING OF FARMERS BANK AND TRUST COMPANY IN 1924. THE FILSON CLUB.

OFFICERS AND DIRECTORS OF BANK. THE FILSON CLUB.

he was crossing the railroad tracks at St. Matthews Avenue with one of his sons, his automobile stalled. When they could not push the vehicle, Professor Moore tried to restart it. The car was struck by an eastbound freight train, and he was killed. County Patrolman Eugene Blandford, whose family lived in the old St. Matthews Episcopal Church rectory north of the crossing, carried the body to a nearby lot and attempted to console ten-year-old Robert Moore, whom he found "running up and down the railroad tracks hammering on the cars with his fists." The next morning's *Courier-Journal* carried numerous expressions of regret from community leaders and educators. Moore, a New York State native and a graduate of Cornell and Indiana universities, was 52 years old.[12]

The old grocery business of William A. Fehr on the southwest corner of Shelbyville Road and Breckenridge Lane was reopened "in an up-to-date fashion" by Roby & Clemens in 1922.[13] There was continuity as John Clemens had been a delivery boy for Fehr. They occupied only the western section of the first floor. In 1924, an addition was made to the east side of the brick structure that created a separate entrance on the corner for the newly established Farmers Bank and Trust Company of St. Matthews. Former Jefferson County Commissioner Phil A. Hunt was president, and the directors included A. W. Bauer, Charles Ochsner, William Marshall Bullitt, and A. J. Eline.[14]

"Because of recent withdrawals and slowness of collections," the bank's board of directors notified the state banking commissioner that business had been suspended on 16 November 1931. Cashier F. M. Hoagland was confident that depositors and stockholders would be paid in full. A plan to reorganize and reopen was outlined to approximately 500 depositors on 1 April 1932. About three-quarters agreed to the plan; however, it was not until August 1933 that the institution reopened as the Farmers and Depositors Bank.[15] Walter Crady was the new president. When Citizens Fidelity Bank and Trust

Company purchased this institution's stock in August 1951, Crady retired. The bank erected a modern branch next door in 1975, and its old building on the corner was sold. PNC Bank, which took over Citizens Fidelity Bank, repurchased the property in 1993, razed the corner structure, landscaped the site, and added valuable parking spaces.[16]

A block east of the bank remains Plehn's Bakery, opened in 1924 by Kuno Plehn, a native of Kiel, Germany, who had his first bakery on Jefferson Street in 1922. He was a founder of the Associated Retail Bakers of America and served as its president in 1934. When he retired in 1945, the business was purchased by his nephew Bernard Bowling, who was mayor of St. Matthews when Plehn died in 1965 at the age of 82.[17]

STANDING ON INTERURBAN TRACKS AT MERIDIAN AVENUE, LOOKING WEST ON SHELBYVILLE ROAD WITH PLEHN'S BAKERY AT LEFT, OCTOBER 1933. CAUFIELD AND SHOOK COLLECTION 129339, UNIVERSITY OF LOUISVILLE PHOTOGRAPHIC ARCHIVES.

TERMINATION OF MERIDIAN AT SHELBYVILLE ROAD. BETHEL EVANGELICAL CHURCH AT LEFT, JANUARY 1933. CAUFIELD AND SHOOK COLLECTION, 126350, UNIVERSITY OF LOUISVILLE PHOTOGRAPHIC ARCHIVES.

My father got the formula from somebody way back when, and nobody remembers who. That picture was taken about the third one. I think this was when they went up to 500 gallons, because when they started out they made about a hundred gallons, and each year they added some. They were raising money for the new church. My father is on the right and I am sitting on the wood pile. He started it when I was seven or eight years old.

From interview of George Drescher, 21 February 1997.

The cornerstone of Bethel Evangelical Church was laid on 17 August 1924. The congregation had been formed early in 1923 and apparently met in the Greathouse School until the initial phase of construction had completed the first floor.[18] A second floor, housing the sanctuary, was planned for a later time.[19] "The first electric revolving cross was dedicated in 1927 and shortly after that, the church's annual turtle soup supper began its tradition. Preparations for the 1931 event were described in a church newsletter:[20]

> The Turtle Soup and Bratwurst Festival to be given by the Brotherhood Bible Class Saturday, June 27th, is the talk of the town. And when we say "town," we include Louisville and most of Jefferson County. Yes, that's taking in a lot of territory, but last year found in the neighborhood of a thousand people at this Festival...
>
> George Drescher, "The Turtle Soup King" of Jefferson County, will again be chief cook and will be assisted by such men as John Lausman, Fred Westerman, Jr., Frank Mueller, John Stuedle, and others who know the ins and outs of genuine Turtle Soup....
>
> Last year the crowd did away with over 60 gallons of soup and more was wanted. This year, "The Turtle Soup King" is preparing to manufacture about 100 gallons.

As the church approached its 30th anniversary, the congregation studied various plans and costs for building a new sanctuary and relegating the old stone structure to strictly a Sunday-school facility. In June 1953, plans by the architectural firm of E. T. Hutchings were approved for a brick edifice, unpretentious in its Gothic styling, to be erected facing Willis Avenue, that would be connected to the back of the old church.[21]

CAULDRONS OF TURTLE SOUP BEING PREPARED FOR THE ANNUAL SUPPER IN ABOUT 1932. SG 86.18, UNIVERSITY OF LOUISVILLE PHOTOGRAPHIC ARCHIVES.

Not far from Bethel, on the northeast corner of Willis Avenue and Breckenridge Lane, local Baptists erected a church soon after forming a congregation in 1927. St. Matthews Baptist Church was outgrown in two decades, and a new edifice at Grandview and Macon avenues was dedicated in 1949.[22]

The St. Matthews Community Club was formed at a meeting of some one hundred residents in the home of its first president, J. C. Hesse, in June 1924. The initial concerns were erecting warning signals at railway grade crossings and providing better fire protection.[23] One of the club's first functions was a community festival "to bring before the people of the county what St. Matthews has to offer the home-builder and the business man, to show what the community produces and to help the country outside of the city in attracting more residents to the suburbs."[24] Anticipating that St. Matthews would be "within a very short time the center of population of Jefferson County," the club proposed that St. Matthews become the county seat and that a new courthouse be erected in "this spry hamlet." The county commissioners, however, were not duly impressed, but the offer put the public on notice that the city of Louisville was marching eastward.[25]

A short distance west of the Triangle, Kentucky Masons convened on 20 October 1925 to lay the cornerstone of the Masonic Widows and Orphans Home. Instead of a single large structure like the Masons had erected 56 years before in Louisville, the architects Joseph & Joseph designed a cluster of brick structures, Georgian in style, in a campus setting conceived by Olmsted Bros. of Brookline, Mass.[26] When the $1,000,000 project got underway in 1919, it had the distinctive Spanish flavor that the architectural firm had employed designing the old state fairgrounds. By the time the cluster of 14 buildings was dedicated by some 8,000 Masons in October 1927, the cost had escalated to $2 million.[27] Recently, six of the vacant structures were renovated to create over a hundred affordable apartments for the elderly, called Masonic Home Village, by the Louis & Henry Group.[28]

When the campus was included in an aerial photograph on July Fourth 1926, underway in the foreground was a polo match, reportedly Louisville's

Jefferson County's first community festival, patterned after those recently held in other parts of the State, will be staged tomorrow night at St. Matthews, on the tract of land known as the Triangle, where the Lexington and Shelbyville Roads meet....The queen of the county will be crowned, chosen from among 100 girls entered in the popularity contest. Among the leaders is Miss Lucille Manemann. One of the attractions will be the serving of turtle soup from the famous recipe made by Mrs. William Hoertz.

From "County Festival Opens Tomorrow," *The Courier-Journal*, 5 August 1925.

Masonic Home campus under construction at top (south). St. Matthews Triangle can be seen before development at top left. A polo match was underway on 4 July 1926 in the foreground. Caufield and Shook Collection 73879. University of Louisville Photographic Archives.

Aerial view of campus as completed. SG 88.32, University of Louisville Photographic Archives.

first. The polo field, maintained by the nearby Louisville Country Club, was along the south side of Brownsboro Road, east of Chenoweth Lane. The country club "malletmen" were entertaining the "mounted croquet players" from the Memphis Hunt and Polo Club.[29]

The St. Matthews Fire Department and its 1920 vintage Model-T Ford chemical wagon moved out of Eline's Garage and into their own quarters in 1925. Fifteen prominent St. Matthews men had organized "a fire brigade" in 1919 under the name, St. Matthews Voluntary Fire Association. With no capital stock, but authorization to incur liabilities up to $2,000, the group acquired the chemical wagon. Its first real use came in March 1920, when calls came into Eline's Garage and the chemical wagon was on the scene of three fires reportedly in less than eight minutes.[30] The small garage behind the corner drugstore on Breckenridge Lane became quite crowded when a brand new Seagrave pumper was added in 1931. Betsy, as the engine

continues to be called, has pumped water from almost every conceivable source. Milk commandeered from a dairy truck was even used to extinguish one fire in Woodlawn.[31] Fifty years after its founding, the department moved into its fourth quarters.

FIRE STATION ON EAST SIDE OF BRECKENRIDGE LANE BEHIND DRUGSTORE, 1940. BETSY IS AT LEFT. ROYAL PHOTO CO. 5382, UNIVERSITY OF LOUISVILLE PHOTOGRAPHIC ARCHIVES.

"St. Matthews is to have a newspaper...to be known as the 'St. Matthews Booster,'" *The Courier-Journal* noted on 22 November 1925. The weekly was to begin appearing late in December. Unfortunately, only a few issues are extant or have been microfilmed. However, one issue, dated 18 September 1901, is in the archives at The Filson Club. Because this issue is also labeled as volume 5, number 29, the newspaper has been noted as first appearing about 1896. In reality, the 1901 date is a typographic error and should have been 1930, which is quite obvious from the news of the day. Until the *St. Matthews Booster* was issued, the only regular news about the community appeared in a column prepared by Mrs. John Simcoe for *The Jeffersonian*. It first appeared on 13 June 1907, although Mrs. Simcoe, who signed her column simply A. B. C., did not become a correspondent until later.[32] The *St. Matthews Booster* was

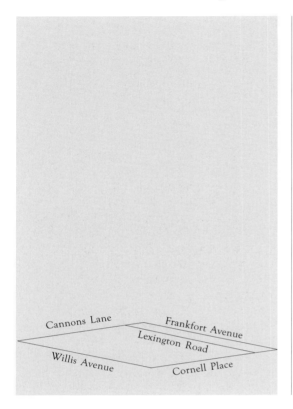

succeeded by the *St. Matthews Sun* in 1935. The *St. Matthews Sun* was published by Tom Jones, who also continued to put out *The Jeffersonian*. In 1940, Peyton Hoge edited a weekly called the *St. Matthews Commuter*.

On 13 July 1949, the first issue of *St. Matthews* was brought out by James K. Van Arsdale. It soon became *The Voice of St. Matthews*, and unfortunately early issues are no longer extant. Van Arsdale began to publish also *The Voice of the Highlands*, but in 1952 was forced to sell his newspapers to Alden J. "Al" Schansberg, who "built the paper from a thin, largely free-distribution paper to a full-fledged, paid-circulation paper of state-wide reputation."[33] Tom Jones's *Jeffersonian* was acquired by Schansberg in 1965, and *The Voice-Jeffersonian* was created. Bruce B. Van Dusen purchased Schansberg's company in 1971. The newspaper, under its present owner and publisher, John H. Harralson, Jr., has been renamed *The Voice-Tribune*.[34]

The Jeffersonian was certainly correct when it reported in 1925: "Many predict that a few years will find St. Matthews one of Louisville's most popular residential districts." Dominic Zehnder's 50-acre dairy farm on the south side of Lexington Road east of Cannons Lane had been acquired by the United States Realty Association as had Norbourn Arterburn's 50-acre tract between Breckenridge Lane and Browns Lane by the Moorhouse Corporation. "City car service is all that is needed to make this locality boom, and it is coming."[35]

RENDERING OF LEXINGTON MANOR SITE, "A HIGH CLASS SUB-DIVISION." INTERSECTION OF CANNONS LANE AND WILLIS AVENUE AT LEFT. 1926, CAUFIELD AND SHOOK COLLECTION 70067, UNIVERSITY OF LOUISVILLE PHOTOGRAPHIC ARCHIVES.

In 1925, Wakefield-Davis Realty Company began offering lots in Fairlawn with a brass band and "handsome presents."[36] The Shelbyville company, composed of James Heady Wakefield, his brother, Mark A. Wakefield, J. F. Davis, and William F. Randolph, had been "up against a bunch of city slickers" in the Louisville real estate market particularly around St. Matthews since 1919. They would develop, among other subdivisions, Druid Hills, Fairmeade, Bellemeade, Rolling Fields, Beechwood Village, and Wexford

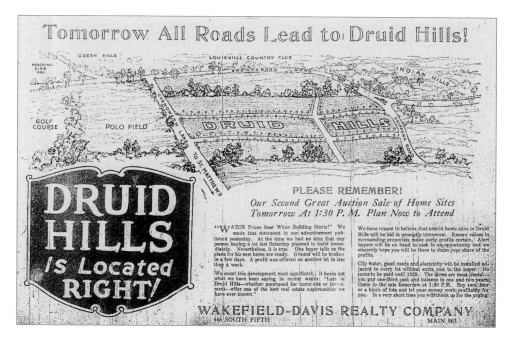

Place. After Mark Wakefield's son, James, and his nephew, Morrie L. McMakin, joined the firm, it became the Wakefield-McMakin Realty Company.[37]

The old Zehnder dairy farm was platted as Lexington Manor, "a high-class sub-division," and advertised in 1926. The interior streets included Eline, Fairlawn, Iola, Oxford, and Cornell, traversed by Wilmington and Willis. The 68.14-acre homestead of the late Henry Holzheimer was platted in three sections in 1926 as Breckenridge Villa, creating Wilmington, Willis, Dayton, Nanz, Wiltshire, Wallace, Wendover, Macon, and Bauer avenues in the process. The Holzheimer property had been purchased by the J. C. Turner Re-

We moved out to St. Matthews in 1926 or 1927. The house was at the intersection of Gilman and St. Matthews avenues. Albert Dick later turned part of it into townhouses. Daddy [Ellerbe W. Carter] had that all the way back to the Kaelins. He owned most of Bonniewood, and he had all the lots between our house and Chenoweth Lane. Daddy had polo ponies and they were characters—Tickletoe, Little Bell, Paleface, and Mondaise were very handsome. Daddy was on the Louisville Country Club team, and they went on polo trips to Dayton or Pittsburgh or down to Memphis. At first the polo field was on Chenoweth Lane across from where the John Welburn Brown place is. We'd all go over there on Sundays. People would bring chairs and they'd sit out in front of the cars. We had one of the first station wagons and it had the name of our place—Glenartney—on it. I don't remember where Mother got the name. There wasn't a glen, but that was a fine name for a place.

From interview of Nancy Carter Farnsley, 1988.

Mr. Thomas Ray, who bought the [Henry] Kraha place, is a nursery man and landscape gardener, does pruning, spraying, shaping, and transplanting. He needs no compliments, his work will stand on its own merit, always satisfactory.

From "St. Matthews," *The Jeffersonian*, 10 November 1921.

alty Company for $110,000 plus tax and interest or some $1,614 an acre.[38] (Turner, like the principals of the Wakefield-Davis firm, was from Shelbyville.) The layout of these massive subdivisions was straightforward. As the ground was level, the streets could be put down in uniform grid patterns and the lots arranged accordingly. The one exception is Norbourne Estates, also conceived in 1926. Its very geometric plan utilized curves and the principal street was a divided boulevard. The design was by Stonestreet & Ford, surveyors, for the Moorhouse Corporation, headed by Leslie W. Moorhouse.

The subdivision was named for land owner, Norbourn Arterburn, although an "e" was added for some undisclosed reason. He had inherited among other tracts, 100 acres of the old Theodore Brown property that wrapped around the Nanz & Neuner nursery. Half the land bordering Shelbyville Road was sold off and Norbourn retained the remaining 50 acres between Browns Lane and Breckenridge Lane.

Taking advantage of the growing suburban trade, Thomas E. Ray purchased a ten-acre plot along the southern boundary of the Ridgeway property in 1921 and created Ray's St. Matthews Nurseries. He had been "planting, pruning, and spraying trees and shrubs" in Louisville since 1906.[39] Sev-

eral Ray descendants remain prominent in the landscape business.

The *St. Matthews Booster*'s headline in its 6 February 1930 issue proclaimed: "Model Home Will Help St. Matthews. Should Bring Many Visitors To This Community; New Home To Be Built In Norbourne Estates." The residence being erected on lot 98 had been designed by an up-and-coming architect, Stratton O. Hammon, as an entry in the Realtors' Home Show. The winning competition entry was awarded $350 and the house was actually erected and put on display in the Jefferson County Armory. After the show, the three-bedroom, two-bath Colonial-style house was dismantled and rebuilt. Hammon became Louisville's most prodigious residential architect, continuing to work for 65 years. When he died in October 1997, *The Voice-Tribune* carried an obituary as well as a full-page pictorial tribute.[40]

Breckenridge Lane went no further than the Lentz family property, which was on the west side south of Hillsboro Road. Lewis A. Lentz, the grandson of Floyd Parks, had been farming the 90-acre tract for years, but by World War I, his bachelor son, Osa W. Lentz, could only claim 14.5 acres. But Osa Lentz was known near and wide for his particular brand of gamecocks. In his comprehensive overview of Kentucky cockfighting, Joseph R. Jones notes: "Osa Lentz's name is connected with an extraordinary event in 'cock' fighting, namely, a 'hen main' between himself and Fred Booker of Louisville. Lentz's vicious Irish hens, with specially made short gaffs, crowed and killed like cocks."[41] When Lentz died in 1928 at the age of 73, his obituary said he was "known nationally as a breeder and fighter of game chickens."[42] When John D. Stengel undertook his extensive retrospective on cock fighting in *The Courier-Journal* on 20 December 1936, he wrote:

> No reminiscence would be complete without mention of the famous "old fighter" Osa Lentz of St. Matthews, and his internationally known strain of gamecock. Friends tell us that during his life Mr. Lentz was the foremost authority on breeding and gaff [spur] problems. His quick wit and interesting stories delighted a host of friends. At that time several pits were in operation in and around St. Matthews.

At the end of Breckenridge Lane (before it was extended as Beauchamp Road to Dutchmans Lane), the huge Bethel Veech property was being sold off.[43] One parcel of some 164 acres on the south side of Beargrass Creek, accessible from Cannons Lane, was purchased by a group of prominent golfers headed by A. L. Terry and Harry Dumesnil. Big Spring Golf Club was ready for play in May 1927. The 18-hole course was laid out by superintendent George Davies, who had "remodeled" the Louisville Country Club course and designed the one at Crescent Hill.[44] The overall concept for the property was the work of Olmsted Bros. of Brookline, Mass. The celebrated firm was, of course, quite familiar with the area, especially having laid out in 1900 the section along Beargrass Creek that flowed through J. B. McFerran's Alta Vista property as well as Cherokee Park, which was Frederick Law Olmsted's

Fairly young old-timers around the Falls Cities may remember "The Point" as a famous place for cock fights. Some of the best birds in the country were brought there and fought openly, in the good old days. Tradition has it that as much as $100,000 changed hands in the betting in a single night. Latterly, of course, the thing had to be done somewhat under cover; but many now-substantial citizens, in their young days sportively inclined, could tell good stories about cock fights at "The Point."

From Hewitt Taylor, "St. Matthews," *The Herald-Post*, 7 October 1936.

RIGHT: PLAN FOR PARKWAY FROM CHEROKEE PARK TO EIGHT-MILE HOUSE, OLMSTED BROTHERS, BROOKLINE, MASS., DATED 20 OCTOBER 1927. JEFFERSON COUNTY HISTORIC PRESERVATION AND ARCHIVES.

Regardless of the fact that St. Matthews has two of the "biggest nuisances" imaginable, still it is the fastest-growing and most important suburb that Louisville has at the present time. The nuisances are: First, the useless screeching of whistles of locomotives coming into Louisville from the north....Trains coming into Louisville start sounding crossing whistle signals when about a mile north of St. Matthews and keep it up continuously until they pass over the crossing at Chenoweth Lane...then again quite often some of the engineers whistle on into Crescent Hill. The writer has been advised that this is done so that the family of the engineer will know that papa has brought some groceries from the country and a signal for them to come down to Crescent Avenue after said groceries....The second nuisance is: The rate of speed at which interurbans run between the city limits and St. Matthews. Some of these cars run at a rate of speed from twenty-five to forty miles per hour....When St. Matthews was a corn field the present arrangements may have been all right, but why can't the railroad and railway company keep up with development in other ways? The tendency today is keep up or get out. If they can't keep up, I hope that we will soon have nothing but busses and trucks instead of the interurbans and steam railroads.

From J. W. Carter, "St. Matthews Nuisances." *The Courier-Journal*, 14 July 1930.

principal legacy in Louisville.

About the time the golf course opened, Olmsted Bros. undertook to devise a Beargrass Creek parkway that originated in Alta Vista and followed the creek's meanders through the old Von Zedtwitz property, part of which the firm would design as Seneca Park. Then the parkway would skirt Big Spring golf course, cross Browns Lane (at Kresge Way), and pass through the Oxmoor property to Eight-Mile House on the Shelbyville Road.[45] The section of the parkway through Seneca Park was included in the Major Street Plan prepared by Harland Bartholomew & Associates of St. Louis as part of the first city and regional master plan in 1929.[46] The parkway's entire length would be projected in the completed master plan in 1930 and would be carried forward on subsequent master plans. It was "advanced" in a 1944 study undertaken for the Louisville Area Development Association, and then made the basis for the location of the proposed Eastern Expressway.[47] However, by that time it was not met with the favor it presumably received twenty years before. An alternate route down Frankfort Avenue was suggested, but such a course would have destroyed much of St. Matthews and Crescent Hill and would have divided the Louisville Water Company's reservoir functions and

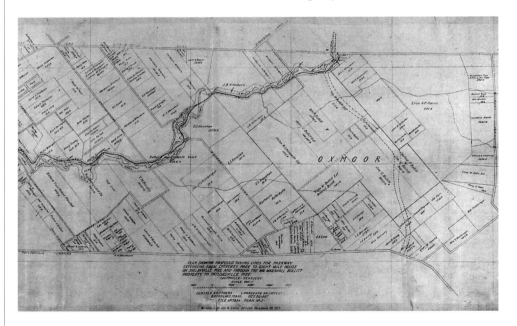

would have forced the L & N Railroad to reroute its track system east of the city.[48] The debate festered into the early 1960s.[49]

It was only a matter of time, once the Crescent Theatre opened in the Masonic lodge on Frankfort Avenue in 1927, until St. Matthews would have its own movie palace. While not quite a palace, it did have a sort of moat—well, really poor drainage. Carolyn Rudy Barth recalls that a good rain would cause a pool of water to form in front of the screen where the children would like to wade. The theater was a concrete block affair with a brick front. A modest marquee protected the entrances and the ticket window. Musical accompaniment was provided by an organ rebuilt by the upstart Louisville Pipe Organ Company.[50] The Evelann's proprietor was William Wallace

"Dixie" Wiegleb, a baseball pitcher of local note, whose daughters, Evelyn and Betty Ann, were the inspiration for the theater's name. After about a decade as a movie theater, the Evelann was converted into the Grog Shop. Wiegleb later converted an old Arterburn home on Shelbyville Road into the Maples Home for the Aged.[51]

It is not every day that one stands on a flagpole, but there was only one day, 24 June 1928, when 500 fans from St. Matthews turned out at old Parkway Field to honor one of their own—Clarence "Wiggles" Nachand. Aware of the attention that former University of Kentucky football great "Shipwreck" Kelly had received the month before for standing atop a flagpole on the old *Courier-Journal* building downtown, Jimmy Jones took a similar stance

on the Schuler building to promote Nachand Day. Jones normally occupied a chair in Bert Nally's barbershop, and forever after he was known as "Barberwreck" Jones. When Nachand first appeared at the plate, he was presented "a diamond ring, a diamond stick pin, a travelling case, a shotgun, and a shotgun case." Tommy Fitzgerald noted in the next day's *Courier-Journal*, "'Clarence Nachand Day' should occur more frequently."

"The Colonels seemed stirred by the frenzied delegation from St. Matthews, Ky., which gathered at Parkway Field Sunday afternoon to honor their native hero, and battered the ball to all corners of the lot to bruise Casey Stengel's [Toledo] Mudhens by 10-2 and 8-0 in a double-header."[52]

Jacob Heskamp had erected the brick garage (now the site of White Castle) in 1917 to the south of his old blacksmith shop that fronted Chenoweth Lane next to the railroad tracks.[53] The St. Matthews Garage faced Shelbyville Road, but was shaped to allow Westport Road to also merge in front. It was run by F. X. Schuler and C. E. Bauer, agents for Dodge and Chevrolet cars. Soon they switched to handling Hudsons and Packards, as well as the Mitchell—"the greatest value in the Light Six field today."[54] By game time in 1928, the agency was Xavier Schuler's outright.

Joseph Oechsli (pronounced Exly) was about 75 years old when he decided to give up farming for the life of a developer. By 1893, he had assembled a 37-acre tract that encompassed the old Dr. John N. Lewis house on Westport Road where it crosses the railroad tracks. The property extended to Shelbyville Road and included land the Grimes family had owned since the 1830s where Abraham Grimes, an early postmaster, lived in a log house.[55] Some frontage was provided for the Greathouse School. In 1927, Oechsli subdivided a significant part of his potato farm as Excella Place. For a sales office, he acquired the old post office on Chenoweth Lane near the railroad station that had been converted into Crowder's barbershop, moving the small frame structure to Ridgeway Avenue. It would serve various family functions in other locations, including that of a carpentry shop for Oechsli's son-in-law, Frank Ratterman. Joseph Oechsli died in late 1935 at the age of 83.[56] The Lewis/Oechsli house is now occupied by Oechsli's granddaughter, Mary Eliza-

ABOVE AND RIGHT: SCENES ON THE JOSEPH OECHSLI FARM ABOUT 1915.

PLAT ON A 1927 SALE BROADSIDE SHOWS LEWIS/OECHSLI HOME ON WESTPORT ROAD AT TOP RIGHT, AND THE SITE ON SHELBYVILLE ROAD OF THE GREATHOUSE SCHOOL THAT HAD ALREADY BEEN SOLD BY OECHSLI AT BOTTOM LEFT. COURTESY OF MARY ELIZABETH RATTERMAN RUCKRIEGEL.

ADVERTISEMENT FOR LOTS IN EXCELLA PLACE. *THE COURIER-JOURNAL,* 10 JULY 1927.

beth "Bessie" Ratterman Ruckriegel.[57] The old post office structure remains behind the house.

By the mid-1920s, the automobile had become part of the landscape, providing a more convenient means of transportation to escape the confines of Louisville. A clear indication of the car's (then simply called the machine) proliferation in suburbia was the appearance of gas stations. Before, garages were outfitted with gas pumps, but as gasoline sales multiplied, the refining companies began to build and supply their own outlets. The Aetna Oil Company advertised in 1926 that it had built the first service station in St. Matthews, "because we are boosters for St. Matthews."[58] It was located on the north side of Shelbyville Road west of St. Matthews Avenue. The Gulf Refining Company and the Standard Oil Company followed suit. Schultz's blacksmith shop

and an adjacent cottage, characterized as old landmarks, were razed to make way for the $30,000 Standard station, which was expected to be the "best looking station in St. Matthews."[59] A dozen years later, a more modern Stan-

EVERYBODY WANTS
REAL ESTATE
AT
St. Matthews

WE HAVE HOUSES LARGE AND SMALL. SOME OF THE MOST DESIRABLE LOTS THAT MONEY CAN BUY FROM $10 TO $40 PER FOOT. A LARGE LIST OF EVERYTHING IN THIS VICINITY. EASY TERMS.

TWO SPECIALS

5-room bungalow with 2 acres; city water; $7,000.

5 rooms, modern in every respect; lot 50x200; $6,000.

ELINE REALTY CO.
Belmont 1487.

dard station would be located across Shelbyville Road just east of the Lexington Road triangle.

    The announcement of St. Matthews' first and only industrial plant came in June 1930 and from Chicago. Lawrence Bernard Palmer-Ball, formerly of Essex, England, and the husband of Louisville native Virginia Vogt since 1914, had determined to invest $1,000,000 in four units of a plant that would employ two hundred men and manufacture principally asbestos for automobile brake linings. The Palmer Asbestos & Rubber Company's production would mainly be purchased by the Palmer Equipment Company of

THE HEART OF ST. MATTHEWS, ABOUT 1940. PALMER ASBESTOS & RUBBER COMPANY ALONG NORTH SIDE OF WESTPORT ROAD, WEST OF ST. MATTHEWS AVENUE, IS AT UPPER RIGHT. BEARGRASS-ST. MATTHEWS HISTORICAL SOCIETY.

PALMER ASBESTOS & RUBBER CORP. WAREHOUSE, PARTIALLY BUILT IN 1941 ALONG ST. MATTHEWS AVENUE, WHEN PLANS FOR COMPLETION WERE DEVELOPED IN 1947. ZV 67-47U, JEFFERSON COUNTY PRESERVATION AND ARCHIVES.

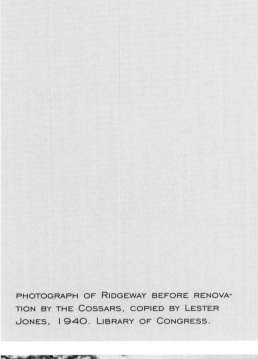

Chicago.[60] The Palmer name became a landmark emblazoned on the 100-foot tall brick smokestack, lighted by "red obstacle lights" so the "intrepid aviators who fly low over this section of the Louisville-Cleveland air mail route" would be warned.[61] In a *Courier-Journal* interview published on New Years Day, 1931, Palmer-Ball said he was impressed with the quality of worker in Louisville—"98 per cent are American born and educated." Despite the depression, he pointed to his factory as evidence of his faith in the future.[62] As the plant grew along the railroad with the advantages of a siding, the large Palmer-Ball family moved to a farm, named Surrey Hill, on Westport Road at Ormsby Lane.[63] Palmer-Ball continued to serve as president of the company until his death in 1961 at the age of 76.[64]

In 1931, street signs and house numbers were required in St. Matthews for the first time in order to facilitate mail delivery.[65] Residents and business concerns had previously trudged to the post office whenever they wished to check their particular slots for mail. Aubrey Cossar changed all that when he became postmaster of Louisville. He was well aware of the needs of St. Matthews, having owned Ridgeway. After the death of its builder, Mrs. Helen Bullitt Massie Martin Key, Ridgeway remained in the Bullitt family until 1911, when the residence was sold to Louis Bauer.[66] Aubrey and Maude Woodson

PHOTOGRAPH OF RIDGEWAY BEFORE RENOVA-
TION BY THE COSSARS, COPIED BY LESTER
JONES, 1940. LIBRARY OF CONGRESS.

Cassedy Cossar acquired the property in 1922. Mrs. Cossar had been society editor of *The Courier-Journal* and a columnist for *The Louisville Herald* before becoming active in Republican politics and serving as city treasurer in Huston Quin's administration, the first woman to hold such a city office. Mr. Cossar had also been associated with newspapers before establishing an advertising firm, and twice had been elected sheriff of Jefferson County.[67] The Cossars retained local architect Frederic L. Morgan to undertake a substantial renovation of the brick house. The landscape plan was prepared and executed by Arthur W. Cowell, Jr., of State College, Pennsylvania, who did other land-

WHISKEY AND BEER SIGNS WERE ALREADY PROMINENT IN THE COMPLEX EAST OF ELINE'S GARAGE IN JULY 1935. CAUFIELD AND SHOOK COLLECTION 138860, UNIVERSITY OF LOUISVILLE PHOTOGRAPHIC ARCHIVES.

scape work for prominent people in this area.[68]

Aubrey Cossar did not have an opportunity to enjoy the postal delivery he created in St. Matthews. He died in December 1931, a month following his wife's death. Raymond H. Heskamp, the former postmaster of the unincorporated suburb, became superintendent of the branch, which employed three mail carriers and two postal clerks, as well as two rural route carriers.[69] Ridgeway was purchased by Judge and Mrs. Churchill Humphrey and it remained in the Humphrey family until Carole and Ben Birkhead moved in and began a careful and systematic restoration in 1977.[70]

In April 1933, the sale of "non-intoxicating" 3.2 beer was permitted by Congress in anticipation of the ratification of the 21st Amendment to the Constitution repealing the 18th Amendment that outlawed the production, distribution, and sale of beverage alcohol. Although the distilling industry moved quickly to bring old facilities out of mothballs, once production was in full swing there remained a waiting period while the new whiskey aged. In the 1936 city directory, John Gerstle was still listed as selling soft drinks at 3801 Frankfort Avenue, as were Greenwald & Hatten at 3821 Frankfort; M. F. Stich at 3922-3924 Frankfort; and the Blue Bird Inn at 4039 Frankfort Avenue. Then the Evelann, St. Matthews' first movie theater, succumbed to temptation, and in 1937 was known as the Grog Shop. Miller Prentice moved his liquor store up from Mellwood Avenue and opened Miller's Liquor Store at 3932 Frankfort Avenue. By 1938, Marvin F. "Dutch" Stich had converted his soft drink establishment into Dutch's Tavern, which would become a popular spot, but Dutch died in 1946 at the age of 41.[71]

What was unique about St. Matthews, it being such a small place, were the bars. We had some neat bars there. The Grog Shop was wonderful. Jutt's and Dutch's and Gerstle's were there and on out the road was the Eight-Mile House, which was a famous place.

From interview of Robert Michael Kirn, 15 December 1997.

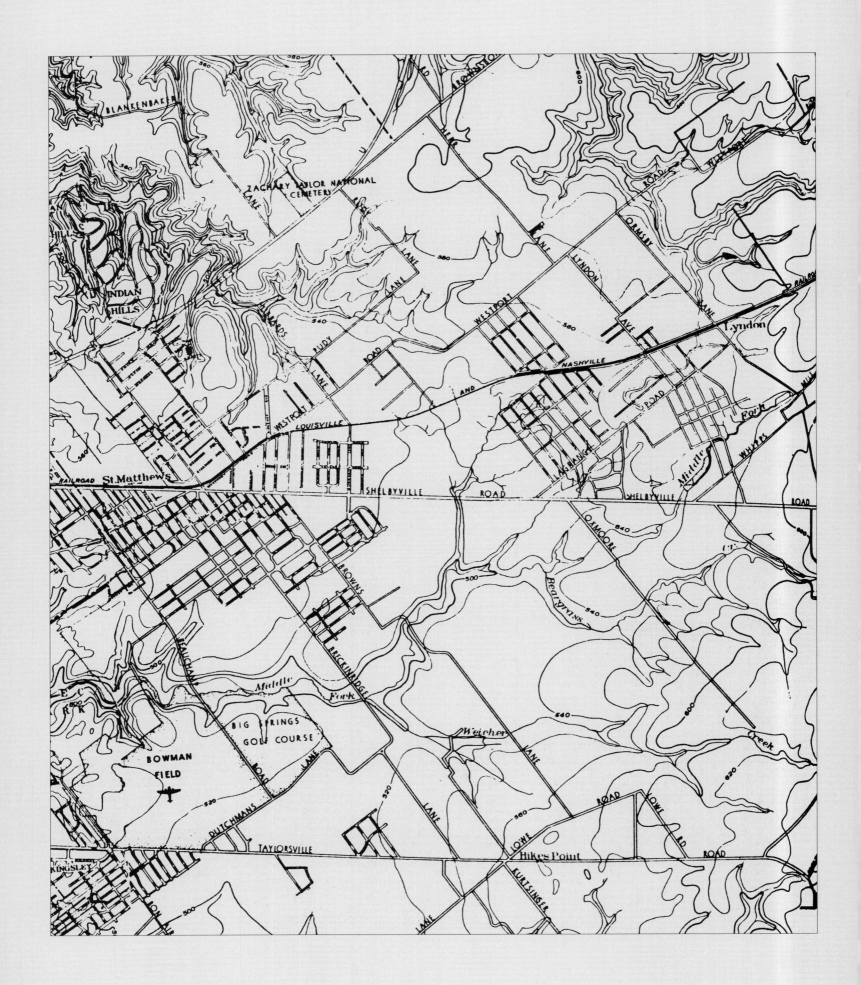

"If the pioneers were coming west today," Hewitt Taylor began his St. Matthews segment of his series, "Salubrious Suburbia," in *The Herald-Post* of 7 October 1936, "they'd stop, most likely at St. Matthews, where five roads come together....They'd see no point in going on to Louisville for St. Matthews has everything, or near so." Taylor noted: "Traffic lights for example. Two, to be exact; there were three, but this was conceded to be a little too swanky. And two banks, and two drug stores, two dry goods emporiums, two five-and-tens, three chain groceries and five beauty parlors." There was no denying that the community had history, as Taylor covered in what must be its first published in-depth retrospective, but the essential ingredient he overlooked (perhaps on purpose) was St. Matthews' lack of any kind of government. However, it was being rectified, if only temporarily.

St. Matthews was incorporated as a sixth class city on 4 December 1936 after a petition had been filed in Jefferson Circuit Court stating that the community was in need of police and fire protection as well as laws "for the maintenance of proper sanitary conditions."[1] The town's board of trustees was comprised of Dr. James E. Winter, Henry K. Nanz, C. T. Hyre, Paul H. Fleming, and Fielding W. Koch.[2] The area incorporated was roughly four square blocks with its northeast corner at the intersection of Breckenridge Lane and Shelbyville Road. This comprised only about a fourth of the community, and in May 1937 the board of trustees passed an ordinance setting up debate on annexing the remainder. Those who opposed annexation by St.

CHAPTER VII

BRING ON THE FLOOD

After the 1937 flood, people were moving out here from the West End. Father didn't have any trouble selling houses. As fast as he laid out a subdivision, they would close it. He didn't start selling cars again until shortly before the war.

From interview of Henrietta Sara Eline Breeland, 20 November 1996.

This is a very fittingly pioneer project on a pioneer road. Lafayette traveled over this road when he visited Kentucky. Andrew Jackson passed over it when going from Nashville to Washington.

From remarks by Eugene Stuart, secretary-manager, Louisville Automobile Club, *The Courier-Journal*, 25 June 1937.

We never called it Shelbyville Road. It was always Shelbyville Pike. They were all pikes.

From interview of Alice O. Monohan, 3 October 1996.

RIBBON CUTTING CEREMONY AT SHELBYVILLE ROAD AND ST. MATTHEWS AVENUE, 16 JULY 1938. *VIEWS OF LOUISVILLE SINCE THE TWENTIES*, 134.

Matthews believed it would be cheaper to the taxpayer to be annexed by the city of Louisville. The proponents said they could not wait for the wheels to turn in Louisville.[3] The opponents responded by filing suit to prevent the board of trustees from levying taxes as well as to annul the city charter.[4] When attorneys for both sides could not compromise, Circuit Judge Churchill Humphrey, whose own home, Ridgeway, was just outside the proposed annexation boundary, ruled that the matter would be decided by popular vote, to be held at "the regular voting place" on Macon Avenue, on 18 September.[5] When 151 of the 286 eligible residents voted to end incorporation, Judge Humphrey dissolved the charter of St. Matthews on 3 December 1937.[6]

The sixth-class city had existed precisely only one year, but 1937 was a turning point in the community's development. The charter controversy had practically drowned out the natural event that would have the most profound influence on its future development. The Ohio River's flood of the century forced residents of the West End to flee to higher ground, many never to return to the flood plain. And there was also an increasing amount of air pollution spewing on the West End as nearby Rubbertown was industrialized. St. Matthews was inviting, on high ground, and its air was clean.

Governor A. B. "Happy" Chandler and local officials (including Dr. James E. Winter representing the St. Matthews board of trustees) congregated at Eight-Mile House on 24 June 1937 to mark the beginning of construction "on Louisville's new gateway." Chandler told the crowd that Jefferson County had been "step-children all these years...promised roads time and time again." "To my positive knowledge," he pointed out, "this road here, your gateway to the Bluegrass, was surveyed eleven or twelve years ago. It is one of the most important roads in the whole State, yet it has been like a

duck's back all the way from Louisville to Lexington." Two twenty-foot traffic pavements of reinforced concrete, divided by a twelve-foot, landscaped median, with eight-foot shoulders, sloped to the inside, with crossovers every 800 feet, would extend 6.5 miles from the Louisville city limits and cost a half million dollars.[7]

Happy Chandler returned on 16 July 1938 to kick off his U. S. Senatorial nomination campaign against Alben Barkley in Jefferson County. He spoke from the front porch of Dr. F. M. Roth's home at 104 Browns Lane. A huge crowd had amassed, but many were there to witness the dedication of the new divided highway to Middletown and beyond. Various events were staged, and the celebration went well into the evening.[8]

Shelbyville Road had been improved by a Republican county administration back in 1918, but it was still merely one lane each way and high crowned.[9]

At the end of 1929, *The Courier-Journal* was calling for replacement of "the Midland Trail, or U. S. 60, commonly called the Shelbyville Road. This dangerous, high-crowned, uneven, surface-treated macadam road" carried the most traffic of any road in the state.

Taking advantage of the favorable publicity the new road generated, James Speed brought out a booklet, *St. Matthews Makes Its Bow*, complete with advertisements and photographs of many business enterprises. In his introduction, Speed wrote: "The big, new highway, which is now the Broadway of St. Matthews, typifies the progressive spirit of this unusual suburb....In

"SHELBYVILLE ROAD, AN EXAMPLE OF WHAT THE COUNTY COMMISSION HAS DONE IN ITS CAMPAIGN FOR GOOD ROADS." THE STRUCTURES AT THE RIGHT ON THE SOUTH SIDE OF THE ROAD BEYOND THE INTERURBAN TRACKS BELONGED TO THE ARTERBURN FAMILY AND WOULD NOW BE LOCATED JUST EAST OF HUBBARDS LANE. FROM BOOKLET PUBLISHED BY THE REPUBLICAN LEAGUE, 1 JANUARY 1919.

The Shelbyville Road, from the city limits eastward, has a right-of-way which will easily permit construction of a highway twice as wide. Traffic demands such a road. In wet weather, the surface treatment is treacherous, the high crown always is dangerous, and the number of hazardous grades and bad curves should be eliminated.

From "An Inadequate Road," *The Courier-Journal*, 28 December 1929.

spite of the heavy traffic on the plainly marked lanes, it is a pleasant and comfortable place in which to transact business. With cars parked vertically to the sidewalk, they move in or out easily and safely. No vacant stores stare gloomily at the passerby in St. Matthews. For rent signs are almost unknown as business is thriving. Even the offices for professional men above the stores are comfortably filled."

Ironically, the first large-scale expansion of the business core in St. Matthews' history would occur not out on the improved Shelbyville Road, but along Lexington Road where it merges with Frankfort Avenue. The strip shopping center was laid out to allow the same vertical parking that had been established along Shelbyville Road when it was widened. Architect Walter Wagner designed the complex which included 10 stores and the 1,100-seat Vogue movie theater. The community had been without a movie theater since the Evelann across Lexington Road had closed in 1935.

Dahlem Construction Company, which had built the first strip center in Jefferson County just the year before, was employed by T. P. Taylor, Jr., and H. A. Taylor, whose drugstore would be an anchor store.[12] The complex would also include a Kroger, Woolworth, and Sears, and "practically double the size of the business district of St. Matthews."[13] A driveway separated the Taylor drugstore from a new Standard Oil Company filling station. A park was planned for the point itself. The Vogue—"the Theater of Tomorrow"— equipped with air-conditioning, lounge seats, a "no-glare screen and RCA

FOR CONTRAST, SAME VIEW ON SHELBYVILLE ROAD IN 1953 AS IN 1926. ST. MATTHEWS SCHOOL OF MUSIC OPERATED BY MRS. MADGE TERRY LEWIS OCCUPIED THE SECOND FLOOR OF BUILDING AT RIGHT IN THE 1950s, WHILE PENDERGRASS CHEVROLET SOLD CARS BELOW.[10] NOW IT IS PART OF RECENTLY RENOVATED TAFEL MOTORS. 94.17.012, UNIVERSITY OF LOUISVILLE PHOTOGRAPHIC ARCHIVES.

OPPOSITE: POWER LINE REPAIR, 20 FEBRUARY 1926. HOUSE IN THE BACKGROUND WAS LISTED AS BELONGING TO C. ARTERBURN ON THE 1858 BERGMANN MAP AND 1879 ATLAS. IN 1950, THE FRAME HOUSE WAS BLOCKED FROM VIEW BY A SHOPPING COMPLEX.[11] THE INTERURBAN TRACTS WERE SPLIT INTO TWO SETS EAST OF ST. MATTHEWS.

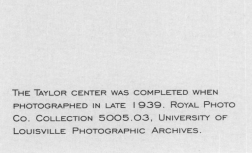

THE TAYLOR CENTER WAS COMPLETED WHEN PHOTOGRAPHED IN LATE 1939. ROYAL PHOTO CO. COLLECTION 5005.03, UNIVERSITY OF LOUISVILLE PHOTOGRAPHIC ARCHIVES.

television sound" held its grand opening just before Christmas, 1939.[14] Dahlem had also just completed an A&P Super-Market across Lexington Road.

Stores came and went in the Taylor's triangle, but the Vogue continued as the mainstay. In 1977, film buff Marty Sussman interjected new life into the "old-fashioned theater," by introducing a novel concept, "The Best of the Movies."[15] But as movie complexes sprang up all around, the days of neighborhood theaters became numbered. On 18 September 1998, *The Courier-Journal* reported, "Vogue has its last picture show." Its run had been nearly 59 years, and it was the last of its kind.[16]

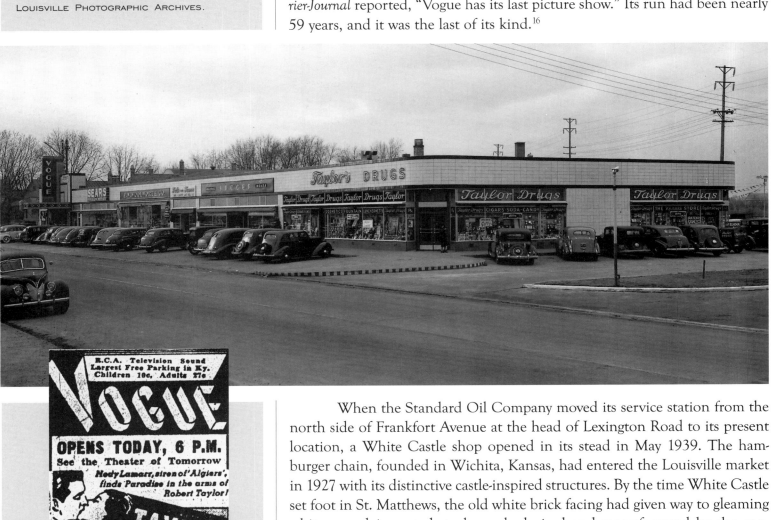

When the Standard Oil Company moved its service station from the north side of Frankfort Avenue at the head of Lexington Road to its present location, a White Castle shop opened in its stead in May 1939. The hamburger chain, founded in Wichita, Kansas, had entered the Louisville market in 1927 with its distinctive castle-inspired structures. By the time White Castle set foot in St. Matthews, the old white brick facing had given way to gleaming white porcelain-coated steel panels devised and manufactured by the construction component of the company.[17] Thirty years later, the 1939 White Castle was replaced by more parking and a larger version placed on the Chenoweth Lane corner.

Within a year of its opening, White Castle had competition in the form of the Third Little Mansion, erected by Chester A. Hoover on the southwest corner of Bauer Avenue and Lexington Road. Hoover had scoured the country "looking at hamburger joints." Walter B. Rueve, a local architect and an associate of Ossian P. Ward for 38 years, designed the structure in an "early American Colonial" style, and Albert Pick of Chicago made the grills and interior accessories. The operation could serve 700 hamburgers a day.[18] Evidently, Mr. Hoover was ahead of his time and the Little Mansions were

R.C.A. Television Sound
Largest Free Parking in Ky.
Children 10c. Adults 27c

VOGUE

OPENS TODAY, 6 P.M.

See the Theater of Tomorrow

*Hedy Lamarr, siren of 'Algiers',
finds Paradise in the arms of
Robert Taylor!*

TAYLOR
LAMARR
LADY OF THE
TROPICS

Plus 2d Big Feature
Nan Grey, Robt. Cummings
"UNDERPUP"

FROM *THE COURIER-JOURNAL*,
22 DECEMBER 1939.

WHITE CASTLE #9, 3809 FRANKFORT AVENUE, WAS LOCATED AT THE WEST END OF THE PRESENT PARKING LOT FROM 1939 TO 1969. IT WAS REPLACED BY THE LARGER AND MORE STREAMLINED STORE ON THE CORNER OF CHENOWETH LANE. WHITE CASTLE SYSTEM, INC. ARCHIVES AT OHIO STATE UNIVERSITY, COURTESY OF DORIS EDLIN, ASSISTANT AREA MANAGER, WHO WORKED IN OLD #9 DURING ITS EXISTENCE.

soon vacant. Kentucky Acres Dairy Store moved in later, and then Jefferson Dairy Queen; now a St. Matthews Seafood establishment occupies the site. Nearby, on the opposite side of Lexington Road, a Memphis hamburger chain opened Toddle House No. 3 early in 1948. According to a historian of the fast food industry, the Toddle Houses' "more sedate" architecture allowed them to thrive in "both working-class and more affluent neighborhoods."[19] By 1971, the Toddle House had been converted into the Magic Inn; today the Danish Express is at that location, 3713 Lexington Road.

The day is sunny, but nippy. Some 30 men stand or shuffle for several yards between Westport Road and the parallel railroad siding near Chenoweth Lane in St. Matthews. Three or four are huddled around a fire of wood scraps....Unemployed men throughout Louisville have learned they may find a day's work there....If a man stands there, he's available for work. Everybody knows that. It's a St. Matthews custom. Job-seekers began congregating there in the early 1930s, available for the unloading of trucks at the Potato Exchange which no longer exists....The Big Flood hit Louisville in 1937, and many residents decided to build on higher land in suburban St. Matthews, far from the Ohio River. Suddenly the building boom was on. More and more job-seekers congregated along Westport Road. Hungry for labor, building contractors would hire as many as 100 men by 8 a.m.—and wish there were more. Job-seekers have been congregating there ever since, but jobs are harder to come by these days.

I carried water when I was a boy and the circus came to St. Matthews. It was always in the point where the first shopping center was built in St. Matthews—where Taylor Drugs and the Vogue are. For carrying water, they would give us boys some free rides on the Ferris wheel. That was every summer. I have been told that they used to have a ring and if you could throw this guy out of the ring you would get a prize. Old Buttermilk Hahn and Snow Kaelin got in the ring and threw this guy out and they got the prize.

From interview of Earl Combs Stich, 25 March 1997.

James Goble wrote about this continuing St. Matthews institution and the individuals looking for work in *The Courier-Journal*'s Sunday Magazine on 22 January 1961. "As long as I can remember," recalls Alice Monohan, who was born in St. Matthews in 1912, "if you wanted any extra help, you went over behind the grocery store on Westport Road. They would come out on the interurban or walk or whatever, and they would stand back there. Anytime I would want someone I would go to the hardware store and ask George Hammer to get me a good one—not a wino. Then all the newcomers came out and they didn't think that was a good idea having those men standing back there. They didn't hurt anybody. If they were not picked up then they had to be gone by a certain time."[20]

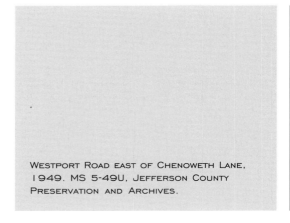

WESTPORT ROAD EAST OF CHENOWETH LANE, 1949. MS 5-49U, JEFFERSON COUNTY PRESERVATION AND ARCHIVES.

Great Britain and France declared war on Germany when Hitler invaded Poland in September 1939. A year later during the Battle of Britain, Congress authorized induction of the National Guard, and compulsory military service was approved. On 25 January 1941, men of Headquarters Company and Anti-Tank Company, 149th Infantry, departed with ceremony from St. Matthews destined for a year's training at Camp Shelby, Mississippi. An advance group from the 138th Field Artillery regiment had already gone, and the main part would leave by truck and train a few days later. The 109 were bid farewell, as they marched from Holy Trinity School, where they had been encamped because the nearby armory was just under construction, through St. Matthews to the L & N station where they boarded trains. The armory, designed as were others in Kentucky by local architect Maj. Edd R. Gregg, who was serving with the 138th Field Artillery, was completed in July 1942.[21] The armory is now part of Trinity High School.

NATIONAL GUARD UNIT MARCHING WEST ON
SHELBYVILLE ROAD AND TURNING NORTH ONTO
CHENOWETH LANE, 25 JANUARY 1941. FROM
LOUISVILLE SINCE THE TWENTIES, 152-153.

SOLDIERS CONTINUE TO MARCH EAST BEHIND
ST. MATTHEWS BANK AND TRUST COMPANY ON
WESTPORT ROAD. IN THE BACKGROUND ARE THE
LANDMARK PALMER SMOKESTACK (LEFT) AND
MERCHANTS ICE & COLD STORAGE (CENTER).
FROM *LOUISVILLE SINCE THE TWENTIES*, 152-
153.

WELL-WISHERS LINE THE RAILROAD TRACKS EAST OF CHENOWETH LANE FOR SEND OFF. REMNANTS OF BABYTOWN CAN BE SEEN ON WEST SIDE OF CHENOWETH LANE BEYOND WHERE CARS ARE PARKED. THIS HAS BEEN THE SITE OF THOMAS'S CAR WASH FOR MANY YEARS. FROM *LOUISVILLE SINCE THE TWENTIES*, 152-153.

It was interesting to watch Fort Knox personnel come up Breckinridge Lane (we spelled it the right way) in convoy with a big caravan of tanks on flat boys and soldiers who were going overseas. We would get on our bikes and follow them into St. Matthews. The train would come in and they would unload the German prisoners of war right there in front of the depot with all the MPs around. They would stand on Westport Road in platoon fashion, sometimes all the way to St. Matthews Avenue. Then the army would take over the train and load the soldiers up that were going out to fight. The vehicles that brought them were loaded up with the prisoners of war and taken to Fort Knox. We got to see this fairly often in the early days of the war.[22]

From interview of Robert Michael Kirn, 15 December 1997.

A temporary wooden memorial honoring the fallen dead of World War II from the St. Matthews area (Brownsboro Road, MacArthur Avenue, Beargrass Creek, and Cannons Lane) was placed in the little triangle point park on Armistice Day, 1943. By then, eight names were painted on the shaft.[23] The memorial was replaced by a stone version in 1946 bearing the names of 29 men who had died during the war.[24] When a fountain was dedicated on 19 July 1967, the site became known as Fountain Point Park. Responsibility for the park was assumed personally by John B. O'Leary, whose plumbing and heating company was a St. Matthews institution.[25]

Without much fanfare a new movie theater opened along Shelbyville Road on 29 August 1941. The newspaper advertisement noted you could come and leave as you please and parking would be no problem. That particular claim was put to the test that night, however, when more than 600 carloads of movie-goers pulled into the field "graded in ripples to form earth ramps" and headed to stanchions that held car speakers. The place was simply called the Drive-In Theatre.[26] Although outdoor theaters had been in existence for eight years, around Louisville there was no reason to be too specific because this was "Something New Under The Stars." Later it would be designated the East Drive-In, and by 1961 there were ten such places in Jefferson County. Twenty years later, they were a thing of the past and as civilization moved into their once outlying locations, the land was put to better productivity. The East Drive-In became the parking lot for a strip center that included Service Merchandise.[27]

In the fall of 1941, the St. Matthews Civic Club revisited the conten-

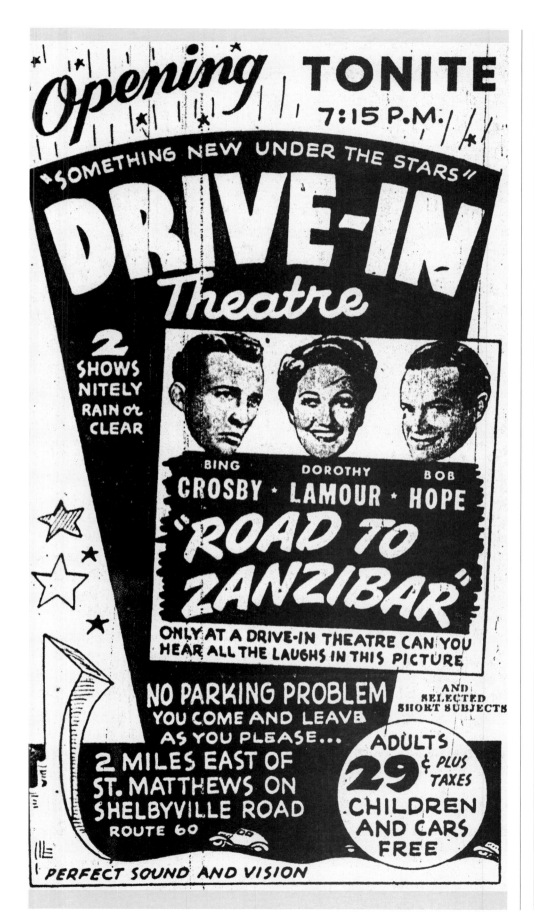

FROM *THE COURIER-JOURNAL*, 29 AUGUST 1941.

St. Matthews, Louisville's most congested suburb, still has 40 per cent of the land vacant or in farms. Robert Russell, planning engineer for the City-County Planning and Zoning Commissioned announced this finding yesterday as he worked on a comprehensive plan for the development of the suburb… Russell confined his analysis to the area known as St. Matthews proper. It includes territory north and south of Shelbyville Road between the Louisville city limits and Hubbard's Lane….

"The area has many problems and the earlier we get a definite plan going the better it can be developed. One is the heavy traffic….

"Coupled with a review of the zoning, there are other studies that should be made. One is the need for a community center involving schools and recreation. Streets need redesigning to eliminate grade crossings and traffic congestion. And smoke control is a paramount problem."

From "Russell Says St. Matthews Is Still 40 Pct. Vacant Land," *The Courier-Journal*, 15 December 1946.

For the second time within five years, St. Matthews residents are split into two camps over the question of incorporating the suburb of 15,000 persons—described by Robert L. Ripley recently as the "largest non-corporate group of people in the United States."

From "300 Want St. Matthews To Be 'As Is,'" *The Courier-Journal*, 29 October 1941.

Acquisition of all except 626 shares of the St. Matthews Bank, a total of 4,374 shares, was revealed yesterday in the annual report of the First National Bank...Based on a total cost of $97,158, the 4,374 shares represented an investment of approximately $22.22 a share.

From Donald McWain, "First National Acquires St. Matthews Bank Control," *The Courier-Journal*, 22 January 1944.

St. Matthews Bank was not formally merged into First National Bank until 24 July 1954. The original Bank of St. Matthews, later called the St. Matthews Bank, had been razed in late 1937 or early 1938 when the second bank building, dating to 1921, was remodeled and enlarged. That structure was removed in 1966 to provide parking on the corner of Shelbyville Road and Chenoweth Lane for the present First National (now National City) Bank branch.

tious question of incorporation or annexation. At the initial meeting on September 24th, there was consensus to avoid incorporation again, and to investigate the merits of being annexed by the city of Louisville.[28] A separate group of residents, including Kuno Plehn, James J. Butler, Jr., and John Monohan, Jr., met a month later and advocated incorporating as a sixth-class city to block annexation.[29] A third group of some 300 residents then met, opposed to either incorporation or annexation, and favoring "leaving St. Matthews 'as is.'"[30] All the bases were full, and the opposing managers sent up pinch hitters in an attempt to score. Andrew Broaddus, then president of the Louisville Board of Aldermen appeared before the civic club to say the city had no plans to annex the village. But he did impart the veiled threat that a new mayor and board might initiate some action.[31]

To many this seemed the case when the General Assembly convened in January 1942, and a bill was introduced easing the process for annexing of suburban (unincorporated) territory. At yet another village meeting at Greathouse School on January 18th, retired contractor John W. Kamper stepped forward to galvanize the effort for incorporation.[32] "We have waited to see what Louisville would do at this session of the legislature, and now we know what they will do." Then appealing perhaps more to civic pride than reason or merit, he asked: "Do you want to incorporate St. Matthews or be annexed by the city of Louisville?" Kamper also produced a map of the district proposed for incorporation as well as a petition for signatures.[33] The civic club decided to invite Louisville Mayor Wilson W. Wyatt to a meeting "to ascertain what annexation of the community by Louisville would involve."

Wyatt did not, however, wait for the invitation, and made known on radio that he did not regard the legislation as fair and "asked that action on it be deferred by the General Assembly pending preparation of 'an entirely new proposal.'"[34] In immediate response, a "fact-finding committee" was organized in St. Matthews "to study problems of annexation."[35] The conciliation simply pushed any decision making further into the future.

In April of 1943, the question of annexation arose again when Jefferson County's Planning and Zoning Commission was about to adopt a master plan as required by state law. The St. Matthews Chamber of Commerce protested that the plan did not allow for industrial areas east of the community that would be needed "to aid in sustaining the added population."[36] It appeared to the chamber that the zoning plan was being tailored so St. Matthews could not be self-supporting, and that would aid the city of Louisville in its attempt to annex it. The Planning and Zoning Commission responded that the master plan was fluid and an attempt to "prevent developments that will be regretted by the great majority of the people later on."[37] Despite the submission of an alternate zoning plan by the St. Matthews Chamber of Commerce, Jefferson Fiscal Court adopted the master plan that had been promulgated, but with the caveat that it could be modified as warranted.[38]

By the first of 1944, Mayor Wyatt and the leaders of the St. Matthews Civic Club were in general agreement as to how new annexation legislation would be worded. The city of Louisville would have to show cause for annexing St. Matthews rather than St. Matthews having to prove why it should not be annexed. Other concessions were also made dealing with delivery of services and who could oppose annexation in court.[39] The civic club told Wyatt the plan would be explained to the residents and public opinion would be measured. The community's mind was already made up. In a personal survey, County Commissioner Elliott P. White found that 97% of the residents adjacent to Louisville opposed being annexed.[40]

At the end of 1944, hearings were held relative to modifying the county's zoning plan in the St. Matthews area. The commission's planning engineer, Carl Berg, recommended that "St. Matthews remain a single-family residential district with commercial and industrial development limited to its needs."[41] Berg suggested that provisions be made for "suitable neighborhood shopping centers where need for such exists or develops." At the same time he discouraged "zoning of long stretches of main highway frontage as commercial." His voice was to be drowned out by projects that seemed impossible to imagine at the time.

When the war ended, there was another influx of housing in St. Matthews, and a substantial increase in residents who liked what they had and did not want to pay additional taxes or city taxes to make improvements. As Louisville concentrated its planning efforts on getting its own house back in order, once more there was a grass roots movement in St. Matthews to incorporate and avoid being annexed.[42]

The 275-member St. Matthews Civic Club, of which Bud Andriot was president, voted in favor of annexation rather than incorporation. But 1,004 residents (out of some 9,700) in a 7-square-mile area petitioned Jefferson Circuit Court to be incorporated as a third-class city. A third world war was erupting, but fortunately it would be contained in the St. Matthews Armory. A thousand or so witnessed the face-off, moderated by a former adjutant general, on April 9th, but when it was over, the matter remained far from decided. The main question seemed to be, why was the business district being excluded from the territory proposed for incorporation?[43] And to dampen some incorporation sentiment, the potential tax rate for a new third-class city was published, based upon a comparison with Kentucky cities of a comparable size—Winchester, Hopkinsville, Corbin, and Mayfield. It was projected at between $2.30 and $2.75 per $100 assessed valuation.[44] The rate already being paid to state and county was $1.18 per $100. In a carefully researched article, "St. Matthews Isn't Just a Place—In Reality, It's More a State of Mind," Robert Doty spelled out in *The Courier-Journal* on 21 April 1946 the various services that the community received and the costs entailed. It came down to whether the proposed third-class city could provide the services required and desired from its projected income of $106,700.

Despite frequent assertions that this was a battle for St. Matthews to resolve by itself, the city of Louisville was preparing to take matters into its own hands. "We can't sit by," declared Mayor Leland Taylor, "and let the city be hemmed in by a great many small incorporated areas which derive ben-

The general outward movement of residents seeking more favorable and pleasant places to live, to escape the dirt, noise, blight, obsolescence and taxes of the central city has been stimulated by the increased use of the automobile, the improvement of streets and highways, the extension and provision of better suburban bus and transit service, and the extension of the city's public utility lines....

The growth of the area has been phenomenal. From a mere station stop and a small group of residences and cross-road stores of 30 years ago, St. Matthews today is a community of over 10,000 persons centered upon a thriving business district at the intersection of U. S. Highway no. 60 and Chenoweth and Breckinridge Lanes....

During the 1920's, there was considerable subdivision activity and development, but during the economic depression the growth of the area was slow. From 1940 to the present there has been a most spectacular expansion of the area....

A complete population and land use survey, made by the office of the Commission during October and November 1944, reveals that today of 3513 Building Lots, 2661 or 76% are built up and 852 or 24% are vacant or devoted to agricultural use. The 2661 developed parcels of land are used for the following purposes: 2534 or 95.00% for Residential; 36 or 1.35% for Commercial; 30 or 1.13% for Industrial; and 27 or 1.00% for Public or Semi-public. Thus it appears that St. Matthews is primarily a residential community.

From "Planning Engineer's Report on the Proposed Adjustment of the Zoning Plan in the Vicinity of St. Matthews, 5 December 1944.[45]

Bernie Gratzer is the prophet who 26 years ago predicted that St. Matthews' postwar growth would outdo anything ever before witnessed in home building anywhere. His predictions about the future of this small suburban community in 1944 were unbelievable but nevertheless they all came true...and then some. The "some" includes a tremendous commercial growth that is still booming. Incorporation was to be the answer to control and regulate what was happening in what was once the largest potato-growing area in this section of the country. "As I saw it, we got in just in the nick of time to prevent another Dixie Highway," Gratzer said.

From Marilyn Frederick, "Midwives At The Birth Of A City," *The Voice-Jeffersonian*, 9 April 1970.

When I was in the eighth grade, Mayme Waggener used to have a dance for the kids one Friday night a month. She would open the old school across from Beargrass Christian Church and she would pull the partition curtains back and the boys would move the desks out of the way and we would have a dance. Mayme Waggener could sure tickle those keys. She could really play the piano. She was a wonderful person. I never had a teacher who was as good as Mayme Waggener.

From interview of Sue Hall Arterburn Stich, 2 January 1997.

efits from the city but pay no city taxes." In special session on 24 April 1946, the Louisville Board of Aldermen passed an ordinance proposing to annex the business district of St. Matthews that had been omitted from the incorporation area. It was hoped that the petition in circuit court to incorporate the surrounding St. Matthews area would be abandoned, at which point, it too would be annexed.[46] This attempt at incorporation by St. Matthews was further damaged when residents of the Richlawn subdivision decided to withdraw from St. Matthews' petition for incorporation, and they petitioned to incorporate Richlawn as a sixth-class city.[47]

Then in September 1946, Chancery Judge Scott Miller declared the law that allowed as few as 500 voters to compel incorporation to be unconstitutional.[48] Those wishing to incorporate, represented by Franklin P. Hays, appealed the decision of Jefferson Circuit Court to the Court of Appeals, then the state's highest court. On the periphery were James T. Robertson representing the St. Matthews Civic Club which preferred annexation by the city of Louisville, Lawrence Grauman representing Sevier Bonnie and others on Brownsboro Road who were opposed to annexation and incorporation, and Bemis Lawrence representing Richlawn residents who wanted to incorporate themselves.[49] When the Court of Appeals upheld Judge Miller's decision, the city of Louisville immediately moved to annex a large block of St. Matthews from Cannons Lane to beyond Hubbards Lane and from Brownsboro Road south to Brownlee Road.[50] Druid Hills immediately filed suit for incorporation.[51] When Jefferson Circuit Court Judge William H. Field ruled in November 1948 that the city of Louisville could annex St. Matthews, Druid Hills was excluded, as was Richlawn.[52] However, the Kentucky Court of Appeals reversed Judge Field's decision in January 1950, stating the city of Louisville had acted improperly within the two-year waiting period prescribed by law.[53] The slate was again clean, but not for long.

On 22 March 1950, through the efforts of Joe Hughes, Bernie Gratzer, and Jim Noland, the sixth-class city of St. Matthews was incorporated. It consisted of only three and a half blocks between Chenoweth Lane and St. Matthews Avenue, north of the railroad tracks, but it was a beginning. As Jim Noland, petitioner for incorporation, was quoted, "the new city would welcome adjacent areas that wished to be annexed."[54]

While the questions of annexation and incorporation bounced in and out of the courts, the number of school-age children was multiplying but no new schools were being provided. Jefferson County was not willing to build a school in an area that the city of Louisville wanted to absorb or St. Matthews might incorporate. Finally, in a move probably designed more to ingratiate than to educate, the Louisville School Board agreed in the fall of 1947 to purchase 34-acres of Monohan property on Browns Lane for $59,500.[55] When the school opened seven years later as a junior high school to be expanded with subsequent classes into a senior high, it carried the name of a revered educator.[56] Mayme Sweet Waggener, principal of the Greathouse School for 28 years, had died early in 1953 at the age of 76. The widow of John M. Waggener had retired in 1946.[57]

In the meantime, the Great Atlantic & Pacific Tea Company had moved twice—first because it really needed additional space and the second time necessitated by fire. Before the war, the A & P was located at 3816 Frankfort Avenue, in the eastern part of a duplex. It was replaced by a Steiden's store. Chism's Hardware occupied the site from 1952 until turning it over to a restaurant, Rick's Cafe Grille, in 1997.[58] Sometime in late 1939, a much larger A & P Supermarket was constructed on Lexington Road across from where the Vogue Theater would soon be built.

Early on a Saturday morning in May 1945, the A & P was destroyed

A & P SUPERMARKET IS AT RIGHT, THE VOGUE THEATER AT LEFT, JUNE 1941. *LOUISVILLE SINCE THE TWENTIES*, 132.

by fire.[59] The $62,000 loss, however, set off a series of positive changes. The supermarket operated out of a part of Eline's garage while awaiting construction of a completely redesigned store at 3929 Frankfort Avenue (now addressed 3929 Shelbyville Road) that was the first in the United States to conform "to the food chain's postwar store blueprint." Under a lease agreement, the Eline Realty Company erected the steel, glazed tile, and glass structure according to company specifications at a cost of $125,000. A year and two days after the fire, a new 15,180 square-foot supermarket, one of the largest in the South, opened. A department was devoted entirely to frozen foods, displayed in open, self-service refrigeration cases. Paved parking was provided for 100 cars.[60] The Bluegrass Brewing Company now occupies the site, which also was the home of a series of restaurants in the 1980s and '90s.

The burned out hulk of the old A & P at 3726 Lexington Road was

They drove cattle through Chenoweth Lane to the Brownsboro Road, and then they would take them into the stockyards. Drovers came through there with lots of cattle many times. There were men on horseback who kept them from running here and there and to keep them in line.

From interview of Cornelia Drescher Stone, 16 December 1996.

FROM *THE COURIER-JOURNAL*, 17 MAY 1947.

replaced by a "merchandise mart," a one story ceramic brick structure designed by Walter C. Wagner and Joseph H. Potts. Various branch shops were to be included, and in December 1946, Byck Brothers and Company and Emory's Baby and Junior Shop were the first to open.[61] Next door, on the corner of Macon Avenue, a Canary Cottage restaurant opened in May 1947, replacing the Louisville institution Richard Menter Wheeler had opened on Fourth Street two decades before. It was fashioned after Wheeler's earlier Canary Cottages in Winchester and Lexington. Others would follow in Cincinnati and Indianapolis. The St. Matthews version became Davidson's Cafeteria in 1970, and now, after considerable renovation, a branch of Bank One.

At the end of World War II, burgeoning St. Matthews was being stifled by the lack of one very necessary but inadequate service—garbage collection. As coal-fired furnaces gave way to smaller and more efficient ones burning oil and natural gas, garbage could not be burned in the basement. The use of paper products, however, was being drastically increased. Garbage pickups were rather haphazardly conducted by men still using a horse and wagon as had the junk collectors of old, or small farm trucks. Two soldiers just back from the war seized upon this opportunity and built a thriving business. Guy Redmon, Jr., and Clyde Poynter formed the St. Matthews Sanitation Service in April 1946. Within months they had signed up 550 customers who welcomed their once-a-week, rear-door pickup for a monthly charge of $1.[62] Soon additional open trucks with sides that let down were needed. Early on Saturdays they also cleaned the streets in the commercial area of St. Matthews, finishing up their wide-broom and shovel work by 4 or 5 o'clock in the morning. Within five years the partners separated their interests and expanded their territories. Redmon remembers a revolutionary change taking place in the business when the old, open trucks were replaced by rear loading, compactor types in the early 1950s. With "packer" trucks, heavy cans no longer had to be hoisted up to a loader, and more trash could be accumulated. Then came the roll off box that businesses and contractors could use. Previously, construction waste had been scooped into a pile on the site and burned. We hauled away everything in those days, Redmon recalls, but "dog kennels were the worst."[63]

The old residences at the south end of Chenoweth Lane have recently been nicely converted into specialty shops with snappy names. They all owe a debt of gratitude to the street's first nonconforming use, which was such a necessity to local residents with lawns and gardens that no one complained. Actually, the venerable St. Matthews Feed & Seed Store started out simply as a feed store operated by George Washington Weaver in his back yard. The lot he initially purchased in the St. Matthews Land Company's subdivision in 1914 was along Chenoweth Lane, but it fronted 3901 Gilman Avenue. In 1920, the adjacent lot on Gilman was added, most likely to house the feed store, which faced Chenoweth Lane. Weaver's 1956 obituary stated that "he operated the store 30 years before retiring several years ago." Presumably, he retired in 1950 when Raymond W. "Red" Davis, who lived across the alley on Elmwood Avenue, took over. In 1958, Davis began building the present store while razing Weaver's old structures. He died in 1987 at the age of 72, but his store remains an institution.[64]

TOP: GEORGE WEAVER'S ORIGINAL WARREN OF FEED STORE BUILDINGS ABOUT 1954. FRAME STRUCTURE IN MIDDLE OF PARKING LOT POINTED WAY FROM CHENOWETH LANE. ABOVE: NEW OWNER RAYMOND W. "RED" DAVIS (LEFT) AND BUDDY MORGAN IN FRONT OF STORE IN 1952. DAVIS FOUND WILD BIRDSEED TO BE A BIG SELLER IN WINTER. HOUSE ON ELMWWOD IS IN BACKGROUND. LEFT: ARRIVAL OF "THE GOAT MAN" ABOUT 1954 WAS GREETED WITH GREAT EXCITEMENT ALONG CHENOWETH LANE. HIS CARAVAN OF JUNK AND POSSESSIONS WAS DRAWN BY A TEAM OF GOATS. PHOTOGRAPHS COURTESY OF THE DAVIS FAMILY.

Probably the "most widely known couple in St. Matthews," according to a 1946 *Courier-Journal* Sunday magazine profile, lived on Chenoweth Lane. "Uncle Lee" and Retta Bartlette, who had been married for nearly seventy years, occupied a small house behind the Frank Hoaglands, at 155 Chenoweth Lane. Retta cooked for the Hoaglands. Even at 97, Uncle Lee was still a familiar sight braving the St. Matthews traffic walking on errands and to Legion Field to see a baseball game, where with his super-senior discount, he never paid admission.[65]

WEST SIDE OF CHENOWETH LANE, NORTH OF THE RAILROAD TRACKS, PRESENT SITE OF THOMAS CAR WASH, WAS OPPOSITE THE PROPOSED DEVELOPMENT, AN ART DECO FURNITURE STORE AND GARAGE DESIGNED BY OTTO D. MOCK, BUT NEVER BUILT. SEE ELEVATION FRONTING CHENOWETH LANE BELOW.[68]

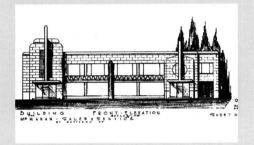

ST. MATTHEWS EPISCOPAL CHURCH, 1999. BY SAMUEL W. THOMAS.

Furthermore, with this property being situated only a "stones throw" from the two banks and the Post Office of St. Matthews and only a "stones throw" from "Five Points" of St. Matthews, or better described as "Times Square" of St. Matthews, this property should be, in my opinion, zoned commercial. Frankly, I cannot see any good and sufficient reason for the people living north of the railroad track being denied the opportunity of doing some shopping simply because all of the commercial property is situated south of the railroad track.

From letter of Joseph E. Hughes, vice president and cashier of Farmers and Depositors Bank to Friend Lodge, secretary, Louisville & Jefferson County Planning & Zoning Commission, dated 17 August 1949, supporting zoning change on the southeast corner of Staebler Avenue and Chenoweth Lane.[69]

The revelation that "St. Matthews Episcopal Church—which gave the town of St. Matthews its name, but ceased to exist in 1910—is to be re-established," appeared in *The Courier-Journal* in 1948.[66] For four years, services were held in the St. Matthews Woman's Club, while land was being acquired on Massie Avenue at Hubbards Lane and a church of rather conventional "modern design" was being devised. However, a dozen years later, Larry Leis of the Hartstern, Louis & Henry firm designed a striking new sanctuary framed by a beaming system that is spanned by a sweeping roof contoured in ridges and valleys.[67]

The first major, post-war office building planned for St. Matthews was the state headquarters of the Kentucky Farm Bureau Federation. A three-story structure, costing $150,000, was authorized to be erected in the 3600 block of Lexington Road "unless a more suitable location is found immediately."[70] A site on South Hubbards Lane was selected and the architectural firm of Otis & Grimes designed a contemporary, two-story edifice with corner-wrapping windows. When it opened in late 1948 at a cost of $180,000, mammoth by St. Matthews' standards, there was already talk of expansion.[71] Eventually, the Kentucky Farm Bureau would erect a larger headquarters visible along I-64, and the Hubbards Lane facility has been renovated to provide assisted living housing.

Having been in the mortuary business for a century, the Pearson family had already moved from downtown to Old Louisville, and there was a growing realization within its fourth generation that their old-line customers were moving to the East End. The Ratterman family had expanded its West Market Street business by opening the St. Matthews Funeral Home at 3711 Lexington Road in 1939. George Ratterman had started as a mortician in 1864, and was later joined by his son, John B. Ratterman, Sr. Seven of John's ten sons followed suit, including John, Jr., and Carl B., who came to St. Matthews.[72] But even before then, Emil A. Bizot had operated a funeral home at 3810 Shelbyville Road for a number of years. In 1951, the Pearsons branched out from the old Ferguson mansion on Third Street (now headquarters of The Filson Club Historical Society) to Breckenridge Lane in St. Matthews. The first Pearson—Lorenzo D.—had moved to Louisville from Shelby County in 1831 to apprentice under James Reed, a cabinetmaker. (Then, an undertaker was obligated to measure the corpse and custom make a coffin.) A series of partnerships began in 1848, eventually leading to the firm of L. D. Pearson & Son. Along the way, he designed the first wood-enclosed hearse decorated with oval windows on either side.[73] The funeral home was moved from Third and Chestnut streets to the Old Louisville location in 1924. Then, following population migration into the east end, Pearson's purchased a part of the Nanz & Kraft tract.[74] A Federal-style brick structure was erected with a colossal, classical entrance portico. Most visitors, however, arrive via the parking lot in the rear.

Before fast-food establishments, drive-in restaurants catered to the needs of a public on wheels. Anticipating the "cruise" generation, veteran downtown restauranteur Austin C. Pryor created the first such drive-in restaurant along Shelbyville Road.[75] His architect, Norman M. Sweet, Jr., began to design a 50' by 42' structure, mostly of glass, for the vacant southwest corner of Hubbards Lane in 1948. Pryor's was an outpost; beyond remained mostly undeveloped old farmland. On the town side, a long building with a Quonset-like roof had been erected by Herbert V. Lancaster and William H. Dohrman for bowling. When Sweet's request to the Planning and Zoning Commission to allow the restaurant to be erected on the same set-back line established by the Landohr bowling alley and Caudill Chevrolet (both are now part of the newly renovated Tafel Motors) was approved, construction proceeded, including erection of a large, gaudy roadside sign. A stone chim-

The explosion at Pryor's Drive-In Restaurant, 4170 Shelbyville Road, hurled a kitchen helper [William Wilson] 25 feet from the building into Hubbards Lane....The blast ripped out the one-story building's east wall. All windows in the modernistic building were shattered....

Lucian Hornback, restaurant manager, said either sewer gas or gas from the heater on the roof over the kitchen exploded...at the same time he saw the restaurant's east wall crumble away from the building "with Wilson following it." He said the $100,000 damage estimate was made by the building's architect.

From *The Courier-Journal*, 13 December 1957.

PRYOR'S, MID-1952. ROYAL PHOTO CO. COLLECTION 13404.01, UNIVERSITY OF LOUISVILLE PHOTOGRAPHIC ARCHIVES.

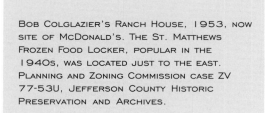

BOB COLGLAZIER'S RANCH HOUSE, 1953, NOW SITE OF MCDONALD'S. THE ST. MATTHEWS FROZEN FOOD LOCKER, POPULAR IN THE 1940S, WAS LOCATED JUST TO THE EAST. PLANNING AND ZONING COMMISSION CASE ZV 77-53U, JEFFERSON COUNTY HISTORIC PRESERVATION AND ARCHIVES.

ney was about all that was left intact when the popular spot was rocked by a gas explosion in late 1957.[76] (Later, after yet another renovation, it became part of the Arby's chain.)

Soon after Pryor's opened, farther out on Shelbyville Road, Robert L. Colglazier strategically located one of his Ranch Houses just beyond the East Drive-In Theatre. Later a carport was added in front of the modest structure. When the property was taken for the extension of the Watterson Expressway north of Shelbyville Road, Colglazier purchased a new site adjoining the St. Matthews Woman's Club.[77] It should be noted that Kentucky Fried Chicken did not open on Shelbyville Road, and then on St. Matthews Avenue, until the late 1960s, and McDonald's came even later.

"Even a superficial examination of plans for new expressways and grade-crossing elimination in Louisville reveals a housing headache for the future," Grady Clay reported early in 1951.[78] What it could have meant for St. Matthews was the demise of the traditional crossroads and a major change in future use of Shelbyville Road. Even before the Second World War had come to an end,

the Louisville Area Development Association was beginning to examine the ramifications of a crisscross system of superhighways being proposed by Congress. The three highways then being discussed would ultimately blossom into I-65, I-64, and I-71. The one resembling I-64, was initially intended "to provide an express route to the southwestern industrial area between St. Matthews and eastern residential sections." While the other two were first envisioned as depressed highways with cross-street overpasses, the one through St. Matthews was to be "more of a park-like boulevard, with divided lanes."[79]

The superhighway system had been revised and expanded by 1947 to include an "innerbelt" that would link Brownsboro with Dixie Highway, connecting in an arc the various communities between St. Matthews and Shively, as well as an "outerbelt" that would swing deeper in the county from Shelbyville Road to Dixie Highway. Eastern Expressway (eventually I-64) was intended to

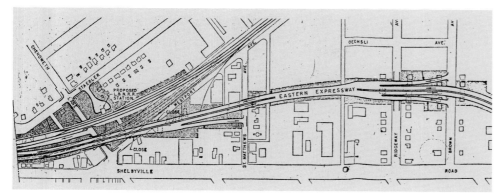

ILLUSTRATION OF PROPOSED (1950) EASTERN EXPRESSWAY THROUGH ST. MATTHEWS IN DOUGLAS NUNN, "WHICH WAY?" THE COURIER-JOURNAL, 6 APRIL 1958.

speed traffic from St. Matthews and the Highlands to downtown.[80] Its proposed route through parts of Cherokee and Seneca parks met with immediate opposition, and the city of Louisville countered with an alternative route down Frankfort Avenue. The main problem was that the L & N Railroad would have to abandon its tracks coming into the city from the east and share tracks with the Southern Railway. The L & N threatened simply to leave the city.[81] To mollify the L & N, plans were made to keep the tracks by depressing Eastern Expressway from St. Matthews into the city. The Louisville Water Company, which had major underground connections between its Crescent Hill reservoir and purification plant under Frankfort Avenue, balked.[82] For some seven years the planning process remained in limbo while Save Our Parks advocates held firm. Then in 1958 as Federal transportation planners began to press for an agreed upon route for the east-west interstate highway through Louisville, Douglas Nunn's comprehensive piece in the 6 April 1958 *Courier-Journal* asked the old question: "Which Way?"

While concern had been voiced about the disruption to traffic and destruction of neighborhoods if the Eastern Expressway route along Frankfort Avenue was selected, the impact on St. Matthews also would have been severe. The interstate would have probably obliterated Hubbards Lane as it merged into Shelbyville Road and then become elevated before passing over Westport Road and Chenoweth Lane. For Louisville Works Director W. W. "Tubby" Sanders, a Frankfort Avenue expressway was "utterly preposterous." He endorsed the route that for the most part skirted the parks as well as Cave Hill Cemetery, Bowman Field, and Big Spring Golf Club. The plan was really a derivative of a parkway devised in 1927 by Olmsted Brothers of Brookline, Mass., "extending from Cherokee Park to Eight Mile House." A branch of the road then continued on through William Marshall Bullitt's property, east of the Oxmoor house, and then southeastwardly to Taylorsville Road (see page 130). This parkway proposal had been included in Harland Bartholomew & Associates' 1930 master plan as well as the firm's updated plan of 1957. It would be the route selected for I-64, which was opened in 1970, two decades after being proposed.[83] The Watterson Expressway partially opened in 1956 and was extended some years later to meet I-71. The highway system was now in place that would facilitate the further decentralization of downtown Louisville and the increased suburbanization of the area east of the original crossroads' core of St. Matthews.

It's a good thing that Planning Engineer Friend H. Lodge is a stubborn man. Without him St. Matthews, and points east, might turn into a nightmare of frustrated truck drivers and honking Florida-bound tourists....It worries him that the Inner Belt is going to swing from the Dixie Highway clear around the city and stop mash-bang against the Shelbyville Road...Turning all these people loose is already choking St. Matthews, or in the maze of cowpaths to the east which baffles even the natives, is the horrible thought that drove Lodge to search for a solution....A couple of years ago, the night club in the angle between the LaGrange and Shelbyville roads burned to the ground. That left a vacant triangle which could be used for a modified traffic circle, cloverleaf or whatever the State Highway Department sees fit.

From Cary Robertson, "A Move's Afoot To Avert An Inner Belt Nightmare," *The Courier-Journal*, 27 October 1951.

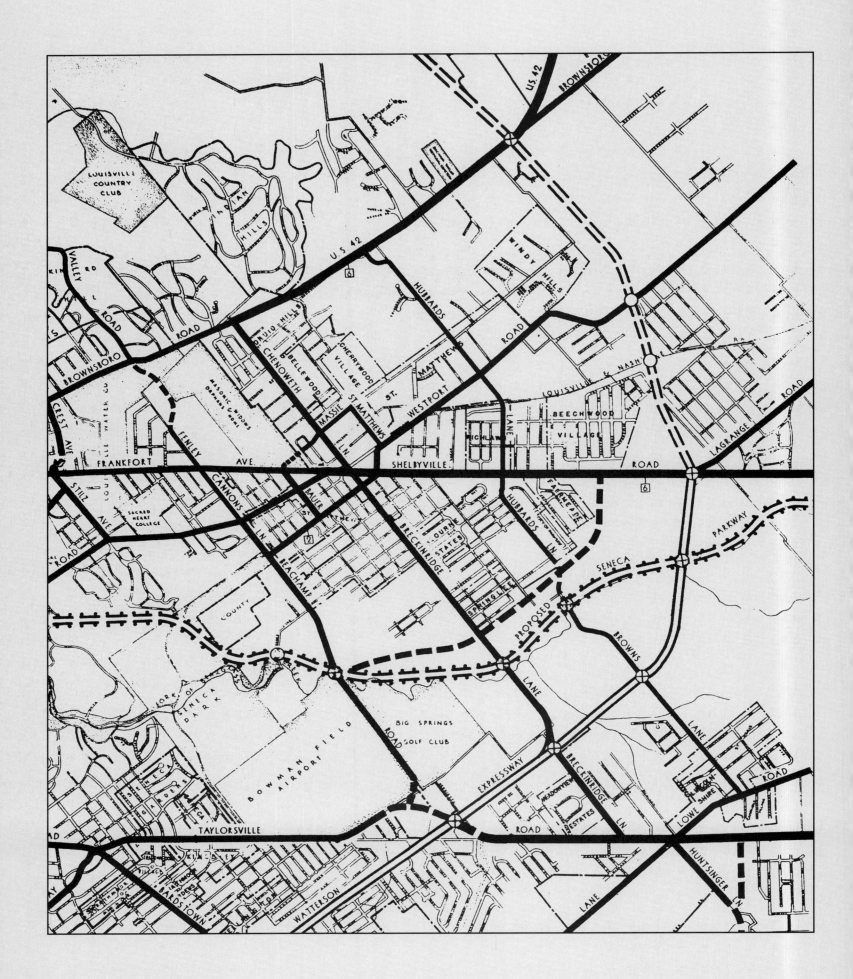

To mark the fifth anniversary of his weekly publication, *The Voice of St. Matthews*, editor Emil Aun prepared a meticulous and factual history of St. Matthews that was so comprehensive it appeared in two issues in July 1954. At the beginning of part two of "The Story of St. Matthews," which focused on the period after World War II, Aun made a most prophetic observation. "Despite the fact that everyone deplored strip and spot zoning, these practices continued. The growing area needed more stores all the time. When Wallace Center was built in 1949 [actually a zoning permit application was not made for the brick structure by Sidney Schneider until early in 1950], everyone hoped it might establish a pattern for St. Matthews. The block of stores sits well off the Lexington Road highway behind Terry Texaco. Traffic is slow and parking facilities good. Perhaps St. Matthews would not become a Dixie Highway, or so people hoped." Aun then concluded: "But it didn't work. Nobody wanted to build homes along Shelbyville Road. They wouldn't sell. So the strip zoning began, out of necessity."[1]

One of R. W. "Buck" Marshall's early real estate endeavors was assembling the ground for a new Buick dealership owned by Fred C. Koster and Darrell W. Swope, who was married to Marshall's sister, Mildred. Swope had worked for Summers-Hermann, a downtown Ford dealership that had a branch in St. Matthews, first in the Eline garage and then in the old Schuler garage. (Later the brick structure at Chenoweth Lane and Shelbyville Road was sold to C. W. Haggard Motor Company, before being occupied by Consolidated Sales. Eventually razed, the site was used for a new White Castle.) Fred Koster was married to Xavier Schuler's only daughter, Florence. He had been a outstanding, all-around athlete at Male High School and the University of Louisville, and during his ten-year professional baseball career, he played one year with the Philadelphia Phillies. Koster-Swope Motors, formed about 1944, was located on East Broadway, but when they became associated with Buick five years later, the location on Frankfort Avenue, just west of the triangle, was selected as the threshold to the burgeoning East End corridor. After Darrell Swope died in 1978 and Fred Koster in 1979, the dealership was acquired by Tom Payette.[2]

In the fall of 1951, J. Bacon & Sons announced that it would build a $1 million department store on land owned by the Henry Bauer estate along Shelbyville Road. That decision, noted Harold S. Johnson, president and general manager of the Louisville firm started by Jeremiah Bacon in 1846, had been made long before General Electric announced it was coming to the city.[3] *The Courier-Journal* also quoted Johnson as saying he was convinced that "suburban expansion won't hurt the downtown shopping center," as long as Louisville is a growing community. Bacon's first major venture out of the downtown was based upon its management's belief that St. Matthews was "the No. 1 suburban market in Greater Louisville." Property on Lexington Road had already been considered, but the site on the north side of Shelbyville Road next to the A & P would have more off-street parking and better ac-

CHAPTER VIII

ON THE ROAD TO RETAIL

I will never forget the night I wrote that story. St. Matthews was having one of the hottest summers in memory....We had no air conditioning, just a small window fan blowing 100-degree air across my face....I finished at 2 am after about 16 straight hours of writing, and the material was published just as it came from my typewriter.... Reading it now 20 years later, I am astounded at how much I wrote and how fact-filled the history is. Its inordinate length required us to publish it two weeks running.

Frankly, I think I wrote more than anyone wanted to know about St. Matthews, dating clear back to pioneer days. I had studied county records, doctors' theses and old newspapers— and had interviewed old-timers like Tony Eline. And I put it all in. But long and rambling as it is, I am proud of one thing. Not a single fact in those thousands of words was ever challenged for accuracy.

From Emil Michael Aun, "How it was— really—back when" *The Voice*, 25 July 1974. Aun sold his interest in the newspaper in 1960 and withdrew as editor after a ten-year association that began while he was a senior at the University of Louisville. He later worked for the U.S. Department of Labor and on the staff of Indiana Senator Vance Hartke.

cess.[4] In fact the layout of the new facility designed by Nevin & Morgan, Architects, provided two fronts, and the building's orientation was clearly toward the 330-car parking lot in the rear on land acquired from Merchants Ice & Cold Storage. Shelbyville Road would never be the same, but Bacon's would be the last large store to be built right on the street. Setbacks to provide automobile parking in front would become the norm.

Steel being in restricted supply, construction was delayed until the fall of 1952. In the meantime, the Spur gas station and Sander's Cleaners relocated and the old Henry Bauer residence was moved to the new grounds of Holy Trinity Church on Cherrywood Road and renovated for its custodian.

Business continued to be brisk, and in 1955 a third floor was added for furniture and home decorations. The general office also moved into the new area. In 1960, Bacon's would announce plans to take over the sites of Bechtel Interiors and the Twig & Leaf Restaurant and expand to the east, matching the old facade. A complete restyling of the exterior would take place decades later as it became Bacon's home store.[6]

FRONT AND REAR ELEVATIONS BY NEVIN & MORGAN, ARCHITECTS, PUBLISHED IN *THE COURIER-JOURNAL*, 8 JUNE 1952. THE EXTERIOR WALLS OF THE 52,000-SQUARE-FOOT STRUCTURE WERE MADE OUT OF A COMBINATION OF WHITE BRICK AND FIELDSTONE.

FLOODING IN FRONT OF BACON'S AND THE A & P, 27 JULY 1955. BY FREDERIC BECK, COURTESY OF SIDNEY W. ELINE, JR.

We opened Kentucky's first major suburban department store on Thursday August 27th, 1953, after a big ad and a lot of giveaways. It was estimated that 25,000 people came to St. Matthews that day. Traffic was stopped, and you couldn't get across the railroad tracks.[5] It was a nightmare. I was co-manager of the store. Harold Johnson told me on opening day that he wanted me to build a Stewart's of St. Matthews. And that is exactly what I did. We got business from people who would not have darkened Bacon's door downtown. But after the initial rush, business fell off, and I told Urban Dischinger, the co-manager in charge of buyers and merchandising, that until we upgraded our product lines, we would not do well out here. I will never forget. He said: "Oh, you people in St. Matthews are snobs." I told him we might not have a lot of money in St. Matthews, but we have good taste. And they started to upscale the merchandise, and from then on look what happened. Bacon's will still be here when the others are gone.

From interview of Georgia Ellinger, 6 March 1997.

Dewey Weyland had been selling DeSotos and Plymouths in St. Matthews for 16 years when his Advance Motor Company moved from a stone-veneered showroom on Lexington Road (now a branch office of Stock Yards Bank & Trust Company) to a sleeker one in aluminum and glass on Shelbyville Road in 1948.[7]

I'm here because I made a most careful study of this town. For several years my business caused me to pass through St. Matthews quite frequently. I observed the steady and solid development business and in building. There was no boom at any time. No cheap construction was indulged in by the real estate men. Under such conditions well-to-do young people come and they need cars.

From statement by D. W. Weyland in James Speed's *St. Matthews Makes Its Bow* (1938).

GILBERT OCHSNER IN FAMILY'S YARD AT 105 FAIRFAX AVENUE (NOW LOCATION OF MIDAS) IN EARLY 1930S, BEFORE INTERURBAN TRACKS ALONG SHELBYVILLE ROAD WERE TAKEN UP. BEYOND IS SITE OF TRINITY HIGH SCHOOL'S ALUMNI HALL AND STANDIFORD FIELD CAR SALES. JUDY OCHSNER EDWARDS COLLECTION, BEARGRASS-ST. MATTHEWS HISTORICAL SOCIETY.

THURSTON COOKE FORD (TRNITY HIGH SCHOOL'S ALUMNI HALL) AND GIL MUELLER AUTO SERVICE (STANDIFORD FIELD CAR SALES), IN 1953. ZV 120-53U, JEFFERSON COUNTY PRESERVATION AND ARCHIVES.

Within a few years, Weyland had given way to a Ford dealership operated by Thurston Cooke, whose massive lighted signage told motorists he meant business. In June of 1960 the lights suddenly went out as his financial

empire unraveled and his four defunct dealerships were disposed of. Cooke had come to Louisville in 1931 from Butler County where he had been born in the crossroads community of Quality. Like his cousins, V. V. and Almond Cooke, he became successful selling automobiles. He was tireless, generous,

personable, and took an active interest in various civic causes, the state Democratic Party, and Broadway Baptist Church. He never recovered from his downfall and died at the age of 57 in 1966.[8] Joe Brown Ford bought Thurston Cooke's remaining assets in St. Matthews.[9]

When Sears, Roebuck & Company began to cast around for a new site to accommodate a larger store with more parking in the fall of 1953, the company had had a presence in St. Matthews next to the Vogue theater since October 1939. Its lease at 3731 Lexington Road was about to expire, and a 5-acre site on the northwest corner of Shelbyville Road and Thierman Lane was selected. The land had been part of a tract owned by the Washburne family, and contained an obviously old, clapboarded house. A residence of L. Washburne appears in that location on the 1858 Bergmann map. Lewis (also spelled Louis) Washburne already had an interest in the "turnpike tract" when he received the remainder from his father's estate in 1853. He also received full title to the 50-acre "home tract," containing a grist mill north of the Louisville & Lexington Railroad tracks that later was subdivided by his son as Warwick Villa. That clapboarded residence, at 711 Fountain Avenue, has been preserved by Judge and Mrs. Macauley Smith. The date the Shelbyville Road house was built has not been ascertained, but even before it was razed, it had indications of being improved before the Civil War, perhaps when Washburne married Mary Ann Rudy in 1853.[10]

For decades, the property on Shelbyville Road west of Thierman Lane had been farmed by the Seiderman family, and in later years by the Seiderman sisters. Carolyn Rudy Barth, who lived nearby, remembers that the sisters worked long and hard on their truck farm. Carolyn was sent by her mother to buy vegetables, and she recalls that the cellar rooms were full of potatoes, turnips, onions, and squash. "They never went to the bank, and they had drawers of money."[11]

The two Seiderman sisters looked about eight foot tall. They wore long, black garb. They did the garden in those black togs all the time. There were just the two women there.

From interview of Frank L. "Tubby" Barth, Jr., 20 January 1998.

SEIDERMAN RESIDENCE AND OUTBUILDINGS ON NORTHWEST CORNER OF THIERMAN LANE AND SHELBYVILLE ROAD IN 1953. 94.17.019, UNIVERSITY OF LOUISVILLE PHOTOGRAPHIC ARCHIVES.

The rezoning process touched off an extended court battle that ended in late 1955 with the Kentucky Court of Appeals ordering the Jefferson Circuit Court to have the City-County Planning Commission zone the property commercial. The plan, prepared in 1953 by the Chicago firm of Dittrich & Gibson, Architects & Engineers, called for the long rectangular Sears structure to front on Shelbyville Road, while to the east, parking would be provided along Thierman Lane for over a thousand cars.[12] The layout was significantly altered to conform to prevailing suburban shopping center setbacks when an additional three acres on Shelbyville Road that had been part of the old potato farm was acquired from R. Lee Durning in 1957. The main, two-story structure was placed significantly back from Shelbyville Road allowing for parking in front of the store. Combined with parking along Thierman Lane, 703 cars could be accommodated. The new, $2-million complex opened at 4121 Shelbyville Road on 1 October 1959. The old Lexington Road store closed after operating for 20 years. In the fall of 1984, when Sears moved to Oxmoor Center, the old building was renovated by developer Frank Metts, and is now called the St. Matthews Pavilion.[13]

RENDERING BY DITTRICH & GIBSON ARCHITECTS & ENGINEERS, CHICAGO, 12 OCTOBER 1953. JEFFERSON COUNTY HISTORIC PRESERVATION AND ARCHIVES.

Some of the initial resistance to the Sears project by residents and planners alike, undoubtedly stemmed from another development being planned to consume an old potato farm farther east on the south side of Shelbyville Road, alongside a part of Sinking Fork of Beargrass Creek, that once belonged to J. B. Dorsey. John E. Bauer purchased the land in 1903. His daughter, Louisa Barbara Bauer, had married Peter Frank Meisner, and he had farmed the land from 1907 until 1950. Then the life-long resident of St. Matthews moved to Brown Avenue where he died in 1956 at the age of 73.[14]

In 1951, Robert Woodrow "Buck" Marshall acquired the Meisner tract with the idea of developing a shopping center.[15] The concept was novel, and the process uncharted. Although he had already been involved in a number of real estate ventures, they paled in comparison to the impact this development would have on St. Matthews. His father, Robert H. Marshall, had moved his family in 1928 from Cannons Lane to 133 Breckenridge Lane, where he had acquired a concrete-block house recently erected in the Magnolia Subdivision by Edward Johnson.[16] Next to it, he established a planing mill to

MEISNER HOUSE AND BARN, NOW SITE OF THE
SHELBYVILLE PLAZA. VIEW FROM SHELBYVILLE
ROAD JUST EAST OF CREEK THAT BORDERS THE
SHOPPING CENTER. PHOTOGRAPH BY WARREN
KELLAR FREDERICK ABOUT 1940. UNIVERSITY
OF LOUISVILLE PHOTOGRAPHIC ARCHIVES.

augment his meager earnings as a mathematics teacher at duPont Manual High School. His father had operated a successful sawmill in Monroe County, but the work was tough, and being sickly in his youth, he determined to pursue an academic career. He graduated from the Western Kentucky Normal School at Bowling Green, where he roomed with the future president of the University of Kentucky, Herman Lee Donovan. He married Flossie Tinsley from Muhlenberg County, and later received degrees from the University of Illinois at Champaign, where a son was born in July 1913. While he was named Robert Woodrow Marshall for Woodrow Wilson, the sitting President and a former university president, his father would call him Buck. The senior Marshall was teaching in Pittsburgh, Kansas, when he accepted a position at duPont Manual, where he taught for 21 years.[17]

Robert H. Marshall supplemented his teaching income by operating the planing mill, and in addition, he would annually build a house. According to the 1938 booklet, *St. Matthews Makes Its Bow*, the mill carried a "complete stock of lumber, doors, windows, built-in cabinets, roofing, shingles and paint products." The sign over the truck entrance promoted millwork and hardware. By then Buck Marshall had taken over the operation for his father, who had done well mainly by obtaining chestnut wood for trim from Monroe County. Then, in 1932, as FDR campaigned to repeal prohibition, the mill began to set up patterns for bars and booths. The work load became staggering, and Buck Marshall dropped out of high school to help out. He never returned.[18] Sawdust was in his blood. Experience would be his teacher.

Marshall's first attempt at gaining approval of the Planning and Zoning Commission for the Shelbyville Road Plaza project was met with great resistance, the main sticking point being the traffic congestion it would cause on Shelbyville Road.[19] Marshall came back to the commission a third time in May of 1953, with another version prepared by architect E. W. Augustus. He also came armed with polished proponents who argued that the St. Matthews business district had grown "jumbled, confused, crowded, and hazardous to both motorists and pedestrians." Commercial expansion east of the old district would provide not only relief, but also a larger commercial base. At the same meeting, Helm Bruce, Jr., presented his plans for commercial develop-

Mother's father Frank Meisner had been a middle manager at American Standard when he took early retirement and began farming full time. We went out there to live for a few years just after the war when I was about four. He was still farming and was basically a potato farmer. He rotated his fields of potatoes and corn. There was a barn in which he kept 12 or 16 dairy cows, and in one of the attached sheds he kept mules. He bought a tractor when my oldest brother got kicked out of the barn. Grandpa built a new house on the east side of the creek and had just moved into it when it burned to the ground and they lost all of their possessions. They moved back into the old, two-story frame house, and we lived on the second floor. It had a large front porch which nobody used because we would come in the long road from Shelbyville Road and then swing around in back. The old house, which was torn down for the plaza, stood about where the Burlington Coat Factory is now. The two big fields that were rotated with potatoes or corn were divided front to back by a grove of mostly pear trees about 100 feet square. There were about a half dozen tombstones in there, but they were so old you could not read them. There must have been records because they satisfied relatives when they were moved to make way for the plaza. They were about where the post office is.

From interview of Richard Leo Schuler, 16 December 1997.

EAST SIDE OF BRECKENRIDGE LANE, NORTH OF WILLIS AVENUE, 1947. THE MARSHALL FAMILY'S CONCRETE BLOCK HOUSE WAS JUST BEYOND THE OLD ST. MATTHEWS BAPTIST CHURCH PROPERTY. ZV 36-47, JEFFERSON COUNTY HISTORIC PRESERVATION AND ARCHIVES.

ment on 15 acres of the Jule B. Arterburn property several hundred feet east of Marshall's project.[20]

Grady Clay, then *The Courier-Journal*'s real estate editor, realized the advent of the "regional shopping center" was the "beginning of a trend" that would bring on "a major change in commercial real estate values."[21] It would also change the face of the traditional arteries feeding the city. These major conduits had long ago been named for their destination points (Brownsboro, Shelbyville, Taylorsville, Bardstown, Dixie), but suddenly they were a focus of commercial growth because they could accommodate automobile traffic—at least in the decade following World War II. Clay would characterize the subsequent highway commercialization as strips in his 1973 look at the American city, entitled *Close-Up*. "On the strip, automobility runs rampant, carrying that valuable cargo called 'accessibility' to be dropped off anywhere along the way," he would describe.[22] Viewing American commercial strips two decades later, Larry R. Ford contends they "are valuable additions to the urban scene because, quite simply, they work." Other observers, he does point out, have been particularly critical of the strip's architectural context. However, he noted that architects Venturi, Brown, and Izenour in their book *Learning from Las Vegas* (Cambridge, 1988), had a positive reaction to the sculptural forms and communicative powers of highway signage. Yet they would say, "if you take the signs away, there is no place."[23]

Marshall's rezoning appeal was successful, but after realizing the time and energy he would have to expend to develop the $1-million project himself, he leased his 34 acres to Ralph Biernbaum of Rochester, New York, for 99 years at $25,000 a year.[24] The young president of Delevan Realty Company and Jacob Gross, Inc., a firm that had focused on strip centers, had been stationed at Godman Field near Fort Knox during World War II and he was familiar with Louisville. One problem he quickly encountered was the existence of a small cemetery on the site.[25]

Biernbaum assembled a mixture of 23 tenants; eleven were national concerns, many of which he had already worked with frequently. Twelve were long-established downtown firms eager to test the suburban marketplace. Sidney H. Morris & Associates was brought in from Chicago to design the shopping center, which would be surrounded by 1,600 free parking spaces.[26] The center was built by the Dahlem Construction Company, headed by Joseph Charles Dahlem, whose son Bernard V. Dahlem, a 1951 graduate of the University of Louisville's J. B. Speed Scientific School, was more directly involved. Joe Dahlem was Louisville's pioneer strip and shopping center developer, whose earliest work included the Vogue theater complex.[27]

The Shelbyville Road Plaza enjoyed success until shoppers were drawn to the enclosed malls that surfaced closer to the Watterson Expressway interchange. A tenant that reversed that trend, however, was Hawley-Cooke Booksellers. In the mid-1970s, two Legal Aid Society lawyers and their wives determined that Louisville was in the market for a totally different approach to merchandizing books. Since 1915, new books and rare editions had been the almost exclusive purview of W. K. Stewart Bookstore on Fourth Street. Providing much the same service was the St. Matthews Book Shop, run by Jessie Clark Speed, with help from Edith Callahan and Mildred Clark. "It was very convenient and they made it a pleasant place to go," Mrs. John Welburn Brown recalled.[28] The Browns moved into the old Chenoweth house on Chenoweth Lane about the same time the bookshop opened on Frankfort Avenue about 1940. Shortly thereafter, its quarters were moved into a small house at 3920 Westport Road. Like W. K. Stewart's, they picked out good books for the customer, whose taste in literature they generally knew. However, Jessie C. Speed, widow of Evarts Speed, Jr., closed the St. Matthews Book Shop about 1964. Then W. K. Stewart's was sold in 1969, and it went out of business downtown in late 1975.[29] A niche was created, but the book-retailing concept Graham and Martha Neal Cooke and Bill and Audrey Schuetze began to devise would simply dwarf its predecessors. Humongous in every proportion, the idea was altogether revolutionary for this region, let alone Louisville. In June 1978 the doors of Hawley-Cooke Booksellers opened in the Shelbyville Road Plaza, and a cultural institution was born. The previously underutilized plaza parking lot bulged with cars from other counties and states. The store became a tourist destination point, like Churchill Downs or Cave Hill Cemetery, where people proudly took out-of-town visitors to show them a sight to be seen. Hawley-Cooke was soon a landmark on Shelbyville Road, a campus for those long graduated in need of the information and pleasure only reading can provide. No other institution has meant more to the cultural uplift of Louisville. Television had finally met its match. In short order, other communities took notice, as did large chains. But local allegiance has remained with Hawley-Cooke, and its proprietors have enlarged and added two stores to keep up with mounting competition.[30] As for the

"I know them by reputation," said Richard Howorth, president of the American Booksellers Association. "I know that they're good, and big; they're very community-focused; among independent book dealers, they are well known and respected....

Three Louisville stores now carry the partnership's name, which borrowed the Hawley from William Schuetze's family history because his last name is too hard for the un-Germanic to pronounce.

...But even as they celebrate success, the four owners profess to have little more idea of what the next several years will bring than they did 20 years ago. "It's a rapidly changing industry; there's probably been more change in the last two years than there was in the first 18," said William Schuetze, 52.

From David Goetz, "Hawley-Cooke opens book on third decade," *The Courier-Journal*, 7 June 1998.

At that time the Shelbyville Road Plaza was a fairly large center. They were all open centers then, not enclosed like later. We built between 80 and 100 shopping centers in the suburbs. We followed where the population was going. St. Matthews was the magnet. It was an affluent community and could stand a good center. It was the first in Louisville of that size.

From interview of Ralph Biernbaum, 9 December 1996.

Shelbyville Road Plaza, by 1995, new owners, THP Development Company, had modernized the center's appearance, and were proposing to expand the center south along Bowling Boulevard.[31]

Endorsing Shelbyville Road's emergence as a retail strip, both Bank of Louisville and Lincoln Bank & Trust Company announced in 1954 construction of branches along the corridor east of Hubbards Lane.[32] Each branch would feature a drive-in window and plenty of parking in front. Bank of Louisville got the jump by moving a cottage onto the site to provide temporary quarters while a brick-clad structure was razed and the new bank facility, designed by Wagner & Potts, was erected.[33]

THE TEMPORARY STRUCTURE WAS POSITIONED
TO THE LEFT (EAST) OF THE STRUCTURE BEING
DEMOLISHED TO MAKE WAY FOR THE NEW
BRANCH DELINEATED ON THE SIGN IN BETWEEN.
1954, CAUFIELD & SHOOK COLL. 284831,
UNIVERSITY OF LOUISVILLE PHOTOGRAPHIC
ARCHIVES.

Local government finally emerged from the confines of the court system. Back in March of 1950, the sixth-class city of St. Matthews had incorporated. Immediately, the tiny, three-and-a-half block municipality set its sights on annexing two-and-a-half square miles surrounding it. The additional area was projected to have a population of between 15,000 and 20,000 persons, which would make the brand-new and bigger St. Matthews the largest sixth-class city in Kentucky. A remonstrance suit was brought to block the annexation, but on 2 June 1951, Judge Scott Miller ruled it could proceed. While opponents then went to the Kentucky Court of Appeals, the trustees of St. Matthews (James H. Noland, Gilbert Flack, B. W. Gratzer, Henry Leathers, and T. S. Rudy) began to establish various boards and a police force, in addition to mailing out tax bills. At the same time, the YMCA housed in the old rectory of the original St. Matthews Episcopal Church was renovated for a city hall. The first ceremony held in city hall was the swearing in of zoning commissioners by City Attorney C. Maxwell Brown on 17 January 1951.[34] A few days later, *The Courier-Journal* aptly characterized the situation: "St. Matthews May Not Know Where It's Going—But It's Going."[35] When the Court of Appeals ruled in August 1951 against the annexation, St. Matthews was relegated again to measuring itself in blocks, not miles.

James H. Noland, who had been chairman of the trustees since St. Matthews had become a sixth-class city in 1950, continued as chairman of the council. Although he again reiterated that annexation would only be pursued where favored, in the fall of 1953 the city of St. Matthews moved to annex the business district as well as the adjoining 2-square-mile area.[36]

Based upon its increased population, the city of St. Matthews was upgraded from sixth class to fourth class by the Kentucky General Assembly in 1954, the legislation taking effect on 17 June.[37] At a luncheon meeting of the St. Matthews Committee of the Louisville Chamber of Commerce at the

St. Matthews' city hall, by Thomas V. Miller, Jr., from *The Courier-Journal*, 21 January 1951. From its style, the structure appears to have been erected about 1880. It had been leased, along with 2.5 acres, by the St. Matthews YMCA branch beginning in the fall of 1948. The old rectory on the east side of St. Matthews Avenue, north of the railroad tracks, was razed as part of a fire-fighting exercise in November 1969.

Canary Cottage on Lexington Road on June 21st, Mayor James H. Noland outlined six projects the city would undertake by virtue of its new powers, including establishing a police force, appointing an alcoholic beverage administrator, contracting for fire protection with the existing St. Matthews Volunteer Fire Department, and engaging in planning and zoning matters.[38] The government, itself, would be substantially altered from its previous five-member board of trustees to an eight-person council, presided over by a mayor.

At the city council's first meeting, in July 1954, Ronald C. Kelsay, a former member of the Louisville police force who was attending the University of Louisville, was sworn in as police chief.[39] Prior to the establishment of this bare bones department, Jefferson County's police had responsibility for law enforcement in St. Matthews. Familiar in that capacity to residents was

Charles King Osborn, who became a county policeman in 1907 and was later chief.[40] The St. Matthews police force has grown from a chief and two patrolmen with one patrol car into a sizeable operation employing 37 with an annual budget of $1.6 million.[41]

The business district takeover was predicated upon the city of Louisville's being denied to do so by the Kentucky Court of Appeals. However, in 1957, after the question of annexation had been litigated for 11 years, the Court of Appeals failed to act, allowing both the city of Louisville and the city of St. Matthews to press forward.[42] Finally, early in 1964, Louisville obtained the old St. Matthews business district along Lexington Road and Shelbyville Road, from Eline Avenue to Fairfax.[43]

"Mayor Jim" resigned in September 1958, after eight gratuitous years formulating a governmental entity in St. Matthews, all the while keeping the city of Louisville at bay. He had been in the bedding business all his life, and had moved to St. Matthews in 1929, after which he was active in the Beargrass Christian Church and the Boy Scouts, as well as various other civic endeavors. He died on 21 June 1960 at the age of 65.[44] His hand-picked successor was Bernard F. Bowling, a civil engineering graduate of Notre Dame University and owner of the bakery founded by his uncle, Kuno Plehn. As mayor, Bowling watched over St. Matthews like a hawk for nearly 26 years, 21 years without pay. He concentrated on relieving drainage problems, oversaw construction of a city hall, helped establish a community center, persuaded the James Graham Brown Foundation to donate land for a park, and worked tirelessly and successfully on annexation matters including the Mall property.

Bowling's first official duty as mayor-elect in 1958 was to turn a spade of dirt on Church Way to mark the groundbreaking for the Sidney Eline Memorial Library. The youngest son of A. J. "Tony" and Elizabeth Eline was 23 years old when called into active duty during World War II. On his 13th

In the middle 50s, St. Matthews decided it needed a police force. A friend, Ron Kelsay, wanted a job as patrolman so he could continue his education at the University of Louisville. He asked me to write a letter for his signature to send to Mayor Jim Noland....A few days later Jim Noland stopped by and asked me about Kelsay....

"We're thinking about making him chief of police," Jim said.
"But you can't," I said. "He's just a kid and he's still going to school."

"Yeah," Jim said. "But you should see that great letter he wrote me."

From Emil Michael Aun, "How it was—really—back when," *The Voice*, 25 July 1974.

Mr. W. C. Winchester was robbed about a week ago. The thief seems to have watched until the family went to supper; then entered the sitting room, taking a watch, which was an heirloom, and twenty dollars. No information has been gained as yet. We are sorry, indeed, for this loss, but can only advise Mr. Winchester to pull down the shades after nightfall, and also lay up his treasures in Heaven where thieves cannot break through and steal.

From "St. Matthews," *The Jeffersonian*, 28 January 1915.

The role for which he probably received the widest recognition outside his own city was as champion of the cause of metropolitan government during his early years as mayor....Several years ago, Bowling built a reputation as a champion of annexation—at least the annexation of territory to St. Matthews. The fact that so many sixth-class cities have mushroomed east of Louisville, is due in part to the reluctance of some suburbanites to become St. Matthewsites.

From Anne Moore, "A Baker Makes St. Matthews Bubble," *The Courier-Journal*, 30 July 1968.

bombing mission over Germany, Sidney Eline's plane was shot down on 1 April 1943. He was survived by his wife and their three-month-old son. When efforts were being made to replace the totally inadequate, one-room, 5,200-book library on St. Matthews Avenue, the Elines provided the land and $10,000 to do so. The rest of the money to build the modern structure designed by Ed Augustus was raised through a public fund drive spearheaded by Emil Aun, J. Price Webb, and particularly Mrs. Harriet Cowman, a newcomer to the area who thought the existing library's 10' by 14' space was totally inadequate.[45]

To operate the new facility, the unique arrangement with the Louisville Free Public Library was continued by which it would staff the new library and supply the books, but the building would be erected and maintained by the St. Matthews group. A branch of the Louisville Free Public Library had existed in the Bank of St. Matthews at least as early as 1922.[46] A branch was operated at 3832 Frankfort Avenue from 1938-1946, and then at 133 St. Matthews Avenue.[47] It was the only public library in the East End outside the city of Louisville, the bailiwick of Mrs. A. W. Schumann for ten years before she continued as librarian of the Sidney Eline Memorial Library Free Public Library, which was dedicated in April 1959.[48] The St. Matthews/Eline branch library moved into a section of City Hall in 1994.

When Mayor Bowling died suddenly at the age of 62 in 1984, city councilman Arthur Draut was named mayor of the fourth largest city in Jefferson County following Louisville, Jeffersontown, and Shively, with a population exceeding 13,000. Draut had been on the council since 1976, but he was probably better known in the community through his association with Waggener High School, first as dean of students in 1954, then as assistant principal and principal from 1959 until retirement in 1983. As St. Matthews' third mayor, he was embarking on his third career. He had served in the Navy for 24 years, attaining the rank of commander, and had obtained degrees from the University of Louisville. Various programs and public improvements have been initiated since an occupational tax was established in 1986, including the purchase and renovation of the Greathouse School for a larger city hall.[49]

Georgia Ellinger, who was co-manager of Bacon's from its opening until leaving for a banking position in 1958, recalls that the store had a toy department in the basement that was "unusual." Toys were generally handled on a limited basis by hardware stores or by department stores only before Christmas. But "Uncle Jim" Thornbury was gearing up competition. " I think we got out of the toy business because of Thornbury's," Ellinger remembers. "They were really a successful store, one of the best."[50] In 1954 when the McCormick spice company closed its Louisville office, regional sales manager James G. Thornbury went looking for a small business. He decided to open a bicycle shop in St. Matthews at 117 Breckenridge Lane, in direct competition with the St. Matthews Cycle Shop that had been operating for five or so years on Frankfort Avenue west of the old White Castle location. Around Christmas, he soon began to stock toys also. Then as the economy improved and memories of Depression days faded, toys became year-round commodities. Effectively using Saturday morning television, Thornbury Toys became a local institution, moving into a larger store in the commercial building that replaced the old Greathouse School.[51] Thorny, the store's wooden monkey mascot, became a celebrity in his own right.[52] With his family participating, Uncle Jim's single store multiplied into 17, located in Kentucky and various other states.[53] Thornbury retired in 1983, and within five years all but the original store had been sold. Before he died in 1991 at the age of 75, even that had been purchased by St. Matthews Schwinn Cyclery.[54]

"Busy, growing St. Matthews will get its fifth branch bank," *The Courier-Journal* announced on 28 May 1961. The Louisville Trust Company's modest brick and glass structure replaced a service station outlet of the National Oil Corporation, whose president was Clarence E. Bauer. There he, and later Martin A. "Motz" Bauer, had marketed their familiar Continental Oil Company gasoline, Conoco.[55] The bank building now houses Edwards Photo.

We were on bicycles until we were in high school. We got to know every nook and cranny of St. Matthews. There wasn't a place that we didn't know about. That is what we explored all the time. We got our parts from the old cycle shop near Gerstle's. I can see that man right now.

From interview of Robert Michael Kirn, 15 December 1997.

NATIONAL OIL CORP. SERVICE STATION PUMPING CONOCO GASOLINE ON SHELBYVILLE ROAD EAST OF MERIDIAN, WHICH RUNS DIAGONALLY IN THE BACKGROUND, 1950. ZV135-50U, JEFFERSON COUNTY HISTORIC PRESERVATION AND ARCHIVES.

The land between the Shelbyville Road Plaza and William Marshall Bullitt's 1,000-acre Oxmoor tract had been in the hands of the Arterburn family since 1830. In that year, Branham Arterburn purchased 287 acres, excluding the one-acre burying ground where William Christian was interred that had been set aside as a family cemetery by Alexander Scott Bullitt.[56] Thomas W. Bullitt, who was born at Oxmoor in 1838, would later write: "Two forks of Beargrass cross the front of the place—one across the pasture in front of the house, the other through the Evinger field at the foot of the graveyard. They unite in the (now) Arteburn (formerly Christian) place, a quarter of a mile or more below the graveyard."[57] (Bullitt consistently spelled Arterburn phonetically, leaving out the middle "r.") According to the obituary of Norbourn Arterburn, who died in April 1878, he was born on Beargrass Creek in 1813, the son of William and Rachel Smoot Arterburn.[58] Jefferson County tax returns do not reveal where on Beargrass Creek the Arterburns were then living. Little is known about William, but he came to Louisville with his father and various brothers about 1800.[59] His wife, Rachel (also spelled Rachael), was born in Shenandoah County, Virginia, on 13 July 1775, and perhaps the Arterburns, too, were from that region. After William died or departed, Rachel purchased an additional 107 acres from the estate of John Evinger.[60] When she died on 6 March 1872, her burial took place in the family cemetery, which still exists west of the log house she lived in much of her almost ninety-seven-year life.

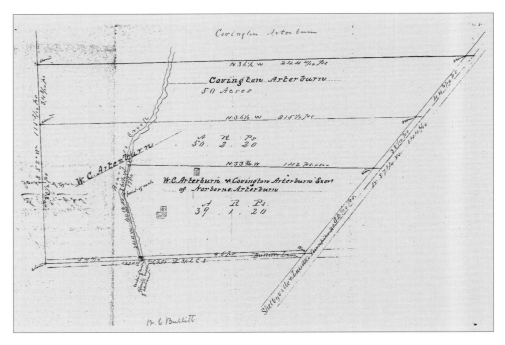

FROM A 1878 DIVISION PLAT OF ARTERBURN FAMILY PROPERTY. BULLITT LANE THEN DIVIDED OXMOOR FROM THE ARTERBURN LAND TO THE WEST. THE ELL-SHAPED RESIDENCE WEST OF BULLITT LANE IS THE LOG HOUSE WILLIAM CHRISTIAN BUILT. IN 1786, HE WAS KILLED BY INDIANS AND BURIED IN FRONT OF HIS RESIDENCE. THE CHRISTIAN-BULLITT FAMILY GRAVEYARD IS NOT SHOWN, BUT IT IS IMMEDIATELY NORTHWEST OF THE INTERSECTION OF BULLITT LANE AND THE CREEK. THE ARTERBURN FAMILY GRAVEYARD IS SHOWN BEHIND THE CHRISTIAN HOUSE, WHICH THE ARTERBURNS ACQUIRED. PLAT, DATED 27 NOVEMBER 1878, IS FILED IN JEFFERSON COUNTY COURT CASE 121.

Norbourn Arterburn's inheritance from his mother's estate reportedly helped make him one of the richest men in the state. His marriage to Ann Herr, daughter of John Herr, in 1840 was a contributing factor. He was a director of the Farmers and Drovers Bank and maintained controlling interest in the Brownsboro turnpike. His reputation was not sullied by brothers Jordan and Tarlton Arterburn, who were notorious slave dealers.[61]

Norbourn Arterburn's eight brothers included Covington and William Crawford Arterburn. Together the three had tremendous farm holdings on both sides of Shelbyville Road. Wm. C. Arterburn died of typhoid fever at the age of 85 in January 1901.[62] His obituary said he owned "one of the best farms in the county, and had valuable interests in Louisville." He was survived by a son and his brother, Covington, who was described as "the prominent horseman." Wm. C. Arterburn's homestead, noted on the north side of Shelbyville Road on the 1879 county atlas as Walnut Grove, was inherited by his only child, Norbourn Arterburn, who had been born in 1857 in the spacious two-story house designed in the prevailing Italianate style. Norbourn Arterburn married Sue Hall and later Sallie C. Tucker, and had five children including William Norbourn Arterburn, a graduate of Yale University, who with his father owned the Louisville Nurseries that later was subdivided as Fairmeade.[63] When Norbourn Arterburn died in July 1937 at the age of 80, followed only a few weeks later by his son, William Norbourn Arterburn, at the age of 55, a great deal of land along Shelbyville Road was being readied for market.

A year later, Norbourn's nephew, Jule B. Arterburn, considered the oldest resident of St. Matthews, died at the age 82.[64] A deaf mute, the son of Covington Arterburn was a retired farmer. He had lived in a brick house far down a long drive on the south of Shelbyville Road, on property known as Beechwood Gate.[65] Later he built a newer house nearer the road, opposite where the Howard Johnson's restaurant was erected. When the property was being cleared for development in 1964, the stone entrance columns were moved to the Locust Grove restoration on Blankenbaker Lane.

Wm. C. Arterburn's brother, Covington, died only seven months later at the age of 83.[66] He was the youngest and last living of the nine brothers, "one of the main pillars of Beargrass Christian Church," and had served

as president of the Jefferson County Turnpike Company. He was survived by his wife, Annie, and son, Jule Bernard Arterburn. His residence on the south side of Shelbyville Road was very prominent east of Hubbards Lane until obscured by development. A brick facade was added to the rear, which now constitutes the front on Norbourne Boulevard, part of the Parkside subdivision.

Rachel Arterburn supposedly settled on Beargrass Creek in that cabin there near Oxmoor with those seven sons. They all grew up from there. The old Arterburn cemetery is back of the log house near there. We used to go up there and drink the spring water. They had a springhouse. Daddy [William Norbourn Arterburn] would take us up there as kids.

From interview of Sue Hall Arterburn Stich, 2 January 1997.

OLD COVINGTON ARTERBURN RESIDENCE IN 1950 BEFORE DEVELOPMENT TOOK PLACE ALONG SHELBYVILLE ROAD. ZV40-50U, JEFFERSON COUNTY HISTORIC PRESERVATION AND ARCHIVES.

The Planning and Zoning Commission has been asked to rezone two tracts of land south of Shelbyville Road and west of Watterson Expressway for construction of shopping centers. On the surface, the idea sounds logical and attractive. Further study, however, indicates that a shopping center at either of the two proposed locations would not best serve the needs of residents in the St. Matthews area or the sound development of the eastern section of Jefferson County....

It is also the duty of the commission to correct a weakness in zoning regulations which was brought to light during discussion of the proposed shopping centers. Under existing regulations there is no way to require a developer to abide by the details of the plan on which the commission bases its approval of his application.

From "A Shopping Center Is Needed, But Not Here," *The Courier-Journal*, 25 May 1953.

The heirs of Jule B. Arterburn subsequently leased the 67-acre tract to developer Helm Bruce, Jr., and landscape architect Campbell Miller for 99 years, and in 1957 they in turn leased a 50-acre portion to a new Baltimore firm, Community Research and Development (CRD), Inc. Bruce, the son of a distinguished Louisville lawyer, had developed Cherokee Gardens as well as the "Pink Palace" property in Memphis (estate of Piggly Wiggly grocery chain founder Clarence Saunders).[67] The Baltimore outfit had acted as an owner's representative in the creation of one of the country's first regional malls, but it had yet to do one on its own. CRD's chairman was the experienced Baltimore shopping center developer, Jack Meyerhoff. Its president was James W. Rouse, and executive vice president Williard G. Rouse. The latter would be the point man for the Mall St. Matthews.[68]

Four years after the lease announcement, ground was broken and plans were unveiled for a $10-million mall to house 50 to 55 stores in the 300,000 square-foot center amidst an air-conditioned, botanical garden atmosphere. Recognizing that 42 percent of Jefferson County's population lived within a 15-minute drive, parking would be provided for 2,500 cars. The Baltimore architectural firm of Taliaferro and Lamb would design the facility, while Lewis Clarke of Raleigh was the landscape architect.[69] Among the guests at the groundbreaking was St. Matthews Mayor Bernard Bowling. While St. Matthews had considered annexing the Mall site, Bowling dodged answering the question of whether annexation would be considered in the future.[70]

When the Mall opened in March 1962 with 40 stores, patrons were invited to browse a shopping street "lined with cages of tropical birds." While James W. Rouse attended the Mall opening, he had an opportunity to discuss with Grady Clay, then urban affairs editor for *The Courier-Journal*, an even more ambitious project. (He subsequently obtained from Clay materials on

Aerial view of the Mall after its opening in the spring of 1962. Edge of Oxmoor farm is in background. Billy Davis Collection, University of Louisville Photographic Archives.

new towns.) In late 1963, Clay was able to reveal that Rouse had been envisioning Columbia, Maryland.[71] Rouse would also develop the "festival market places," Faneuil Hall in Boston and Inner Harbor in Baltimore, before turning his attention to affordable housing.[72] After slipping in popularity to the newer mall at Oxmoor, the Mall St. Matthews was enlarged and renovated by the Rouse Company beginning in 1992, and by mid-1994 it had regained its perch "among the region's most popular retail venues."[73]

At the same time Helm Bruce, Jr., and Campbell Miller were leasing Arterburn-owned land to the Rouses, they entered into an agreement with

VIEW OF COMMEWRCIAL DEVELOPMENT IN PLACE ALONG SOUTH SIDE OF SHELBYVILLE ROAD WEST OP WATTERSON EXPRESSWAY BY FEBRUARY 1967. ACROSS ROAD, EAST DRIVE-IN WOULD BECOME SITE OF SERVICE MERCHANDISE AND STEIN MART. BEYOND, AT END OF TEN PIN LANE, IS THE COMMUNITY RECREATION CENTER, NOW UNDERGOING EXTENSIVE REVITALIZATION. BILLY DAVIS COLLECTION, UNIVERSITY OF LOUISVILLE PHOTOGRAPHIC ARCHIVES.

A. L. Entwistle for 3.5 acres on which the Louisville-area agent for the Howard Johnson chain intended to build a 100-unit motel and a restaurant. Evidently that deal fell through, but by 1959, Entwistle had found other suitable Arterburn property across Shelbyville Road east of Beechwood Village on

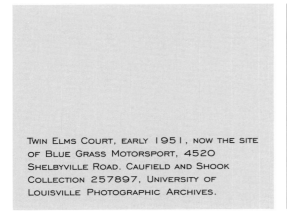

Twin Elms Court, early 1951, now the site of Blue Grass Motorsport, 4520 Shelbyville Road. Caufield and Shook Collection 257897, University of Louisville Photographic Archives.

which to build Howard Johnson's first motor lodge in Louisville. The land was leased from R. W. Marshall, who in turn had a 99-year lease from the Arterburn family. The restaurant with its "eye-catching orange porcelain shingles" was designed in the familiar Howard Johnson style by the company's architect Joseph Cicco of Walliston, Mass. The architect for the 120-unit, two-story motel component was Perry C. Langston, who worked for a subsidiary of Bank Building Corp., a St. Louis firm that was also consulting on the design of the new Liberty National Bank & Trust Company headquarters on Jefferson Street.[74] The first motel along Shelbyville Road was a far cry from the cottages of the Twin Elms Court, owned and operated by Guy B. Jones since about 1940.[75]

Heinrich (Henry) Albert Holzheimer had been born at the crossroads in St. Matthews in 1878. He had grown up on Breckenridge Lane on the 68-acre tract his father had farmed since turning over the tavern and grocery he had purchased from Daniel Gilman to the Bauer brothers. His father died in 1919 and in 1926 his farm was sold to realtor J. C. Turner. The son received $28,443 as his portion of the sale. He purchased land along Westport Road and continued to farm before working in real estate. His father had died at the age of 92; he died in 1963 at the age of 84.[76] On the 8th of March, the day Henry Albert Holzheimer was interred in Cave Hill Cemetery, *The Louisville Times* reflected on his passing and the changes that had occurred in St. Matthews during the period he and his father had lived and labored there.

The observations were quite profound:

> Death of Henry A. Holzheimer at his home on Westport Road breaks a link between the busy St. Matthews area and its rural past. For Holzheimer was 84 years old, and the 68-acre potato farm he sold in 1928 [1926] covered most of what is now St. Matthews's business and residential area.
>
> Sale of the Holzheimer farm, in fact, marked beginning of the end of the potato-growing area for St. Matthews, because Breckinridge Villa, built on the farm, became one of the first big subdivisions there and erased the rural atmosphere.
>
> Henry Holzheimer's father moved to St. Matthews soon after the Civil War. After operating a general store where the First National Lincoln Bank now stands, he became one of a number of men—mostly of German origin—who developed the surrounding land into farms. Jefferson County reputedly was the biggest potato producer next to Aroostook County, Maine, early in this century, and St. Matthews became one of the nation's biggest shipping points.
>
> St. Matthews still bears the marks of its transformation, in a relatively few years, from farm land to suburb. The individual farms have become a collection of individual subdivisions, and the business district clusters around what were intersecting county roads beside a railroad grade crossing. Since the change was innocent of any urban planning, the area presents a study in the advantages and handicaps of haphazardhood. Traffic is an insoluble problem, but there is a certain charm in the variety of big stores and small shops, parking lots and walkways, and the devious traffic patterns that have grown up out of necessity.
>
> St. Matthews potatoes now come from Idaho and Maine by way of the supermarket, and Henry Holzheimer must often have found the whole thing hard to believe.

The Holzheimer family was recognized by the city of St. Matthews in 1997, when the small park created where the railroad station and a parking area used to be was named in the family's honor.[77] The sliver of ground was once part of Henry Holzheimer's vast property holdings in St. Matthews that included 26.5 acres along the west side of Chenoweth Lane from the railroad tracks north to George L. Herr's subdivision, Elmwood. Elmwood's southern boundary is marked by Thorpe Interiors, with its distinctive earmarks of the Prairie School made famous by Frank Lloyd Wright. And in fact, the design was executed by the Frank Lloyd Wright Foundation, operating out of the Wright studio, Taliesin West, near Scottsdale, Arizona.

Nell Thorpe had been an interior designer for about ten years when she was joined in 1957 by her son, Norbourne "Skip" Thorpe, who was fresh

---

Lighted hamburgers. Revolving buckets of fried chicken. An advertising slogan blazing at night in red letters. Spotlights on roofs. Flashing. Blinking. Lightbulbs, on and off, chasing each other around the top of a building. The widespread use of outdoor lighting by businesses is one of dilemmas facing officials who are trying to cope with the energy shortage....

On one block of busy Shelbyville Road in St. Matthews one can see a lighted ice cream cone, roast beef sandwich, time and temperature sign (there's another two blocks up the road), and a lighted pizza.

From Bill Cox, "The energy that lights up the night," *The Courier-Journal*, 14 December 1973.

out of the University of Louisville School of Law. They purchased a *ca.* 1910, story-and-a-half, frame house at 224 Chenoweth Lane in 1959, and set up shop.[78] Several years later, Skip was asked by a family friend to negotiate a contract with the Wright Foundation for a substantial project, and in doing so, he became acquainted with Kenneth B. Lockhart, an architect representing the Taliesin West group. During one of Lockhart's visits to Louisville, Mrs. John Acree happened into Thorpe Interiors. Her son, Jack, and Skip Thorpe were best friends in high school. In an aside, she told Skip that Mr. Acree was going to New York the following week "to see if he can engage an architect to design a building so instantly recognizable that he will not need to have a sign." Skip wondered if Mr. Acree would like to talk to Frank Lloyd Wright Foundation architect Kenn Lockhart while he was in town and staying at his in-laws' house. Lockhart made a successful presentation to John Acree and his board of directors of the Lincoln Income Life Insurance Company, and he departed with contracts in his pocket for both large projects. In addition, Skip Thorpe asked Lockhart if he "could do something" for the front of the simple frame structure they had converted for their establishment. Six months later, a roll of beautifully articulated drawings and plans arrived in the mail from Taliesin West. The exterior of Thorpe Interiors would be radically altered. Later, a display window, sketched by architect Wes Peters at Taliesin West, was added. Some years later, the Thorpes acquired the old residence next door, and it was given a complementary Prairie School treatment.[79]

DISTINCTIVE GALLERIES OF THORPE INTERIORS, 224 CHENOWETH LANE, 1999. BY SAMUEL W. THOMAS.

On 17 July 1963, William Wesley Peters placed his stamp as a registered architect on a completed set of plans for the home office building of the Lincoln Income Life Insurance Company and applied his signature and the date. Four years after famed architect Frank Lloyd Wright had died at the

age of 91, his first apprentice in the fledgling Taliesin program had come into his own. Wes Peters had attended MIT for a year before joining Wright in 1932, and three years later becoming his son-in-law. (Later, the widowed Peters would marry the daughter of Josef Stalin.) In the Wright scheme, Peters became essential as a structural engineer and project architect in making Wright's innovative designs work and then getting them built. After Wright's death in 1959, Peters became head of the successor firm, Taliesin Associated Architects, and it was to this group that John T. Acree, president of Lincoln Income Life Insurance Company, turned in 1961 when his fast-growing company acquired 17 acres of the Golden Maxim Farm in the northwest quadrant of the Watterson Expressway/Breckenridge Lane interchange from Virginia and Clayton Moore for $125,000.

Although Virginia Murphy had grown up on the east side of Browns Lane, her father, Thomas M. Murphy, purchased part of the old Bethel Veech property along Beargrass Creek west of Breckenridge Lane where he established Beargrass Stud. His mare, Layol, foaled in 1920, birthed Golden Max by Golden Maxim—thus, the name of his farm.[80] Murphy had come to Louisville from Henryville, Indiana, and become involved in the horse business. In his later years, he also headed the Tip Top Baking Company.[81] His daughter Virginia married Clayton Moore, who worked for the baking company. When Murphy died in late 1929, the Moores took over Golden Maxim Farm. After the wholesale bakery business was sold, Clayton Moore devoted his attention to racing horses in partnership with Louis J. Hollenbach, Sr. When I-64 split the farm, the 25 acres north of the interstate were developed by a Columbus, Ohio, firm as "a garden-apartment community," Jamestown of St. Matthews.[82] Clayton Moore died at the age of 91 in 1985, and when the remaining 109 acres were acquired in 1986 by NTS Corp. for development, Virginia Moore was given a life tenancy on a four-acre tract that included the family residence.[83] Later the house, which the Moores reportedly had erected after moving onto the farm in 1939 "from the creek-stone foundation of an old hotel," was removed to make way for The Springs development.[84] The hotel had belonged to the Lewis Smysers, who had purchased the land from James B. Burks, but the high-walled Burks family cemetery was not disturbed.

Lincoln Income had been formed in 1930 by a merger of the Income Life Insurance Company of Louisville and the Lincoln Life & Accident Insurance Company of Oklahoma City. The company had continued to do a great deal of business in Oklahoma and the southwest, and very probably Acree and others were familiar with Wright's "needle on the prairie," the Price Tower at Bartlesville. In any case, when the announcement was made of the proposed office structure in late 1961, Acree already had in mind "a modern curtain-wall building" emanating from "a true park-like atmosphere" to be called "Lincoln Park Land."[85] There was no other suburban office tower even on the horizon at that time, but before Lincoln Income could get the project out of the ground, Kemmons Wilson, chairman of Holiday Inns of America, had placed the first suburban tower in Watterson City.[86]

The problem of annexation resurfaced. St. Matthews had already

Once church steeples were the tallest structures in Suburbia. But today scores of house-wives can see some of the Louisville area's newest tall buildings from their kitchen sinks....Some suburbanites couldn't care less about the presence of the skyscrapers—if the buildings keep their distance. For others, the towers are reminders of the city they left behind when they moved to the greener areas....

While they have watched the "lace-covered" tower go up with inordinate curiosity, nearby residents interviewed last week expressed no objection to the building itself. Some feel that the landscaping will enhance the area if the builders follow through on original proposals to build fountains and man-made waterfalls.

From Simpson Lawson, "Are Skyscrapers Spies In The Sky To Suburbia," *The Courier-Journal*, 25 July 1965.

View of Golden Maxim barn from Lincoln Tower, May 1967. From Georgia Ellinger collection, Beargrass-St. Matthews Historical Society.

Lincoln Income Insurance Company tower rising between the Watterson Expressway and the Clayton Moores' Golden Maxim Farm, on the west side of Breckenridge Lane. *Ca.* 1965, Billy Davis collection, University of Louisville Photographic Archives.

moved to annex both the Golden Maxim and J. Graham Brown farms, separated by Breckenridge Lane. Louisville, too, cast its eye on the golden egg. However, when the Moores indicated they did not appreciate being annexed by St. Matthews, and Lincoln Life preferred being in Louisville where fire protection for the tower was considered better and the required zoning changes would be "easier to get," a compromise was struck.[87] In late July 1962, Acree unveiled Wes Peters' elevation of the proposed $2.5 million, 15-story "Gold Tower." Besides its radical appearance, the building was to be constructed by a novel method. A central concrete core containing elevators and restrooms would support an upper terrace under which cantilever trusses would extend out on three sides to support the suspension of the first twelve floors. The curtain wall was to be entirely of glass. To reduce heat loads from sun penetration, Peters had devised an outer sunscreen panel of gold-anodized aluminum, designed in a curved and circular filigreed motif to prevent birds from nesting.[88] An aluminum prototype was tested but when its durability could not be guaranteed, concrete was substituted and the building took on a very different color than the gold originally envisioned. At the same time, the center concrete core was not painted the originally intended turquoise color.[89]

When Mrs. Frank Lloyd Wright came to inspect the Lincoln Tower when it opened in March 1966, *Louisville Times* reporter Moyra Schroeder remarked that the "outside colors—elusive shades of pink, echoed and varied throughout the inside, were Mrs. Wright's choice."[90] And so, the southern exposure of St. Matthews was to have "one of the most-discussed buildings in this region" as its defining landmark, bursting out of bluegrass fields where horses continued to graze, visible from every direction for miles.

Acree's insurance company became a subsidiary of Indianapolis-based Conseco, and in 1986 the Lincoln Tower at 6100 Dutchmans Lane was acquired by the Kaden Group. The structure's systems were upgraded, and Wes

Peters was brought back to advise particularly on the controversial exterior paint color, which he had once described as dusty copper. He opted to paint the core "Taliesin tan" and the concrete doilies white, but before the much-heralded new color could be applied, Peters had a change of heart—pink.[91] A restaurant was added on the top floor, providing a magnificent view of the countryside. Such a facility had been envisioned initially, but when Clayton Moore complained to John Acree that a cocktail lounge might attract drunks who would drive through his fences and allow his horses out, Acree dropped the idea.

In his customary far-sighted wisdom, *Courier-Journal* Urban Affairs Editor Grady Clay pointed out in his Sunday piece marking the opening of the Lincoln Tower in mid-March 1966: "Assuming the normal workings of decentralization, this will be only the first of many tall buildings to be built in this area. The Moore farm still has 140 acres, J. Graham Brown and the Monohan families own several hundred acres to the east, and still farther east lie the 3,000 acres of Oxmoor, Hurstbourne and Plainview Farms. Once Interstate 64 is finished, this will become a 'natural' for site-seekers."[92] While each of these holdings would be developed as Clay envisioned, construction of high-rise structures was restricted so as not to conflict with the flight patterns of nearby Bowman Field.[93]

Expressways help define St. Matthews' boundary as well as much of its land use. I-64 is the major east-west corridor through the state. The Henry Watterson Expressway, first proposed by Harland Bartholomew & Associates in 1929, is the primary ring road around the state's principal metropolis. They intersect only a short distance south of Shelbyville Road. In the fall of 1956, the Henry Watterson Expressway (I-265) terminated at Shelbyville Road, just east of the where LaGrange Road branched off.[94] The location had been known in interurban days as Beechwood Junction, where interurban cars

So he [William Wesley Peters] took his tile and the new, brown-pink-bronze color he'd made back to Scottsville, and he revised it....Finally, Peters said, "Hey, I've got it!" And he painted his real *final* final color for the Kaden Tower on a piece of concrete—the same kind used in the building—and sent it by Federal Express to Louisville...and when they pulled the piece of concrete from within, they saw it was...PINK!

...Over the years, the original "dusty copper" has faded and the building—though still eye-catching—hasn't demanded as much attention. The new coat of paint to be applied this week, will likely change all that.

From Glenn Rutherford, "Architect of 'doily' tower may raise the hue and cry with his choice of tint," *The Courier-Journal* 18 May 1987.

THE COLONEL BOARDING KENNELS ON THE NORTH SIDE OF SHELBYVILLE ROAD, EAST OF LAGRANGE ROAD, 1945. THE SITE IS UNDER THE NORTHEAST QUADRANT OF THE WATTERSON EXPRESSWAY--SHELBYVILLE ROAD INTERCHANGE. ZV227-45U, JEFFERSON COUNTY HISTORIC PRESERVATION AND ARCHIVES.

Norwood Gardens was kind of notorious. I think all they had a license to sell was soft drinks, but they sold everything. Saturday nights would get wild over there. We were always prohibited from going over there until we got a little older. A woman ran it. They may have made the nightclub out of the kennels that were there. It was going during and after Prohibition.

From interview of Frank L. "Tubby" Barth, Jr., 20 January 1998.

diverged, continuing on to Anchorage or Shelbyville. La Grange Road first appears on the 1913 atlas of Jefferson County as "Sisson or Zimmerman Lane," evidently built for access to the Southern Addition to Warwick Villa. In the triangle created by this lane and Shelbyville Road was a roadhouse, first known as the Peacock Inn. After Prohibition it was called The Colonel, run by Rudy Kirchdorfer, who had worked at the Sada San, and his wife Marie. During World War II, she used it as a dog kennel, and in 1946, they reopened the restaurant and nightclub.

As the Mall came under construction in 1961, the elaborate Watterson Expressway-Shelbyville Road cloverleaf and overpass was built, allowing the expressway to continue northward and tie into US 42 and then I-71. The Watterson was a hodge-podge of engineering, unsafe at even modest speeds, and totally inadequate to handle the traffic that depended on it. When a 1972 proposal to widen it to ten lanes met with resistance augmented by a gasoline shortage, the widening plan was scaled down to eight lanes scheduled for construction around St. Matthews beginning in 1988. In addition, there were massive new interchange modifications, particularly at Shelbyville Road and I-64. The latter superhighway, initially called Eastern Expressway, opened in 1970 after being bogged down for years by controversy over its usurping parkland.

When Sam Swope's brand new Pontiac dealership opened at 4311 Shelbyville Road in 1966, he sold more new Pontiacs than any other dealer sold any brand, including the traditional best sellers Chevrolet and Ford, anywhere in the region. He combined testimonial advertising with "Nobody Walks Away," a slogan he had thought up in 1961 and brought with him from his old headquarters at 126 Breckenridge Lane. Swope, a Cleveland native and Ohio State University graduate, had increased sales of a Dodge-Plymouth dealership in Elizabethtown tenfold when he purchased the DeSoto-Plymouth operation of George and Bob Riggs on Breckenridge Lane in 1960. Soon after, he had the opportunity to change franchises to Pontiacs, which he recalls "as about the best day of my life." He began to look for more space and exposure along Shelbyville Road. The property he purchased was owned by the Ford Motor Company, which actually wanted his dealership next to one they were planning to build in the 4300 block.

At the tract's center was the Maples Home for the Aged, a nursing home run by William Wallace "Dixie" Wiegleb for a decade. The 14-room, brick facility had been William C. Arterburn's home. A century before the property was known as Walnut Grove. Early in 1964, J. Staten Brown, president of Joe Brown Ford, announced the purchase of the property at McArthur Drive.[95] Brown sold the land to Ford. Joe Brown Ford's vice president, Al J. Schneider, designed the agency's new headquarters and his construction firm would build it. Blue Grass Mercury would be the first occupant at 4301 Shelbyville Road. Next door Sam Swope enlisted Garst-Receveur to build his Pontiac dealership. Both "stores" opened in 1966. Swope remembers St. Matthews Mayor Bernie Bowling paying him a visit to request that no flags or pennants be put up along Shelbyville Road. Swope continues to honor

their verbal agreement. The success of Sam Swope has been immense. While he employed about fifty people on Breckenridge Lane in the early 1960s, Sam Swope Auto Group, Inc. presently employs in the Louisville market alone some 550 persons.[96]

In October 1963, a long-range development plan for the 1,094-acre Oxmoor farm was filed in the old Planning and Zoning office by Thomas W. Bullitt, son of William Marshall Bullitt, and co-trustee of the William Marshall Bullitt Trust property.[97] As Grady Clay pointed out in his Sunday *Courier-Journal* piece on the rezoning request, Oxmoor "has long been recognized as the most valuable single-family ownership of undeveloped real estate in Jefferson County."[98] With the massive farm being bounded by the Watterson Expressway (I-265) and Shelbyville Road, and being transected by I-64, it certainly had to be the most valuable acreage in the Commonwealth. The comprehensive development plan had been prepared by the landscape architectural firm of Miller, Wihry & Brooks, a local firm recognized and respected within the region. The main features in the plan described by Grady Clay included: "a shopping center, 'office campuses,' garden and elevator-apartment districts, a 'historic site' including the 176-year-old house, a golf course and country club, a greenway system following the creek lines, and about 1,200 single-family lots."

Far down the list in the development sequence was the proposed shop-

From "A Master Plan for the Development of Oxmoor Farm," 15 November 1963, p. 12.

Wings were added to the old Oxmoor house as well as a second floor, 1999, by Samuel W. Thomas.

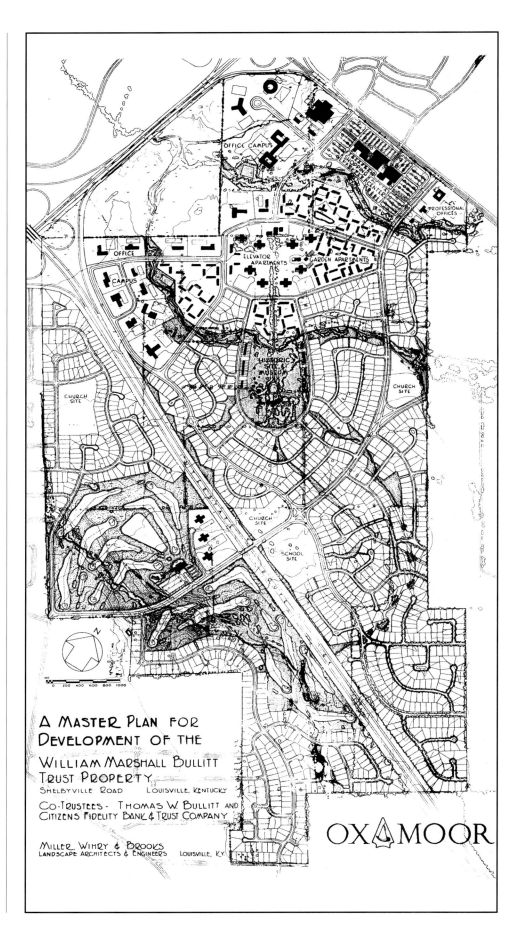

A Master Plan for Development of the

William Marshall Bullitt Trust Property
Shelbyville Road   Louisville, Kentucky

Co-Trustees - Thomas W. Bullitt and Citizens Fidelity Bank & Trust Company

Miller, Wihry & Brooks
Landscape Architects & Engineers   Louisville, Ky.

OXMOOR

ping center. The Mall St. Matthews had only recently opened and Bullitt was projecting a "relatively small" center, but "of the highest possible quality, housed in the most attractive building possible." At the core of the development was a 35-acre preserve—"a green around the house, its slave cabins, and other outbuildings." This was part of a 166-acre parcel which Thomas W. Bullitt had been left by his father, although his mother had a life interest in it and continued to reside in the house, which she and her husband had reopened in 1906 and had made substantially larger and more elegant.

The initial improvements to the frame and brick house, all painted white, were carried out by the prominent local architect George Herbert Gray. The gardens and grounds were laid out by Marian Cruger Coffin (1876-1957).[99] Then in 1926, F. Burrall Hoffman, Jr., best known for his design of Vizcaya, the Deering villa near Miami, was brought in to make the 1829 brick addition into a full two stories. In doing so, the recessed portico was removed and a new brick front was put on. A year later, Bullitt wrote the noted architectural historian, Rexford Newcomb, that Hoffman was adding a wing for his extensive library. The 60' by 28' room, painted a shade of green that Bullitt had admired in Hoffman's New York office, is without equal in Kentucky.[100]

VIEW OF OXMOOR PROPERTY SOUTH OF SHELBYVILLE ROAD, *CA.* 1939. IN CENTER IS BULLITT LANE THAT RUNS BACK PAST THE OLD ARTERBURN FARM AND THE BULLITT FAMILY CEMETERY BEFORE DOGLEGGING BACK THROUGH AN AVENUE OF TREES TO THE BULLITT RESIDENCE. BULLITT FAMILY PAPERS.

The rezoning proposal was immediately challenged by the trustees of Bellemeade, the sixth-class city across Shelbyville Road. But the chief complaint was uttered by none other than 82-year-old Nora Iasigi Bullitt, widow of William Marshall Bullitt, who initially had been a party to the rezoning request. She wished that Oxmoor could be kept as a working farm.[101] A comprehensive plan for the St. Matthews to Middletown area was adopted by the planning and zoning commission in the spring of 1966. It limited commercial development along Shelbyville Road and in particular on the Oxmoor property.[102] However, in the fall of 1970, Oxmoor Center, developed by the

Winmar Company, the same West Coast outfit that had erected the Citizens Plaza tower, was ready to open.[103]

The master plan envisioned in 1963 had given way to piecemeal development. Tracts were sold off to residential developers, and the shopping center was enlarged by nearly a million square feet in 1984, principally for a Sears store. However, 890 acres of fertile farmland remained cultivated in wheat, soybeans, corn, and hay, with some acreage in bluegrass sod and some for grazing 230 head of beef cattle. "It's too good to build houses on," farm manager Eugene Allgeier observed when interviewed in 1984.[104] An interesting comparison can be made with the assessment of the farm operation that Harry Toulmin made in 1793. Alexander Scott Bullitt's Oxmoor then consisted of 500 acres, 150 acres of which were "under fence and cultivated." Bullitt had 14 laboring hands, eight male and six female; four horses and a wagon, five plows, 14 hoes, and two scythes. (In 1984, 890 acres were tended to by a crew of four with various pieces of equipment.) He had a modest herd of 30 head of "black" cattle and 50 hogs, but concentrated his farming efforts in producing Indian corn, wheat, hemp, flax, and tobacco. In 1984, Oxmoor was yielding 160-185 bushels of corn per acre compared to 120 bushels in 1793.)[105]

The next phase of development, west of Oxmoor Center, produced a new road system through the property. Access to Oxmoor Place was achieved by a new road that broke off Oxmoor Lane at the Bullitt family cemetery and then wrapped around the Christian/Arterburn log house and the A'Sturgus Station springhouse, as well as the Arterburn family cemetery. This part of Oxmoor had been in Arterburn family hands until William Marshall Bullitt acquired it in 1931.[106] This road also provided access to additional Arterburn property that been landlocked by the expressway. Paragon Group would lease that 66-acre tract from the heirs of Covington and Shelton (sons of Jule Bernard Arterburn), and develop City Place.[107]

Just east of Oxmoor on the Shelbyville Road as well as a branch of Beargrass Creek was the Soldier's Retreat property of Richard Clough Ander-

son, Sr. He built a massive stone house in the 1790s, but unfortunately it did not stand the test of time, and after his death, the Anderson family sold off the land. In the mid-1850s, John J. Jacob, Jr., a Harvard University graduate, whose brother, Charles D. Jacob, would serve four terms as mayor of Louisville, had architect Jacob Beaverson design a brick house in the prevailing Gothic Revival style.[108] On Bergmann's 1858 map, the Jacob property is called Lynnford, probably in reference to William Linn's station, which had been located nearby at the headwaters of the creek. (Bland Ballard was residing temporarily at the station when Linn was killed by Indians on his way to county court in March 1781. He later recalled that his body was recovered "about a mile from the station and near the place of residence of the late Colonel [Richard Clough] Anderson."[109]) Pattie Anderson Ten Broeck (no relation of Col. Anderson) and her husband, the internationally known horse breeder and trainer, Richard Ten Broeck, purchased the property in 1868. They called it Hurstbourne in recognition of his friend, the Duke of Portland, whose estate was named Hurstbourne.[110]

Pattie Ten Broeck helped raise her niece, Mary Martin Anderson, whose parents had died. Mary was the great-granddaughter of John Lewis Martin, the second husband of Helen Scott Bullitt, who had been born at Oxmoor and who owned Ridgeway. When John L. Martin died in 1854, he was considered one of the richest men in Louisville. His wealth passed on to Mary Anderson. On 26 April 1871, she eloped with Meriwether Lewis Clark, Jr., and they were married in Jeffersonville, Indiana, before returning to Hurstbourne. Five days later they were remarried by the Rev. James Craik in the St. Matthews Episcopal Church. Lutie Clark, as the grandson of the co-leader of the Lewis and Clark expedition was called, was a fledgling banker, but Richard Ten Broeck introduced him to the world of horses and provided access to horsemen. The Clarks traveled to Europe in 1873 and with his uncle, John Churchill, witnessed the Derby at Epsom Downs. They returned with a firm idea of establishing a new jockey club and building a race course on Churchill land south of the city.[111]

RICHARD CLOUGH ANDERSON, SR., BROTHER-IN-LAW OF GEORGE ROGERS AND WILLIAM CLARK, AND FATHER OF ROBERT ANDERSON, BUILT SOLDIER'S RETREAT. COL. ANDERSON WAS A REVOLUTIONARY WAR VETERAN AND SURVEYOR. THE FILSON CLUB.

LYNNFORD/HURSTBOURNE BEFORE EXTENSIVE RENOVATION BY THE HERTS. PHOTOGRAPH APPEARED IN *THE COURIER-JOURNAL*, 25 AUGUST 1918.

The man chiefly responsible for the future physical shape of the 984-acre Hurstbourne Estate on Shelbyville Road…is Robert M. O'Donnell, a landscape architect whose Denver-based firm prepared basic plans for the rolling Jefferson County farmland….On a one-day trip… O'Donnell noted some beauty spots in Louisville's landscape…. He also recognized the pattern of plantings along roadways leading to Lyndon Hall, the Hurstbourne mansion, as the work of pioneer landscape architect Frederick Law Olmsted.

From Simpson Lawson, "Hurstbourne Planner O'Donnell Covers A Lot Of Ground—And Sea," *The Courier-Journal*, 24 January 1965.

Hurstbourne was later purchased for a summer home by Joseph L. Harris, a native Kentuckian residing in New Orleans, placing the farm operation in the hands of his son Norvin T. Harris.[112] The 15 July 1915 issue of *The Jeffersonian* announced the purchase of the Harris and adjoining W. C. Winchester places comprising 750 acres, by A. T. Hert. The former superintendent of the Indiana Reformatory at Jeffersonville, who became well-to-do as president of the American Creosoting Company, reportedly intended to erect a "handsome residence" and use it as his country home.

Instead, the Herts took over the old Jacob house and created a park-like setting, perhaps with the help of the Olmsted firm.[113] After Alvin Tobias "Tobe" Hert died in 1921 at the age of 56, Mrs. Hert became a power in her own right within the national Republican Party. In 1928, she retained architect E. T. Hutchings to substantially modify the house, which included veneering its old painted brick surface in new red brick.

During World War II, hemp had a resurgence at Hurstbourne. Rope was being substituted for wire wherever possible, but the Japanese controlled the source of Manila hemp, which had decades before replaced domestic hemp as the cordage fiber of choice. However, the hemp fields became inviting at harvest time. *The Courier-Journal* reported on 11 September 1942: "Hemp is known to the narcotic addicts as marijuana, and it is smoked as 'muggles' in cigarette form. It is a powerful narcotic when smoked. The state has long been the source of seed for hemp, which is a source of cordage, oakum and other products. At the instigation of the U.S., 16,000 bushels of seed were produced in the state last year and the yield this year is expected to be 350,000."

HEMP FIELD ON THE HURSTBOURNE FARM, BY H. HAROLD DAVIS, SEPTEMBER 1942. *LOUISVILLE SINCE THE TWENTIES*, 128.

The land, bought for less than $700 an acre shortly after the war, is now selling at more than 20 times that for individual lots. "That was the foresightedness of my dad," the 56-year old Highbaugh observed.

He explained that 30 years ago, before the metropolitan area had spread down Shelbyville Road, and before anyone knew that an interstate highway would be built through the area, his father [L. Leroy Highbaugh, Sr.] believed urban growth would make the acreage valuable.

From Ben Z. Hershberg, "In eastern Jefferson, long-developed drama has matured into a hit," *The Courier-Journal*, 4 March 1979.

The district supervisor of the narcotic bureau reported that "we have been practically free of narcotic violations....The great fields of the hemp are magnets now, but we intend to keep violations down." The hemp-growing effort was soon terminated.

After Mrs. Hert died in 1948, the property was purchased by the L. Leroy Highbaughs, Sr. and Jr., and called Highbaugh Farms, while the house became Lyndon Hall.[114] In a 1979 *Courier-Journal* retrospective of development along the Shelbyville Road corridor, the Highbaugh acquisition was characterized as "the most important single event that has shaped the current scene in eastern Jefferson County."[115] Senior Highbaugh was a native of Hart County, who after a varied professional career, got into the real estate business, first in rental housing and then in the development of subdivisions, many in the St. Matthews area.[116] When he moved into the Commodore Apartments in the early 1960s, and the development of Oxmoor was being explored, it seemed only a matter of time before Hurstbourne/Highbaugh

PART OF SOLDIER'S RETREAT'S FOUNDATIONS
DISCOVERED DURING ARCHAEOLOGICAL
EXCAVATION IN 1972. BY SAMUEL W. THOMAS.

Bob Bayersdorfer and his father, Stanley, also sensed that Hurstbourne [Parkway] was the place to be when they closed The Fashion Post in St. Matthews and moved to The Forum off Hurstbourne a year ago…. Bayersdorfer also said he misses the more "pedestrian-friendly streets of St. Matthews. "I miss being able to run to Karem's or to Stan's Fish Shop for a sandwich at lunch," he said. "Here, you gotta get in your car."

From Nina Walfoort, "Hurstbourne area thriving on 'edge,'" *The Courier-Journal*, 2 September 1997.

Farms would follow suit.

Early in 1965, the development plan for Hurstbourne Estates was filed with the City-County Planning and Zoning Commission by the Senior and Junior Highbaughs, calling for some 2,000 dwelling units, including lots for 1,494 single-family residences. Schools, churches and office and shopping centers were also proposed on the 984-acre tract that centered on a 27-hole golf course with the Highbaughs' former residence serving as the clubhouse.[117] The plan for the historic property had been devised by landscape architect Robert M. O'Donnell of Harman, O'Donnell & Henninger Associates, land planners from Denver.[118]

A small section of the tract along Hurstbourne Lane was designated a "Historical Park." This included the site of Richard Clough Anderson's stone house, various stone outbuildings and a springhouse, and the family graveyard. In the back of Leroy Highbaugh, Jr.'s mind was the notion of determining the exact location of the old house and reconstructing it. The foundation was uncovered below grade by Dr. Joseph Callaway and a team of his archaeology students from the Southern Baptist Theological Seminary. The outline conformed with room dimensions noted by Charles Anderson in his recollections of growing up at Soldier's Retreat, where former President James Monroe and a young Andrew Jackson visited in 1819, and the Marquis de Lafayette was entertained by his former aide-de-camp in 1825.[119]

The initial phase of the proposed $50,000,000 Hurstbourne Executive Park, on the southwest corner of Hurstbourne Lane and Shelbyville Road, across from land the Highbaughs had donated for the Kentucky Southern College (later the University of Louisville's Shelby Campus) got underway in the summer of 1970.[120] By 1997, the Hurstbourne area had taken on most of the characteristics of a so-called edge city as popularly defined by Joel Garreau in his 1991 book, *Edge City: Life on the New Frontier*.[121]

In the fall of 1970, the Falls Region Health Council approved the construction of two hospitals in St. Matthews, one by Extendicare, Inc., the other as a satellite of the old Kentucky Baptist Hospital on Barret Avenue. Demographic studies had indicated to H. L. Dobbs, head of the hospital system run by the Baptist church in Kentucky, that St. Matthews was fast becoming the geographical center of Louisville's migrating population. The area had no hospital, and its doctors were urging him to build one. Dobbs initially tried to establish a satellite hospital system similar to one in Texas, where he had also become acquainted with the Blue Cross concept, which he had introduced to Louisville. A site on Breckenridge Lane appeared ideal for a hospital, and Almond Cooke, then president of Kentucky Baptist Hospital, made contact with its owner, J. Graham Brown, and an agreement was made for 52.3 acres at $15,000 per acre. Brown also offered to sell the smaller portion of his farm that contained the residence, but Dobbs thought the hospital would never need the additional space for expansion. However, Brown indicated that he might give the land to the hospital later. About six weeks later he died, and the land reverted to the James Graham Brown Foundation, which later gave it to St. Matthews for a park. Baptist Hospital East opened in March

1975.[122] Extendicare, which had evolved into Humana, had already opened Suburban Hospital.

A 97-acre portion of the J. Graham Brown Farm was zoned for what St. Matthews Mayor Bernard F. Bowling termed "one of the finest shopping areas in the country." Commercial development would take place on 67 acres, and 30 acres were rezoned in two tracts for office buildings. Dutchmans Lane was to be extended through the shopping center, connecting Breckenridge Lane and Browns Lane. Mayor Bowling wanted to have an exit of the Watterson Expressway feed directly into the shopping center. He liked the development's location, believing it would siphon traffic off Shelbyville Road. Details of the project were not made known, although mention was made of tentative plans for a motel, theater, and car dealership in conjunction with the office buildings, shopping center, and huge G.E.S. Store that already fronted Breckenridge Lane on Brown's land.[123]

The full extent of Indianapolis developer Warren M. Atkinson's concept was made known in two *Courier-Journal* articles in August 1967. In the initial announcement much was made of the new taxes the project would generate for all levels of government. L. S. Ayres & Co. would be the principal tenant in the 65-store shopping center. The office building was to be 20 floors, as was an adjacent apartment building, both on the north side of the extended section of Dutchmans Lane.[124] A more revealing piece was prepared by John K. Woodruff for the next day's Sunday *Courier-Journal*, headed: "Breckinridge Square: A Host Of Superlatives." The shopping center was to be more than twice as large as the Mall. The L. S. Ayres store was to be only second to Stewart's in size in Kentucky. The project would dwarf Atkinson's Watterson Park under construction on the Watterson Expressway at Bishop Lane. He planned a 40-foot waterfall, while incorporating the "classic, colonial simple design of the Bluegrass area." While objections to the traffic con-

DuPont Square off Breckinridge Lane was the development that first focused the spotlight on Metts. "I caught more hell over that than I like to remember," he says of the busy tangle of streets, shops, offices and traffic. It brought frowns from those who would have liked to see a more 'orderly' development, but Metts defends it. "There are 8,000 people working out there and I haven't had to rob anybody on the rent."

From George H. Yater, "'Ahead of the Pack,'" *Louisville* 36 (September 1985): 25.

gestion continued to be raised, Atkinson, at least publicly, thought the projected new roadwork would provide "easy accessibility." However, in the fall of 1968, Atkinson abruptly abandoned the entire project blaming traffic congestion in the area—in particular that being created by the G.E.S. Store, which he claimed had been built after he had made plans for Breckinridge Square. Mayor Bowling remained steadfast. "Somebody will come along and develop that site. It's just a matter of time."[125]

Frank R. Metts would be that somebody. The product of Louisville's West End had quit school at sixteen, but he had plenty of smarts, nerve, drive, and an incredibly good sense of timing. When he read that Atkinson

RENDERING OF THE VILLAGE PROPOSAL BY HOFMANN & METTS, REALTORS. VIEW SOUTH-EAST FROM INTERSECTION OF I-64 AND BRECKENRIDGE LANE AT RIGHT. EXTENSION OF DUTCHMANS LANE THROUGH MIDDLE. WATTERSON EXPRESSWAY AT TOP. BEARGRASS-ST. MATTHEWS HISTORICAL SOCIETY.

had backed out of the project, Metts went to see J. Graham Brown. Breckinridge Square became The Village, and somewhere along the overall development scheme, the name DuPont Square was introduced. Because the site had already been rezoned for the Breckinridge Square project, there was no process by which plans had to be unified or made public. Compounding the development's disarray, Metts sold some parcels and leased others. In spite of the maze of traffic and dysfunctional architecture, planners were dumbfounded by DuPont Square's public acceptance.

Sunday, July 2nd, 1972 was a watershed day in the local economy. For a decade, debate and protest had raged over the issue of retailers being able to sell merchandise on Sunday. As *Courier-Journal* writer Chris Waddle aptly phrased the radical change brought about by laws passed in the city of Louisville and Jefferson County: "Most of the Louisville area woke up yesterday with the blue washed out of its Sunday closing laws."[126] Stores such as Bacon's, J. C. Penney, Sears, Levy Bros., Ayres, Stewart's, Gus Mayer, Rodes, and Loevenhart's initially remained closed on Sunday, believing they already provided enough shopping time and not wanting to ask their employees to work on Sunday. However, retailers adapted and eventually found Sundays profit-

Developer Harry Rosen of Executive Properties likes to think of his Executive Park as a horizontal skyscraper. Built on Sherburn Lane at I-264, between Shelbyville Road and Browns Lane, Executive Park is a seven-building complex of one- and two-story office structures around an attractively landscaped man-made hill with a real waterfall....Across the road are the Mallgate Apartments, another Executive Properties development. And within a three-minute walk is The Mall...It's the formula of residential/commercial/professional mix that makes these 'uptowns' successful, says Adolph Horwitz, a vice-president of Executive Properties.

From Anne Calvert, "High-Rises In The Potato Patch: the 'Uptown Downtown,'" *Louisville* 26 (March 1975): 37.

able, especially as women accustomed to shopping during the week entered the work force.

At the center of J. Graham Brown's farm along Browns Lane was a modest brick house that the hotel magnate built for his longtime friend, Sonia Kaufmann Uri. She had been widowed in 1929 when her husband Walter Uri died at the age of 39. Uri had worked for his father's distilling firm in Bardstown until Prohibition, and then had gone into the mortgage business with brother Morris. At his death he was also president of the West Baden Hotel Company in Indiana. Mrs. Uri's home was built soon after Graham Brown purchased the old Veech farm in 1940. In addition, a large barn was erected to stable Brown's horses, and the existing barns and sheds and a tenant's house were torn down. The new brick house replaced the Veech family's summer cottage, a rambling one-floor wooden structure enclosed by sleeping porches and verandas. The summer cottage was itself a replacement built on the ashes of an earlier board and batten Gothic Revival style house the Veeches once lived in year-round. They called it Greyholt, after the place occupied by a distant English ancestor, Lady Jane Grey. The house had been built about 1869 by James V. Prather, and the style had overtones of the Theodore Brown and John J. Jacob, Jr., houses in the area. Prather had purchased nearly a hundred acres along "Brown Avenue" and Beargrass Creek from heirs of James Brown and from John and Eliza Burks.[127] Bethel Bowles Veech obtained it in late November 1881, shortly before he married Eliza Graham Quigley, whose family had been involved in starting the L & N Railroad and tobacco warehousing, as well as private banking. The Veech's daughters were born at Greyholt. They were enjoying Thanksgiving dinner in 1911 when the house was destroyed by fire. *The Louisville Times* carried the

Sometimes the best treatment for a case of stress is a stroll through some woods, no matter how small. Add the soothing sounds of a creek and the lazy pace of a meandering path and you may rediscover the inner peace that you lost while you were driving in heavy traffic.

That's why it is important—maybe even vital—to know about such nearby places as J. Graham Brown Park....It is one of the Louisville area's tiny emeralds—a jewel of a park—that St. Matthews brightly polished this summer.

From Linda Stahl, "An urban oasis," *The Courier-Journal*, 21 November 1997.

GREYHOLT ABOUT 1900. COURTESY OF WILLIAM M. OTTER, JR.

following account on 1 December 1911:

> While the family and friends of Bethel B. Veech were gathered around the table at their Thanksgiving day dinner at Mr. Veech's home, in Brown's lane, near St. Matthews, the crackling of flames was heard, and despite the fact that neighbors joined with Mr. Veech in fighting the flames the house was burned to the ground before the chemical engine from Frankfort and Pope streets, with Chief Lehan in charge, could reach the scene.
>
> All the furniture and household goods, except some clothing stored in the closets, were saved, and no person was injured. The house was built in 1869 and was purchased twenty-eight years ago by Mr. Veech for $15,000. It was one of the most handsome homes in that region of the country.

The property, "excluding the Brown family Burying ground with free ingress and egress," had actually been purchased by Bethel Veech's father, Richard Snowden Veech, in late November 1881 for $10,250.[128] The property was conveyed from father to son. After Bethel Veech's wife died in the summer of 1937, the widower never went back to the summer cottage. It was rented to members of the Monohan family for several years and then in 1940 sold to J. Graham Brown. Bethel Veech, who was chairman of the board of directors of the United States Trust Company, which his father had founded with R. C. Ballard Thruston and S. Thruston Ballard, served as president from 1902 until 1945, when he became chairman.[129] He died at the age of 85 in 1946 at the home of his daughter, Mrs. William M. Otter.[130]

James Graham Brown was 87 when he died of congestive heart failure on 30 March 1969. Through various successful enterprises, he had accumulated $100 million or more. He had placed many of his assets in the James Graham Brown Foundation, Inc., created in 1943, and substantial charitable gifts had been made and would continue to be made in his name. He had but one diversion from a life that centered on business, and that was horse racing. His racing stable on Breckenridge Lane produced more than 700 wins and $3 million in purses. He was the largest stockholder in Churchill Downs and served on its board of directors for 32 years.[131] Mrs. Uri was living in the 800 Apartments when she died in 1975 at the age of 83. She had donated the Felix de Weldon statue of Benjamin Franklin for placement in front of the entrance to the new section of the Louisville Free Public Library.[132] Two years later the James Graham Brown Foundation, Inc. donated the 27.5-acre property set aside for Mrs. Uri to St. Matthews for park purposes.

St. Matthews was extensively featured and profiled in *The Courier-Journal* on 8 January 1979 by Jay Lawrence. The gist of the three separate articles was contained in the front-page headline: "St. Matthews tries to balance commercial, residential life." Retail sales within St. Matthews had long surpassed those in Louisville's central business district, but some had begun to

---

I was born on April 2nd, 1923. I was out at the summer cottage as a baby in arms. Later, my parents would drop me off out there in the summer time and I would spend weeks at a time. My associates and friends were sons of tenants who lived there. G. W. Parr, the son of the tenant, and I would go exploring and build in our imagination, and fish. George Washington Parr's father was a Marine veteran. The previous tenant's name was Douglas, and I wandered around there with his son. They were teaching me country ways—how to fish and dig worms and pull heads off crayfish and all that. When I was about seven, my father bought a rig for me—a miniature donkey and cart, and I drove that around the place a lot. I had a small boat in the creek and I paddled there.

From interview of William M. Otter, Jr., 18 November 1996.

question at what cost to the residential community. Lawrence found tension manifesting as Mayor Bowling, supported by a majority of the city council, continued to court business. While the Metro section headline read: "Neighborhood feeling lasts in town grown 'out of sight,'" a resident voiced her opinion that the community had "gone overboard in trying to commercialize" and it was "driving residential people out." But in a separate article on St. Matthews' politics, Lawrence pointed out that the same group—the George Washington Party—had monopolized locally ever since city government had come to St. Matthews.[133] However, a relatively fresh face in that party, the 48-year-old principal of Waggener High School, Arthur Draut, was beginning to bend: "I will probably constantly be in opposition to any more commercialization in the area." He had supported the purchase of the Monohan property for a park instead of its development as Cypress Station. It was obvious that St. Matthews was beginning to soften its fiercely pro-business stance. Art Draut would become mayor when Bernie Bowling died in 1984. He would have an opportunity to improve the park environment in St. Matthews, particularly along Bowling Boulevard adjacent to the old Monohan place.

For the first decade of St. Matthews' corporate existence, city government was shuffled from pillar to post until construction of a city hall at 201 Thierman Lane was completed in 1960. However, it also would become woefully inadequate. In 1994, St. Matthews' government moved into more spacious quarters in the old Greathouse School, which had been nicely renovated. The red brick schoolhouse had been erected on Grandview Avenue in 1939, and the following fall, Jefferson County's first kindergarten program was sponsored.[134] Now not only are the city's functions including the police department housed in the former elementary school, but so are the St. Matthews/Eline branch library and the Beargrass-St. Matthews Historical Society.

We bought The Sign of the Pine Tree in about 1973. It was an institution on Broadway at Third Street, but that part of downtown could no longer support a store that dealt in fine antiques. We knew that the St. Matthews area was a pretty hot spot, and we first looked at Chenoweth Square, which was being built. The rents seemed steep, so we decided to buy a house and convert it. We purchased Bernie Gratzer's old house at 159 Chenoweth Avenue on the corner of Massie. It took some time to get the property zoned commercial and to completely renovate the house. In the meantime, we purchased the house next door and rented it to Nina Tyler and Harriet Northcutt, who created Animal Crackers. We opened about the same time. Merkley Kendrick, St. Matthews Feed & Seed, and Thorpe Interiors were the only other establishments along Chenoweth Lane then.

From interview of Dace Brown Stubbs, 17 June 1998.

Rendering by architect Thomas J. Nolan of "new Greathouse School." *The Courier-Journal*, 7 May 1939.

THOS. J. NOLAN, ARCHITECT
LOUISVILLE . KY.

The Philadelphia planning firm, Wallace Roberts & Todd, was retained by the city of St. Matthews in late 1995 to devise a plan that would enhance the high ground part of Brown Park already in use and make the lower area along the creek meanders accessible. Since the time when the firm was Wallace, McHarg, Roberts & Todd, and one of its founders Ian L. McHarg, a native of Glasgow, Scotland, wrote a significant and much heralded book, *Design With Nature* (Garden City, 1971), the firm has continued to seek ways to improve our environment as the principal and primary tenet of landscape architecture planning. This shows clearly in the simple but masterful layout of Brown Park, where Beargrass Creek can once more be viewed as it would have been from pioneer times at Dutch Station until early in this century. Work on the new park was completed in May 1997 at a cost of $830,000.[135] As the exemplary design by Wallace Roberts & Todd was recognized by the Louisville and Jefferson County Planning Commission, the city of St. Matthews was about to carry out the firm's plan to improve and enlarge the recreation center on Ten Pin Lane.[136] The playground, sponsored by the St. Matthews Community Center and supervised by the Jefferson County Recreation Board, was laid out with baseball fields and basketball and tennis courts in late 1949. The 29-acre tract, just west of the East Drive-In, was being leased from the Arterburn family using proceeds from the Potato Festival that shared the grounds.[137] The Potato Festival had been initiated after World War II with the performance of "a historical cavalcade" performed by a cast of over 400, entitled "Potato Is King." [138]

Turning into the Potato Festival grounds west of the East Drive-In, 24 July 1948, Lin Caufield Collection, University of Louisville Photographic Archives. Right: View west on Shelbyville Road from interchange. 1999, by Samuel W. Thomas.

A balloon used by a parachute jumper at the St. Matthews Potato Festival, last night plummeted to the roof of the home of Mr. and Mrs. Fred Hausman, Jr., 218 Harris Place, and then slid onto a car in the driveway. The hood of the car was bent to the motor by the weight of a 50-pound sack of gravel attached to the balloon....The balloon, inflated with hot air, was used by Don G. Wood, parachute jumper....The balloon is supposed to descend gradually as the air cools off. Last night spectators reported it fell rapidly.

From "Balloon Hits House, Car In St. Matthews," *The Courier-Journal*, 23 July 1949.

It is ironic that many who fled the flood plain after 1937 for higher ground in St. Matthews have continued to endure problems with water. March 1997 was the second wettest month (17.41 inches of rain) in the annals of weather record keeping, second only to January 1937 (19.17 inches). Sixty percent of March's total fell on the first day of the month. In the days and weeks that followed that Saturday, one could easily determine from the mounds of debris hauled out to curbs where the sewer backup and ground flooding had been the worst. Drainage problems have been an underlying concern in most of St. Matthews' history. The first work to be reported in *The Jeffersonian* was late in 1915. "Bids for drainage work to be done which is expected to relieve serious conditions at St. Matthews" were received by Jefferson Fiscal Court just before Christmas. The low bid was for $2,779.80. "This will be the first drainage work done in the First Magisterial district, where much damage has been done to houses as well as farm lands. This is especially true in St. Matthews…where the town proper is lower than the three roads which form a triangle and from all of which the drainage flows into the homes of the town."[139]

As the population of St. Matthews mushroomed with the 1937 flood, new homes were outfitted with a septic tank and a lateral field that was usually in the front or side yard. Although this leaching system was a step up from the old outhouse, in wet weather raw sewage made its noxious presence known.[140]

After World War II, when Louisville residents got wind of plans being made to build a sewage treatment plant in St. Matthews that would then dispose of the waste in Beargrass Creek, a healthy protest ensued. A deal was struck by which Jefferson County Sanitation District No. 1 would instead build a pumping station to lift St. Matthews' waste into Louisville's Beals Branch sewer main at Wilmington and Cannons Lane at a cost of $2,225,000.[141] Sewer and drainage work has continued ever since, but for those who suffered through the high water and sewer backups in March 1997, the drainage problems continued to persist.[142] Many were understandably and justifiably peeved, but none said they were moving. After all, it was these same conditions that brought many of these people to this high ground in the first place.

In the lifetimes of these flood victims they have seen their community change more than any other in Kentucky. The farms along the meanders of the eastern headwaters of Beargrass Creek were subdivided for the influx of people who thought eastern Jefferson County was a pleasant place in which to raise their families. On their heels came retail development the likes of which had never been seen in the Commonwealth. Shelbyville Road, which had been made into a divided highway at the end of the Depression, was widened to eight lanes to accommodate shoppers. The shopping centers, which were considered massive when built, continue to grow. The expressway system designed to get automobiles to and from Shelbyville Road now has an elevated cloverleaf of such dimension, the original town of St. Matthews could be comfortably nestled within it. However, as long as this area, which has run the gamut from pioneer forts to enclosed malls, continues to work toward bettering itself with parks and public improvements, folks will want to live here. And that is the true test of place.

St. Matthews has resolved to be abreast of the times in every way. Consequently, when the rain descended and the floods came, during the last deluge, we were among the flood sufferers; felt like we were living "on the Point," instead of at the Point. No one was neglected in this distribution of water; all cellars and basements were filled to overflowing. All eatables being pooled, we had to depend on whatever could be brought to the upper floors. No lives were lost and the water seeped away in three days, the same way it came. Hereafter, furnaces must be built in the attic instead of the basement, if they are to be of any use during January.

From A. B. C., "Floods Damage Cellars at St. Matthews." *The Jeffersonian*, 23 December 1913.

St. Matthews has been promoted by real-estate speculators like a dress shirt—all front and nothing in back. Oh, we've got a pretty front, all right, but we've got inadequate septic tanks and laterals that flood our neighbors' basements every time it rains.

E. N. "Bud" Andriot in "Incorporation Move Laid to 'Selfish' Bloc," *The Courier-Journal*, 6 April 1946.

ENDNOTES

INTRODUCTION: PAGES 13-15

1. "Historic Excursion," *The Courier-Journal*, 10 July 1883.

2. Charles Anderson's parents were Richard Clough Anderson and Sarah Marshall Anderson, who married in 1787.

3. "Filson Club Makes Pilgrimage To Historic Shrines Of Kentucky," *The Louisville Herald*, 3 June 1923. Otto A. Rothert, "Historic Excursion a Forerunner of the Founding of The Filson Club," *The Filson Club History Quarterly*," 18 (July 1944): 154.

4. "Charles Anderson," *The Courier-Journal*, 13 October 1895.

5. Charles Anderson's penciled manuscript, "The Story of Soldier's Retreat: A Memoir," is in The Filson Club along with a later typed version. Only a hundred copies of *My Life at Oxmoor* were printed in 1911; however a soft-cover reprint was issued in 1994.

6. "Col. Bullitt Wrote Of His Life At Oxmoor," *The Courier-Journal*, 5 April 1910.

7. Soldier's Retreat was reconstructed based upon these excavated foundations. See George H. Yater, "L. L. Highbaugh Recreates 1793 Pioneer Home in Hurstbourne," *Louisville* 33 (September 1982): 32-35.

8. The trustees of Cave Hill Cemetery offered the Taylor family the highest ground, and for many years the circle in Section N was known as the President Taylor lot. Thomas, *Cave Hill Cemetery* (Louisville, 1985), 15 and 100.

9. "St. Matthews To Become 4th-Class City Tomorrow," *The Courier-Journal*, 18 June 1954.

10. David W. Hacker, "St. Matthews Moves 1 Jump Ahead of Louisville," *The Louisville Times*, 18 June 1957. John Meehan, "St. Matthews Census Called Preposterous," *The Courier-Journal*, 1 June 1960.

11. Estimates issued 18 November 1997 were published in *Business First*, 24 November 1997.

INTRODUCTION: PAGE 15

12. Mark Shallcross, "St. Matthews proposes $6.2 M budget for 1998-1999 fiscal year," *The Voice-Tribune*, 24 June 1998.

I. PIONEER PERIL: PAGES 17-18

1. Copy by Lyman C. Draper in Draper MSS. 17CC186, State Historical Society of Wisconsin. Also reprinted in Neal O. Hammon and James Russell Harris, "'In a dangerous situation,': Letters of Col. John Floyd, 1774-1783," *The Register of the Kentucky Historical Society* 83 (Summer 1985): 217-218.

2. Thomas Perkins Abernethy, *Western Lands and The American Revolution* (New York, 1959), 83. William Preston's daughter, Letitia, would marry John Floyd, Jr., in 1804. John Frederick Dorman, *The Prestons of Smithfield and Greenfield in Virginia* (Louisville, 1982), 68.

3. For an account of Arthur Campbell's role in the creation of the three counties and his antagonism for Floyd and Preston, see James William Hagy, "Arthur Campbell and the West," *The Virginia Magazine of History and Biography* 90 (October 1982): 459-461.

4. Virginius C. Hall, *Journal of Isaac Hite: Surveyor at the Falls of the Ohio, 1773* (Cincinnati, 1954), 5.

5. James Alton James, ed., *George Rogers Clark Papers, 1771-1781*, Collections of the Illinois State Historical Library 8 (Springfield, 1912), 500. Clark was in Richmond, Virginia, when the letter was written on 21 January 1781.

6. The location of the defeat was provided by General Samuel Wells to Richard Clough Anderson, Jr., and recorded in his journal on 17 May 1814. See Tischendorf and Parks, *The Diary and Journal of Richard Clough Anderson, Jr.* (Durham, 1964), 12. An account of the 1781 massacre was prepared by Squire Boone's grandson, G. T. Wilcox, for Thomas W. Bullitt, shortly after the unveiling of the memorial monument at Crestwood, and it was printed shortly thereafter as "Floyd's Defeat" in *The Courier-Journal*, 28 July 1880.

7. Humphrey Marshall, *The History of Kentucky* (Frankfort, 1824), 159.

I. PIONEER PERIL: PAGES 18-19

8. Humphrey Marshall, *The History of Kentucky* (Frankfort, 1812), 182-183. *The Lawyers and Lawmakers of Kentucky* (Chicago, 1897), 12-13 and 65.

9. On 22 February 1843, Laetitia Preston Floyd sent a lengthy family history she had prepared to her son, Benjamin Rush Floyd, who was responding to a request from Lyman C. Draper for information particularly about her father, William Preston, and her father-in-law, John Floyd. Draper MSS. 6J89-108, State Historical Society of Wisconsin.

10. Abernethy, *Western Lands and The American Revolution*, 102-103.

11. Hambleton Tapp, "Colonel John Floyd, Kentucky Pioneer," *The Filson Club History Quarterly* 15 (January 1941): 1-12.

12. Transcribed deposition of Charles Floyd in Robert E. McDowell Collection, volume 13, p. 196, The Filson Club.

13. John May, Jefferson County, to Samuel Beall, Williamsburg, 9 January 1783. Samuel Beall papers, The Filson Club.

14. For an extensive sketch of Floyd and his family see "The Floyd Family," *The Louisville Post*, 12 April 1919.

15. Neal O. Hammon, "The Fincastle Surveyors at the Falls of the Ohio," *The Filson Club History Quarterly* 47 (January 1973): 23. Neal O. Hammon, "Early Louisville and the Beargrass Stations," *The Filson Club History Quarterly* 52 (April 1978): 154-155.

16. Otto A. Rothert, "John Floyd—Pioneer And Hero," *The Filson Club History Quarterly* 2 (July 1928): 169-177.

17. "Early times in Kentucky," copied from issue 123 of the *Commonwealth* by Lyman C. Draper, Draper MSS. 17CC176, State Historical Society of Wisconsin.

18. Laetitia Preston Floyd to Benjamin Rush Floyd, 22 February 1843. Draper MSS. 6J107. State Historical Society of Wisconsin.

I. PIONEER PERIL: PAGES 20-22

19. Most of the letters preserved by Orlando Brown and copied by Lyman Draper were published in Neal Hammon and James Russell Harris, "'In a dangerous situation': Letters of Col. John Floyd, 1774-1783," *The Register of the Kentucky Historical Society* 83 (Summer 1985): 202-236.

20. Based upon this reference, Anna M. Cartlidge, a great-great niece of John Floyd, in "Colonel John Floyd: Reluctant Adventurer," *The Register of the Kentucky Historical Society* 66 (October 1966): 363, states that "he started making plans for a larger and better house and for furniture to fill it." When a hand-made brick was found in the mid-1960s at the site thought to be the location of Floyd's Station, George Yater concluded in "The Stations on Beargrass," *Louisville* 18 (October 1967): 17, that it could be "dated precisely" 1783, as Floyd's house was under construction when he was killed. He now believes that the brick probably came from the foundation of the residence built by the Breckinridges.

21. Hammon and Harris, 234.

22. John Thickston's daughter was living in Cincinnati when interviewed by John D. Shane. Lyman C. Draper later copied Shane's notes. Draper MSS. 13CC12-14. The Thickston family was living at Floyd's Station at the time. Interviewee stated that Floyd was on his way to Clear Station near Bullitt's Lick with a party of eight when attacked. He was shot in the back, and was held on his horse by his brother, Charles, until they reached a tavern, where Floyd died in the night. Interviewee's accounts of various Indian atrocities are quite vivid.

23. "Louisville's First Families: The Floyd Family," *The Louisville Post*, 12 and 19 April 1919. Anna M. Cartlidge, "Colonel John Floyd: Reluctant Adventurer," *The Register of the Kentucky Historical Society* 66 (October 1968): 317-366. For a biographical sketch see George H. Yater's entry on John Floyd in *The Kentucky Encyclopedia* (Lexington, 1992), 330.

I. PIONEER PERIL: PAGES 22-25

24. W. R. Chitwood, "Governor John Floyd, Physician," *Virginia Cavalcade* (Autumn 1976): 86-95. Also for a sketch see entry for Letitia Preston Floyd in John Frederick Dorman, *The Prestons of Smithfield and Greenfield in Virginia* (Louisville, 1982), 68-70.

25. *Biographical Directory of the American Congress, 1774-1961* (Washington, 1961), 898.

26. Carl E. Kramer, "The Strange Genealogy of Louisville's Bowman Field and Seneca Park," prepared for the Beargrass—St. Matthews Historical Society in 1986 and sponsored by R. W. Marshall.

27. Robert and Alexander Breckinridge were half brothers of John Breckinridge, who later settled near Lexington and was elected to the U. S. Senate and served as U. S. attorney general under Jefferson. See Lowell H. Harrison, *John Breckinridge, Jeffersonian Republican* (Louisville, 1969).

28. James D. Breckinridge died in Louisville on 6 May 1849 and was buried in St. John's Cemetery and later reinterred in St. Louis Cemetery. See *Biographical Directory of the American Congress, 1774-1961* (Washington, 1961), 592.

29. Kramer, "The Strange Genealogy," 8.

30. Laetitia Preston Floyd to Benjamin Rush Floyd, 22 February 1843. Draper MSS. 6J106. State Historical Society of Wisconsin.

31. Alexander Breckinridge's will, written 16 May 1797, was proved 15 June 1801 and recorded in Jefferson County Will Book 1, p. 110. Robert Breckinridge's will, written 7 September 1833, was proved 7 October 1833 and recorded in Jefferson County Will Book 2, p. 527.

32. From letter in collection of grandson, J. F. Clarke, Boston, and published by Derek Colville, "A Transcendental In Old Kentucky," *Register of the Kentucky Historical Society* 55 (October 1957): 326-327.

33. For information about Caldwell, see Kramer, 9-11.

34. Kramer, 14-22.

I. PIONEER PERIL: PAGES 25-30

35. William Floyd Parks's death notice appeared in *The Louisville Daily Journal*, 22 April 1865. Jefferson County Will Book 6, p. 314.

36. "For Sale...The Parks Grove," *The Courier-Journal*, 1 January 1876.

37. "Pirtle To Read Paper," *The Louisville Herald*, 26 January 1919. A copy of the 31-page paper is in The Filson Club's manuscript collection.

38. "Louisville Pioneers' Graves Discovered By Filson Club," *The Courier-Journal*, 25 April 1921.

39. Hardin H. Herr, "Governor John Floyd Of Virginia," *St. Matthews Booster*, 16 January 1930.

40. Hambleton Tapp's address of 2 December 1940, published as "Colonel John Floyd, Kentucky Pioneer," *The Filson Club History Quarterly* 15 (January 1941): 23-24.

41. Alexander G. Booth, "Floyd-Breckinridge Graveyard," *The Filson Club History Quarterly* 24 (January 1950): 53-57.

42. Martin Moore, "Group Here Wants Old Fort Restored," *The Louisville Times*, 4 November 1969. Christine Eade, "Clearing of Floyd's Station Site Delayed a Week for Raising Funds," *The Courier-Journal*, 19 September 1967. "Breathitt, Snyder Seek Federal Help For Defenders of Floyd's Station Site," *The Courier-Journal*, 21 September 1967. Christine Eade, "Col. Floyd's Letters Indicate He Despised Beargrass Fort," *The Courier-Journal & Times*, 24 September 1967.

43. Leland Winfield Meyer, *The Life and Times of Colonel Richard M. Johnson of Kentucky* (New York, 1932), 18-21. The family soon moved to Bryant's Station near Lexington, and it is often given as Johnson's place of birth.

44. Jim Adams, "Mistaken edentity: It oughtta be Breckinridge Lane," *The Courier-Journal*, 16 September 1993.

45. Howard M. and Edith M. List, eds., "John M. Shively's Memoir, Part I," *Oregon Historical Quarterly* 81 (Spring 1980): 6-8.

I. PIONEER PERIL: PAGES 30-32

46. Letter written from Wilson's Station, 5 May 1780. Draper MSS. 17CC125. According to Richard H. Collins, "Dictionary of the Stations and Early Settlements in Kentucky," *History of Kentucky* (Frankfort, 1966 reprint), 2: 22, Wilson's Station was located two miles northwest of Harrodsburg.

47. The definitive study by Vincent J. Akers of Bargersville, Indiana, "The Low Dutch Company: A History of the Holland Dutch Settlements of the Kentucky Frontier," was published in three issues (Summer 1980, Fall 1980, and Winter 1981) of *de Halve Maen* by The Holland Society of New York. Mr. Akers also addressed the Beargrass-St. Matthews Historical Society on the Long Run Massacre, Floyd's Defeat, as well as the Low Dutch Settlement.

48. Lease of Floyd to Marders recorded in Jefferson County Deed Book 8, p. 184. For sale to Brown see JF-311 file, Jefferson County Historic Preservation and Archives.

49. Richard and Hugh W. Hawes to W. L. Thompson, Jefferson County Deed Book W, p. 120.

50. "Louisville Pioneers' Graves Discovered By Filson Club," *The Courier-Journal*, 25 April 1921.

51. Hammon, "Early Louisville and the Beargrass Stations," 157.

52. Records supplied author by Ann Sturgess Kostmayer Bradburn of New Orleans, a descendant of Minard A'Sturgus.

53. Draper MSS. 51J89, State Historical Society of Wisconsin.

54. George Yater, "The Stations on Beargrass," *Louisville* 18 (October 1967): 20.

55. Samuel W. Thomas, "Blackacre: Research, Reminiscences, and Recommendations for Its Reuse as Part of Blackacre Nature Preserve," 1981.

56. Floyd to Clark, 8 March 1782, Draper MSS. 52J9.

57. Christian family papers among Bullitt family papers on deposit in The Filson Club.

I. PIONEER PERIL: PAGES 32-34

58. The paper was published as "Bullitt's Lick: The Related Saltworks and Settlements," *The Filson Club History Quarterly* 30 (July 1956): 240-269. The article and two historical novels were based upon an extraordinary collection of court documents, now housed in The Filson Club, that Bob McDowell and his wife, Audrea, meticulously researched and transcribed.

59. Filson's 1784 map shows Bullitt's Lick, but the Christians always referred to the site as Saltsburg.

60. From an extensive biographical sketch of William Christian in William H. Whitsitt, *Life and Times of Judge Caleb Wallace* (Louisville, 1888), 73-79. Caleb Wallace's second wife was William Christian's sister, Rosanna.

61. Anne Henry Christian to Susannah Henry Madison, 4 November 1785. Draper MSS. 5ZZ80, State Historical Society of Wisconsin.

62. Anne Henry Christian to her mother-in-law, Elizabeth Starke Christian, 13 November 1786. Hugh Blair Grigsby Papers, Virginia Historical Society.

63. Walter H. Kiser, "Neighborhood Sketches: Home of Mr. and Mrs. Clifton Duncan, Near Louisville." *The Louisville Times*, 11 January 1938. "Purchase of Landmark For Auto Agency Fought," *The Louisville Times*, 20 January 1967. Joe Creason, "Christian Home Was First 8-Mile House," *The Courier-Journal*, 10 March 1967.

64. Ramona Whaley Marsh, "What will be fate of Eight-Mile House Depends on its value," *The Voice-Jeffersonian*, 6 July 1972. Blaine A. Guthrie, Jr., "The Eight-Mile House—A Search For History," *The Filson Club History Quarterly* 47 (October 1973): 343-348. Becky Homan, "Eight-Mile House to be sold, preserved through restrictions," *The Louisville Times*, 16 August 1974.

65. Mike Brown, "Eight-Mile House sale approved; Preservation Alliance to get money," *The Courier-Journal*, 19 February 1975.

66. Richard H. Collins, *History of Kentucky* (Covington, 1874), 2:106.

I. PIONEER PERIL: PAGES 34-36

67. For biographical sketches of William Christian, see Richard H. Collins, *History of Kentucky* (Covington, 1874):2, 127; *The Biographical Encyclopaedia of Kentucky* (Cincinnati, 1878), 77; and *The Kentucky Encyclopedia* (Lexington, 1992), 184-185.

68. Richard Terrell to Benjamin Sebastian, 24 June 1786, recorded in Jefferson County Deed Book 1, p. 206. Benjamin Sebastian to Alexander Scott Bullitt, 5 January 1787, recorded in Jefferson County Deed Book 1, p. 310.

69. Information was extracted from Samuel W. Thomas, "Oxmoor: The Bullitt House in Jefferson County, Kentucky," *The Kentucky Review* 9 (Autumn 1989): 29-40.

70. Richard H. Collins, *History of Kentucky* 2 (Covington, 1874), 2:106. Ella Hutchison Ellwanger, "Oxmoor: Its Builder and Its Historian," *The Register of the Kentucky Historical Society* 17 (January 1919): 9-21.

71. The family is remembered by Richard Taylor's great-nephew, Samuel Woolfolk, in "The Brave Old Pioneers," *The Courier-Journal*, 16 July 1893.

72. "1792 Zachary Taylor Deed To Beargrass Land Found," undated *Louisville Times* clipping. The land in question was then in the hands of Ambrose Madison, Hancock Lee, Abraham Haptonstall, and Richard Taylor's brother, Zachary.

73. K. Jack Bauer, *Zachary Taylor: Soldier, Planter, Statesman of the Old Southwest* (Baton Rouge, 1985), 28-29. The 324-acre tract that Taylor farmed had been purchased from John Veech in 1814 (Jefferson County Deed Book 10, p. 333). Veech had purchased the same land from Taylor's father in 1806 (Jefferson County Deed Book 8, p. 477).

74. St. Matthews historian Hardin H. Herr thought Floyd Parks was named after John Floyd, born on Beargrass Creek, and as governor of Virginia was a nominee for President in 1832. Parks was the father of Louisa Parks Lentz and Joshua Parks, whose place was later occupied by Henry Tinsley. See Hardin H. Herr, "St. Matthews History," *St. Matthews Booster*, 16 January 1930. Floyd Parks died in 1865.

I. Pioneer Peril: pages 37-38

75. Bauer, *Zachary Taylor*, 314-319.

76. See reports in *The Louisville Daily Journal*, of 31 October and 1, 2, and 4 November 1850.

77. "Zachary Taylor's Remains," *The Courier-Journal*, 19 June 1878. "The Taylor Monument," *The Courier-Journal*, 17 June 1883. "Rough and Ready," *The Courier-Journal*, 21 September 1883. "A President's Tomb." *The Courier-Journal*, 15 March 1891. "Taylor's Tomb," *The Courier-Journal*, 15 September 1895.

78. Homer Dye, Jr., "At the End of the Path of Glory," *The Courier-Journal*, 2 February 1919. Included were pen and ink sketches of the property by Dye.

79. Mike Brown, "Tests may resolve suspicions of murder," *The Courier-Journal*, 14 June 1991.

80. "Digging Up Zach," *People* (1 July 1991): 36-37.

81. Holly Holland, "Crowd strains for glimpse of mystery and history," *The Courier-Journal*, 18 June 1991.

82. Holly Holland, "Theories try to explain Taylor's death," *The Courier-Journal*, 23 June 1991. Holly Holland, "Zachary Taylor was tooth-grinder, not arsenic-taker," *The Courier-Journal*, 27 June 1991.

83. Martin Moore, "Zachary Taylor's Home Is Brought Up To Its Times," *The Louisville Times*, 16 April 1966.

84. These changes are evident in a view of the house published in *The New York Daily Graphic*, 19 January 1875.

85. "President Taylor's Tomb." *The Courier-Journal*, 11 June 1893 and Taylor's Tomb," *The Courier-Journal*, 15 September 1895, both mention that the house "had a recent coat of paint."

86. A. B. C., "St. Matthews," *The Jeffersonian*, 4 May 1911.

87. The deed recorded in Jefferson County Deed Book 1245, p. 448, is confusing because it lists the grantee as Emily A. Overman. She was secretary to Robert Worth Bingham, owner of *The Courier-Journal* and *The Louisville Times*, of which Emanual Levi was vice president and general manager. "Dr. J. A. Brady To Be Buried This Afternoon," *The Courier-Journal*, 13 July 1940.

I. Pioneer Peril: pages 38-41

88. Mary Ann Woodward and John Nation, "Living in the Past," *Louisville* 42 (January 1991): H6-7.

89. Jefferson County Deed Book 8, p. 477.

90. Patricia Rodman, "Indian Hill, The Ancestral Home Of The Veech Family," *The Herald-Post*, 30 November 1924.

91. *The City of Louisville and a Glimpse of Kentucky* (Louisville, 1887), 131.

92. "Death Claims Former Head Of Monon R. R." *The Louisville Herald*, 18 September 1918.

93. *First Annual Catalogue of Trotting Horses Belonging to R. S. Veech, Indian Hill* (Louisville, 1876).

94. "Bethel Veech, Banker, Dies," *The Courier-Journal*, 9 May 1946.

95. For interior photographs, see "Open House In Kentucky," *The Courier-Journal*, 25 April 1948.

96. "'Indian Hill,' Country Home Of Veech Family In New Hands After 118 Years," *The Courier-Journal*, 17 August 1924.

97. "Maternal-, Child-Health Expert Dies," *The Courier-Journal*, 11 July 1957.

98. Patricia Rodman, "Indian Hill, The Ancestral Home Of The Veech Family," *The Herald-Post*, 30 November 1924.

99. "An Old Kentucky Home," *The Courier-Journal*, 22 November 1891.

100. Wilhelmine Franke, "Domestic Pageant In Old Kentucky: Herr Homestead Near St. Matthews," *The Courier-Journal*, 30 June 1935.

101. "Nourbourne O. Rudy," *The Courier-Journal*, 17 April 1977.

102. "'Oldest House In County' Is Sold," *The Courier-Journal*, 18 June 1939. Sarah Lansdell, "Growing Old Gracefully," *The Courier-Journal*, 5 May 1963.

103. "Norbourn Arterburn." *The Courier-Journal*, 11 April 1878.

104. Hardin H. Herr, "St. Matthews History," *St. Matthews Booster*, 18 September 1930 (misdated 18 September 1901).

I. Pioneer Peril: pages 42-43

105. Reminiscences of Charles K. Osborn (1865-1957) collected and recorded by Bonna Holzheimer. Beargrass-St. Matthews Historical Society files.

106. The Wedding Guests," *The Courier-Journal*, 20 April 1891.

107. Hite was a member of the Old Kaintuck Club and best known as a fisherman as his obituary attests. "S. S. Hite Makes Last Cast In Life's Stream," *The Courier-Journal*, 13 September 1911.

108. "Killed By Car," *The Jeffersonian*, 15 February 1923.

109. The basis of information about the Herr family houses is "Windy Hills: A Neighborhood History," a paper prepared in 1972 by Sally Sherwood Keith and updated for the Beargrass-St. Matthews Historical Society in 1986.

II. Antebellum Addresses: pages 45-47

1. Rexford Newcomb, *Architecture in Old Kentucky* (Urbana, 1953), 66-67. Clay Lancaster, *Antebellum Architecture of Kentucky* (Lexington, 1991), 147-149.

2. Samuel W. Thomas, *Churchill Downs: A Documentary History of America's Most Legendary Race Track* (Louisville, 1994), 32-34.

3. Wilhelmine Franke, "Domestic Pageant In Old Kentucky: Ridgeway," *The Courier-Journal*, 2 June 1935.

4. The contract calls for the "work to be in the stile of the finishing of John Bustards house of Louisville." This does not preclude Skidmore's layout from having been influenced by one of Thomas Jefferson's plans, as previously postulated.

5. Samuel W. Thomas, "Oxmoor: The Bullitt House in Jefferson County, Kentucky," *The Kentucky Review*, 9 (Autumn 1989): 29-40.

6. "An Eminent Kentuckian—Death of William C. Bullitt—Reminiscences of the Constitutional Convention," *The Courier-Journal*, 29 August 1877.

II. ANTEBELLUM ADDRESSES: PAGES 47-49

7. Plat of Oxmoor, surveyed November 1875, and letter from William Marshall Bullitt to Fannie B. Chenoweth, 3 October 1914. Family papers of William Heyburn.

8. "Killed By Car," *The Jeffersonian*, 15 February 1923. 1. "Death of W. C. Bullitt, Esq." *The Courier-Journal*, 29 August 1877. " Mr. Wm. C. Bullitt's Funeral." *The Courier-Journal*, 30 August 1877. "Mr. W. C. Bullitt's Funeral." *The Courier-Journal*, 2 September 1877.

9. Mac Griswold and Eleanor Weller, *The Golden Age of American Gardens* (New York, 1991), 1996-1997. Diane Heilenman, "Oxmoor: Simply Grand," *The Courier-Journal*, 19 October 1995.

10. A biographical sketch and portrait of James Brown were published in *History of the Ohio Falls Cities and Their Counties* 1 (Cleveland, 1882), 557-561.

11. Family papers of Kathy McDonald Panther, great-great-great-granddaughter of James Brown.

12. "Succumbs," *The Louisville Times*, 20 November 1901. A letter to the editor of *The Voice-Tribune*, published in the 18 October 1995 issue, claims that when the Forman children were orphaned, they were adopted by Mrs. Forman's brother, Theodore Brown. The writer also stated that Uncle Theodore was the source of the Forman brothers' capital in forming the Brown-Forman company. However, George Forman's two brothers were long dead by the time he was made a partner in the firm.

13. Letter from Louisa Anderson Waters to Brown descendant cousins, dated Summer 1948, Kathy McDonald Panther collection. A trust fund of $2,000 was created in 1951. A list of those buried in the cemetery appeared in "Kentucky Tombstone Inscriptions," *Register of the Kentucky Historical Society* 26 (September 1928): 305.

14. "Death Summons Veteran Banker," *Herald-Post*, 2 May 1930.

15. "William C. Fenley Dead." *The Jeffersonian*, 10 June 1915.

II. ANTEBELLUM ADDRESSES: PAGES 49-52

16. Sarah Lansdell, "Fenley Estate To Give Way To Subdivision," *The Courier-Journal*, 15 October 1961. Included were many photographs of the house and outbuildings. Louise Warren, "Early Lyndon area farm now Camelot subdivision," *The Voice*, 30 November 1983.

17. Leaven Lawrence had operated a water mill on Goose Creek north of the location of Lyndon Station. *History of the Ohio Falls Cities and Counties* 2 (Cleveland, 1882), 47.

18. "Lexington and Ohio Railway," *Lexington Intelligencer*, 18 November 1834. T. T. Shreve to William B. Phillips, Jefferson County Deed Book 49, p. 282, dated 1 July 1837.

19. *The Louisville Morning Courier*, 22 April 1850.

20. *The Louisville Morning Courier*, 2 September 1850.

21. "Final Funeral Obsequies for Henry Clay." *The Louisville Daily Courier*, 12 July 1852.

22. *The Louisville Daily Courier*, 7 April 1854. The newspaper supported this report with an editorial on 10 April 1854.

23. Time schedule, effective 8 July 1865. Reprinted in *The L. & N. Employes' Magazine*, November 1927, p. 92.

24. A plan of the station from the L & N Railroad files in the University of Louisville Archives, noting that the structure was built in 1879, was provided by Charles B. Castner, historian of the L & N Railroad, along with his photograph of the station structure being razed.

25. "Louisville, Cincinnati & Lexington Railroad," *Louisville Daily Courier*, 28 August 1867.

26. "The First Trip....Fastest Time On Record Between The Two Cities." *The Courier-Journal*, 19 June 1869.

27. Samuel W. Thomas, *Crescent Hill Revisited* (Louisville, 1987), 8-9.

28. Alfred Herr to Shelbyville and Louisville Turnpike Road Company, 6 December 1862. Jefferson County Deed Book 113, p. 75.

II. ANTEBELLUM ADDRESSES: PAGES 52-55

29. *History of the Ohio Falls Cities and Their Counties* (Cleveland, 1882): 2, 49.

30. "Funeral Notice," *The Courier-Journal*, 21 August 1878. Dr. Lewis was buried in Cave Hill Cemetery.

31. Joseph Oechsli purchased the property in 1893 and later subdivided it. JF386, Historic Jefferson County (1992), 73.

32. "Grand Democratic Mass Meeting," *Louisville Daily Courier*, 25 October 1856.

33. "Ten Thousand Persons Assembled!" *Louisville Daily Courier*, 29 October 1856.

34. The election precinct was established as part of an act approved 29 January 1830, Chap. 386.

35. Louisville Chancery Court case 7906.

36. Chapter 322, approved 4 March 1850. Hardin H. Herr in one of his series "St. Matthews History," *St. Matthews Booster*, 6 March 1930, stated that an election officer drew a line through an 1847 record for Sale's precinct and wrote above it Gilman's. Obviously, Sale was long dead and probably the county court authorized the change before it was ordered by the Legislature in 1850.

37. "To The Other Shore," *The Courier-Journal*, 24 July 1885. The Gilmans were buried in Section C, lot 107, Cave Hill Cemetery.

38. George Herr to Daniel Gilman in trust for his wife, Ann Gilman, Jefferson County Deed Book 105, p. 284. Daniel Gilman to Alfred Herr, Jefferson County Deed Book 142, p. 307.

39. Clarence E. Cason, "Live Towns Around Louisville," *The Louisville Herald*, 30 March 1922.

40. Jefferson County Court Minute-Order Books.

41. Hardin H. Herr, "St. Matthews History," *St. Matthews Booster*, 6 March 1930.

42. Carrie Morrison, "'Art and Soul' at St. Matthew's Episcopal," *The Voice-Tribune*, 2 December 1998.

II. ANTEBELLUM ADDRESSES: PAGES 55-56

43. Jefferson County Deed Book 55, p. 465. Jefferson County Deed Book 147, p. 54. According to Hardin H. Herr, "St. Matthews History," *St. Matthews Booster*, 6 March 1930, the parsonage was occupied by the Blandford family.

44. On 23 November 1871, Mrs. Helen Bullitt Key gave a note to Redin for $598, however the work was not noted. See microfilm of Bullitt family papers, The Filson Club. According to a 15 April 1912 *Courier-Journal* article, the Gothic, board and batten church was built "about the year 1872."

45. "Effort Is Made To Save Church," *The Courier-Journal*, 15 April 1912.

46. "Site Of Old St. Matthews Episcopal Church Sold," *The Courier-Journal*, 18 February 1913.

47. Donald B. Towles, ed., *A History of Beargrass Christian Church, 1842-1992* (Louisville, 1992), 19. Evidently, Beargrass Christian Church was the result of a merger of Beargrass Baptist Church and Goose Creek Church of Christ in 1842.

48. Chapter 135, approved 5 February 1842. *Laws of Kentucky* (Frankfort, 1843), 156-157.

49. *History of the Ohio Falls Cities* (Cleveland, 1882): 2, 48.

50. Jefferson County Deed Book 9, p. 408. A copy of the 1 July 1803 agreement is in the Bullitt family papers, Southern Historical Collection, University of North Carolina.

51. Caleb Noel and others to trustees of Beargrass Baptist Church, 1 July 1809. Jefferson County Deed Book 9, p. 408. Major Noel to John Veech, 14 August 1810. Jefferson County Deed Book 9, p. 62. On the 1879 *Atlas of Jefferson and Oldham Counties Kentucky*, the lot would have been between a pond behind Covington Arterburn's residence and a road that is shown separating Arterburn and Bullitt property and land owned by Theodore Brown, Arthur Brown, and the Monohan family.

52. Towles, 37. The church lot is located on a plat recorded in Deed Book 164, p. 255 (4 June 1872).

II. ANTEBELLUM ADDRESSES: PAGES 56-59

53. "St. Matthews," *The Jeffersonian*, 9 October 1919. Towles, 61.

54. Robert M. Rennick, *Kentucky Place Names* (Lexington, 1987), 261. Hardin H. Herr researched this matter for an article in the *St. Matthews Booster*, 6 March 1930, and the first post office he could find in the area was created in 1854 and called St. Matthews.

55. From "Review of the Life of Theodore Brown, 1821-1899," in the papers of Kathy McDonald Panther, great-great-granddaughter of Theodore Brown. The Harvard graduate B. B. Huntoon (1836-1919) was instrumental in the development of the school, and his history of its first 50 years is contained in the *Report of the Kentucky Institution for the Education of the Blind* (Frankfort, 1891).

56. John Esten Cooke, M.D. (1783-1853), a graduate of the University of Pennsylvania, began teaching in the medical school at Transylvania University in 1827 and ten years later moved to Louisville when the Louisville Medical Institute was founded. When retired, he settled at Woodlawn, but went to Trimble County where he died. See *The Biographical Encyclopaedia of Kentucky* (Cincinnati, 1878), 57-58.

57. Advertisement in *The Louisville Daily Journal*, 26 December 1842.

58. John Esten Cooke to Henry W. Gray, Jefferson County Deed Book 69, p. 669. "Mr. George Gray Dead," *The Courier-Journal*, 30 December 1890. "Old Age," *The Courier-Journal*, 18 July 1903.

III. THE CIVIL WAR AND ITS AFTERMATH
PAGE 61

1. "Major Anderson, U. S. A., Commanding At Fort Sumter," *Harper's Weekly*, 12 January 1861. "Alarm At Charleston," *Louisville Daily Courier*, 17 April 1861.

2. *The Louisville Daily Journal*, 9 October 1861.

3. "Obituary. Major-Gen. Robert Anderson," *The New York Times*, 28 October 1871.

III. THE CIVIL WAR AND ITS AFTERMATH
PAGES 61-68

4. Reminiscences of Henry Massie Bullitt (1842-1908), written 2 October 1906. Bullitt family papers, The Filson Club.

5. Three journals by Cora Owens (1848-1939) for the Civil War period are in The Filson Club. Excerpts made and edited by her were published in an eleven-part series in *The Courier-Journal*, beginning 20 September 1936.

6. "Reorganization of Shelby College." *The Louisville Daily Journal*, 14 July 1852.

7. Owings to Beckett, 3 February 1854, recorded in Jefferson County Deed Book 85, p. 598. Beckett to Page, 25 August 1865, recorded in Jefferson County Deed Book 123, p. 328.

8. "St. Matthews, An Old Area Grown Young," *The Courier-Journal*, 29 June 1941.

9. "St. Matthews Triangle," *The Courier-Journal*, 6 July 1941.

10. Diaries of Cora Owens Pope Hume, The Filson Club.

11. Samuel W. Thomas, *Churchill Downs*, (Louisville, 1995), 24.

12. *The Courier-Journal*, 10 and 13 June 1872. The subdivision plat was recorded in Jefferson County Deed Book 166, p. 639. For information about the subsequent development of the Woodlawn site, see John C. Scheer, *The History of Woodlawn Park, Kentucky* (1977).

13. Interview of Elizabeth Adair Arterburn Baker, 30 July 1998.

14. Reminiscences of Charles K. Osborn, collected and recorded by Mrs. Russell Holzheimer. He would serve in various capacities in law enforcement including chief of the Jefferson County police department from 1933-1937. He died on 14 April 1957 at the age of 91.

15. Jefferson County Court Minute Order Book 25, p. 375.

16. 5 July 1866, Jefferson County Deed Book 128, p. 296.

17. Jefferson County Deed Book 56, p. 597. Jefferson County Minute Order Books 26, p. 218 (dated 20 September 1866) and 28, p. 497 (dated 24 January 1870).

III. The Civil War and Its Aftermath
pages 68-71

18. Samuel W. Thomas, *Crescent Hill Revisited* (Louisville, 1987), 98.

19. Jefferson County Deed Book 123, p. 328.

20. "The Theaters," "The South and History," and "Thomas Nelson Page," *Louisville Commercial*, 15 April 1891.

21. Harriet R. Holman, "The Kentucky Journal of Thomas Nelson Page," *The Register of the Kentucky Historical Society* 68 (January 1970):1-6.

22. Theodore L. Gross, *Thomas Nelson Page* (New York, 1967). Stephanie Yuhl, Duke University, to Samuel W. Thomas, 11 December 1996.

23. Acts approved 27 January 1866 (Chapter 242); 25 January 1868 (Chapter 240); and 5 March 1869 (Chapter 1746).

24. Printed as Appendix III in Thomas W. Bullitt, *My Life at Oxmoor* (Louisville, 1911).

25. Acts approved 21 March 1871 (Chapter 1799); and 6 February 1874 (Chapter 207). Beargrass Railway Company to Smyser and Burks, and Burks to Smyser, Jefferson County Deed Book 185, pp. 15-20.

26. Mrs. Jarvis was perhaps Sarah Bright Jarvis, the second wife of retired pork merchant William Jarvis.

27. "Death of Lewis Smyser," *The Courier-Journal*, 3 August 1877.

28. There were several Burks family residences in the area, including one amidst Bowman Field which was converted into a library during World War II. See "Old House Earns Its Wings," *The Courier-Journal*, 7 February 1943.

29. Nicklies to Nanz, 9 November 1872. Jefferson County Deed Book 167, p. 172.

30. James B. Burks had sold 30 acres of the old Breckinridge tract known as Woodville to Jacob Nicklies, on 6 December 1856 for $9,000. Jefferson County Deed Book 96, p. 635.

31. "Prominent German Dead." *The Courier-Journal*, 19 June 1900.

III. The Civil War and Its Aftermath
pages 71-76

32. "Henry Nanz Dead." *The Courier-Journal*, 27 April 1891.

33. File ZV 10-45U. "Zoning Board Grants Permit To Greenhouse," *The Courier-Journal*, 16 February 1945.

34. Ken Loomis, "Blaze heavily damages florist shop and offices," *The Courier-Journal*, 22 November 1976. Agnes S. Crume, "Here Comes the Bride—Adorned with Flowers by Nanz & Kraft," *Louisville* 34 (January 1983): 74-76.

35. W. C. Winchester's deed, dated 14 February 1916, is recorded in Jefferson County Deed Book 846, p. 193. Walter H. Kiser, "'Kentwood,' Near Louisville," *The Louisville Times*, 29 December 1938. Martha Elson, "Model makeover," *The Courier-Journal*, 24 August 1994.

36. "Assignee's Sale In Bankruptcy Of 121 Acres of First-class Beargrass Garden Lands, Five Miles from the City of Louisville, near Gilman's Point, subdivided into Lots." *The Daily Louisville Commercial*, 11 October 1874. Assignee W. W. Gardner to Tinsley, dated 15 October 1874, Jefferson County Deed Book 195, p. 264.

37. See "Inventor Of Dry-Cleaning Equipment, W. M. Cissell, Is Dead At Age Of 68," *The Courier-Journal*, 25 July 1959.

38. In a family division, S. S. Hite conveyed 50 acres to William Wallace Herr on the west side of "Breckenridge lane" on 8 April 1874. Jefferson County Deed Book 180, p. 206. Herr sold the property, designated in the same way, to Henry Holzheimer on 4 February 1879. Jefferson County Deed Book 222, p. 508.

39. Approved 11 February 1874, Chapter 256, *Laws of Kentucky* (1874), 293-297.

40. Philip Collingwood, "The Old Stone Fort," *The Courier-Journal*, 18 June 1893. Blaine A. Guthrie, Jr., "Captain Richard Chenoweth—A Founding Father of Louisville," *The Filson Club History Quarterly* 46 (April 1972): 147-160.

41. "Death Of Mrs. Dr. Chenoweth," *The Courier-Journal*, 30 March 1896.

42. From a *ca.* 1910 biographical sketch of John Henry Chenoweth in family papers belonging to his great-grandson, William Heyburn.

III. The Civil War and Its Aftermath
pages 76-81

43. "Death Claims Dr. Henry Chenoweth, of St. Matthews," *The Courier-Journal*, 17 April 1905. "Dr. James S. Chenoweth, 82, Dies...," *The Courier-Journal*, 11 January 1950.

44. A photograph of Mrs. John Welburn Brown and son, Hewett, in front of the old Chenoweth house appeared in "St. Matthews, An Old Area Grown Young," *The Courier-Journal*, 29 June 1941.

45. "John Stites, Lawyer and Financier, Dies," *The Courier-Journal*, 2 December 1938.

46. A plat of Elmwood subdivision was filed in Jefferson County Deed Book 392, p. 638.

47. *The Courier-Journal*, 1 May 1892.

48. See Jefferson County Office of Historic Preservation and Archives file JF383.

49. Hardin H. Herr, "St. Matthews History," *St. Matthews Booster*, 18 September 1930. (This issue was misdated 18 September 1901 and was microfilmed as such.)

50. "New Church," *The Jeffersonian*, 8 April 1915.

51. "New Church At St. Matthews," *The Evening Post*, 15 May 1915.

52. The boy was later a suspect in various fires and robberies in St. Matthews. "Bond Set At $1,800 For St. Matthews Firebug," *The Courier-Journal*, 7 February 1939.

53. *Souvenir Dedication and Blessing of New Holy Trinity Church and School*, 15 November 1936. "Fire-Swept Church Will Be Rebuilt, *The Courier-Journal*, 22 September 1937.

54. *Holy Trinity Church, 1882-1982* (Louisville, 1982), 19. "110 Enroll In New Catholic High," *The Courier-Journal*, 7 August 1953.

55. "Holy Trinity High School To Alter Name," *The Courier-Journal*, 24 March 1956.

IV. BEARGRASS BECOMES INDUSTRIAL
PAGES 83-88

1. "The Grease-Skimmers," *The Courier-Journal*, 12-13 December 1869. "Peace! Peace!" *The Courier-Journal*, 21 December 1869.

2. John May, Kentucky County, to Samuel Beall, Williamsburg, 28 May 1780. Transcribed by Charles Hayes Young, a descendant of Samuel Beall, and given to The Filson Club.

3. "Our Wholesale Whisky Trade. Newcomb, Buchanan & Co.—The Largest Dealers in the United States." *The Courier-Journal*, 22 February 1874.

4. "The Newcomb-Buchanan Company," *The Courier-Journal*, 17 May 1876.

5. *The Industries of Louisville* (Louisville, 1881), 83-84.

6. "From His Own Lips." *The Courier-Journal*, 8 October 1884.

7. *Illustrated Louisville: Kentucky's Metropolis* (Chicago, 1891), 121.

8. "Beargrass Afire," *The Courier-Journal*, 11 February 1907.

9. Jefferson County Court Minute Order Book A, p. 161.

10. Otto A. Rothert, "Origin of the Names Beargrass Creek, The Point, and Thruston Square," *The Filson Club History Quarterly*, 2 (October 1927): 19-21.

11. Alexander C. McLeod, "A Man For All Regions: Dr. Thomas Walker Of Castle Hill," *The Filson Club History Quarterly*, 71 (April 1997): 185.

12. Lloyd Arnold Brown, *Early Maps of the Ohio Valley* (Pittsburgh, 1959): 95.

13. Virginius C. Hall, *Journal of Isaac Hite, Surveyor at the Falls of the Ohio, 1773* (Cincinnati, 1954), 14.

14. The lane was named for Jacob Zimmerman, who owned the land at the head of the triangle formed by the roads.

15. Jefferson County Plat and Subdivision Book 4, p. 34.

IV. BEARGRASS BECOMES INDUSTRIAL
PAGES 88-89

16. Jefferson County Incorporation Book 40, p. 518. The company was formed by Joseph E. Roth, president, and William F. Ruedeman, secretary-treasurer.

17. Paul Baldwin, "Beargrass Creek's cloudy past could yield a clear future under task-force plan," *The Courier-Journal*, 21 April 1993.

18. Nina Walfoort, "Car dealership wants to cover 300 feet of Beargrass fork," *The Courier-Journal*, 2 March 1998.

19. Ella H. Johnson, "Beargrass Creek in City's History," *The Courier-Journal*, 6 November 1927.

V. TURN OF THE CENTURY: PAGES 91-94

1. Holzheimer to Bauer brothers, 10 January 1887, Jefferson County Deed Book 298, p. 218. "St. Matthews," *The Jeffersonian*, 20 January 1921.

2. "Prominent Citizen," *The Jeffersonian*," 9 December 1909.

3. Holzheimer to Edinger, 3 November 1899, Jefferson County Deed Book 523, p. 581. Edinger was married to Elizabeth Holzheimer.

4. Edinger to Trustees, 25 July 1900, Jefferson County Deed Book 540, p. 273-274.

5. The advertisement in the *Louisville Commercial* of 15 May 1901 was supplied by George Yater.

6. *The Courier-Journal*, 12 January 1901.

7. George H. Yater to Samuel W. Thomas, 12 December 1996.

8. "A Novelty." *The Courier-Journal*, 23 March 1901.

9. "Good-Bye To The Last Street-Car Mule." *The Courier-Journal*, 27 October 1901.

10. "First Car Over The Shelbyville Extension," *The Courier-Journal*, 20 August 1910. Yater to Thomas, 12 December 1996.

V. TURN OF THE CENTURY: PAGES 94-97

11. The 7 August 1910 *Courier-Journal* identified the pictures of "the cozy quarters" of Hooper's farm hands as being near St. Matthews. He owned land on the west side of Bauer Avenue near Shelbyville Road, which was then considered near St. Matthews, but he probably leased farm land elsewhere.

12. "Doing Things," *The Jeffersonian*, 17 August 1911.

13. Irvin A. Young was interviewed by Samuel W. Thomas, 28 June 1979. He died at the age of 97 on 15 November 1996.

14. "Interurbans May Halt Soon," *The Courier-Journal*, 18 July 1935.

15. "The Passing Of The Tollgate." *The Courier-Journal*, 17 February 1901. However, this article contains many errors and discusses a tollgate at St. Matthews that was actually at the Eight-Mile House.

16. When published in *The Courier-Journal* on 27 August 1933, the Orrs were said to be living in Anchorage.

17. Marion Porter, "Modern Toll Highways? Old Time Gate Keeper At 8-Mile House Calls Them 'Silly Notion,'" *The Courier-Journal*, 30 June 1939.

18. The property was owned by Frank Ochsner's daughter and her husband, the Andrew J. Schmitts. "Old Eight-Mile House being razed for store," *The Voice-Jeffersonian*, 25 November 1965.

19. Blaine A. Guthrie, Jr., "The Eight-Mile House: A Search For History," *The Filson Club History Quarterly*, 47 (October 1973): 343-348.

20. James Speed, "Old Stone Cottage Dignifies Work and Taste of Pioneer Generations," *Herald-Post*, 18 January 1934.

21. "Fire Hits 8-Mile House," *Herald-Post*, 4 March 1930.

V. Turn of the Century: pages 97-103

22. A 10-foot passageway for light and air was reserved between the structures. Lease, dated 2 March 1906, is recorded in Jefferson County Deed Book 638, p. 130.

23. Jefferson County Incorporation Book 14, pp. 601-603.

24. "Louis Bauer, St. Matthews Banker, Dies," *The Courier-Journal*, 21 August 1943.

25. "Gilbert Dick, St. Matthews Banker, Dies," *The Courier-Journal*, 16 September 1949.

26. Interview of Cornelia Drescher Stone, 16 December 1996.

27. A. B. C., "From St. Matthews," *The Jeffersonian*, 3 June 1915.

28. "The Indian Weed." *The Courier-Journal*, 11 June 1893.

29. "Cutting Hemp By Machinery." *The Courier-Journal*, 27 October 1901. E. J. Kinney, "Blue Grass Is Returning To Prestige As Home Of Hemp." *The Lexington Herald*, 15 April 1917. "More Hemp," *The Courier-Journal*, 12 September 1925. Vance Armentrout, "Kentuckians In Crisis Return to Hemp, the Ancestral Crop," *The Courier-Journal*, 4 September 1942.

30. "Farmers and Gardeners Please Notice," *The Jeffersonian*, 17 February 1910, notes that the storage capacity was 5,000 barrels and had been so since 1909.

31. 15 August 1908, Jefferson County Incorporation Book 17, pp. 383-385.

32. 2 August 1910, Jefferson County Incorporation Book 19, pp. 323-326.

33. J. C. Fenley, Farmer, Dies," *The Courier-Journal*, 7 December 1946. "Robert W. Hite, Sr., 92, Retired Co-op Head, Dies," *The Courier-Journal*, 13 January 1961.

34. "Big Farmers," *The Jeffersonian*, 8 February 1912.

V. Turn of the Century: pages 103-109

35. "St. Matthews Noted For Potato Yields," *Christian Science Monitor*, 14 December 1925.

36. "Produce Exchange At St. M. Sold," *The Courier-Journal*, 23 December 1952.

37. Souvenir Historical Program, *Sports & Stars: 50 Years of Baseball, 1911-1961*, sponsored by the St. Matthews Merchants Baseball Association.

38. Survey of St. Matthews Avenue, dated June 1916, by County Engineer J. Russell Gaines. Jefferson County Office of Preservation and Archives.

39. "John L. Stich Dead," *The Courier-Journal*, 12 July 1899.

40. Epp Stich died at the age of 73. *The Courier-Journal*, 17 July 1973. The garage has been razed and the land leased by his son, Earl Combs Stich, to Olympco Muffler & Brake and Kentucky Fried Chicken.

41. "Up-To-Date, *The Jeffersonian*, 18 April 1912.

42. *The Courier-Journal*, 15 March 1950.

43. Jefferson County Plat and Subdivision Book 1, p. 140.

44. "Dr. Hopson Dead; Physician 50 Years," *The Courier-Journal*, 22 August 1923.

45. Dudley Gregory to Rosa Eline, 1 July 1912, Jefferson County Deed Book 766, pp. 180-181.

46. The sale was to Arthur Caudill of London, Kentucky, and J. L. Pendergrass of Louisville. "St. Matthews Chevrolet Firm Is Sold," *The Courier-Journal*, 3 August 1954.

47. Evidently these utilities were in place by the spring of 1912. See "Up-To-Date, *The Jeffersonian*, 18 April 1912.

48. $65,000 Blaze Sweeps Eline Building In St. Matthews," *The Courier-Journal*, 4 January 1958.

V. Turn of the Century: pages 109-111

49. *The Jeffersonian*, 14 November 1912 and 5 December 1912.

50. "Presenting The Story Of St. Matthews," *The Voice of St. Matthews*, 15 July 1954.

51. "St. Matthews," *The Jeffersonian*, 22 July 1920.

52. Interview of Henrietta Sara Eline Breeland by Samuel W. Thomas, 20 November 1996. Mrs. Breeland died on 3 April 1997. See *The Courier-Journal*, 5 April 1997.

53. "Fairfax Building to be razed; new KFC restaurant to arise," *The New Voice*, 6 May 1987. The article contains photographs of the home and Fairfax Building. The first KFC in St. Matthews was listed in the 1968 Louisville city directory at 4518 Shelbyville Road. A year later, another opened at 139 St. Matthews Avenue.

54. "Anthony Eline, Real Estate Dealer, Developer, Dies," *The Courier-Journal*, 24 March 1967.

55. The subdivision plan for Louise Neuner, H. A. Kraft, and Sallie D. Kraft was prepared by Stonestreet & Ford, Surveyors, and was recorded on 7 May 1913 in Jefferson County Plat and Subdivision Book 3, p. 52.

56. "A. P. Grieshaber, Sr.," *The Courier-Journal*, 20 May 1959.

57. "A. M. Zaring, St. Matthews Doctor, Dies," *The Courier-Journal*, 29 December 1944. "Pneumonia Fatal To Dr. Abraham Zaring," *St. Matthews Sun*, 29 December 1944.

58. "W. J. Ogden, Druggist, 60, Dies Unexpectedly," *The Courier-Journal*, 7 April 1945.

59. *The Jeffersonian*, 19 September 1912.

60. "At Last," *The Jeffersonian*, 11 December 1913. Joseph Oechsli to Jefferson County Board of Education, 13 December 1913, recorded in Jefferson County Deed Book 799, p. 187.

V. Turn of the Century: pages 111-115

61. Joellen Tyler Johnston, *Jeffersontown, Kentucky: The First 200 Years* (Louisville, 1997), 114.

62. Interview of Cornelia Drescher Stone by Samuel W. Thomas, 16 December 1996.

63. Jefferson County Deed Book 352, pp. 108-109.

64. Lourena Eaton, "Greathouse Will Lose Its Principal On Friday," *The Courier-Journal*, 12 May 1946. Ruth H. Osborne, "Some Contributions of Parents and Teachers to the Development of Greathouse School, St. Matthews, Kentucky," MA thesis, University of Louisville, 1952, 31-32. *The Jeffersonian*, 15 April 1915. Prentice married Allen, 17 December 1884. Jefferson County Marriage Register 13, p. 612.

65. *The Jeffersonian*, 27 June 1918.

66. *The Jeffersonian*, 29 May 1919.

67. "Veteran Teacher, 93, Dies In Shelbyville," *The Courier-Journal*, 18 July 1935.

68. Lucy McGowan, *History of Crescent Hill Presbyterian Church* (Louisville, 1940), 12. "The Story of St. Matthews," *The Voice of St. Matthews*, 22 July 1954.

69. Osborne, 33. Jefferson County Planning and Zoning Commission permit application by Lloyd T. Ray, dated 12 January 1949.

70. Interview of Frank L. "Tubby" Barth, 20 January 1998.

71. "Old Greathouse School Being Razed, *The Louisville Times*, 28 April 1960.

72. "From St. Matthews," *The Jeffersonian*, 3 June 1915.

73. "A. B. C. News Letter." *The Jeffersonian*, 14 October 1915.

74. *The Jeffersonian*, 15 June 1916.

V. Turn of the Century: page 115

75. A. B. C., "St. Matthews," *The Jeffersonian*, 2 November 1916. Donald B. Towles, ed., *A History of Beargrass Christian Church, 1842-1992* (Louisville, 1992), 65.

76. ZV 38-48U, Jefferson County Historic Preservation and Archives. *The Voice of St. Matthews*, 16 July 1959.

VI. Prohibition Enacts Change pages 117-120

1. "St. Matthews," *The Jeffersonian*, 11 November 1920.

2. "St Matthews Bank and Office Building, *The Jeffersonian*, 26 May 1921.

3. "St. Matthews," *The Jeffersonian*, 8 September 1921.

4. "St. Matthews," *The Jeffersonian*, 27 October 1921.

5. *The Jeffersonian*, 10 February 1921.

6. "The Name 'Bauer,'" *The Jeffersonian*, 5 June 1924.

7. "Son of St. Matthews Area Pioneers Dies," *The Courier-Journal*, 25 December 1957.

8. "G. J. Wurster Dies In Lexington Hospital," *The Courier-Journal*, 26 November 1941.

9. Susan McDonald, "Pete Hammer nails it," *The Voice-Tribune*, 29 October 1997.

10. "Miss Virginia Wheatley," *St. Matthews Booster*, 20 May 1926.

11. "New Barber Shop," *The Jeffersonian*, 15 March 1923. "Bert Nally, 54, Ex-Head Of Barber Board, Dies," *The Courier-Journal*, 19 July 1946.

12. "Prof. Moore Is Killed At Grade Crossing," *The Courier-Journal*, 28 March 1923.

13. "St. Matthews," *The Jeffersonian*, 25 January 1923.

VI. Prohibition Enacts Change pages 120-123

14. "St. Matthews to Have New Bank," *The Courier-Journal*, 2 May 1924. The bank was to open May 31st.

15. "St. Matthews Bank Suspends Business," *The Courier-Journal*, 17 November 1931. "500 Depositors Attend Meeting," *The Courier-Journal*, 2 April 1932. "Bank To Open In St. Matthews," *The Courier-Journal*, 14 August 1933.

16. Martha Elson, "Bank razes storefront for parking," *The Courier-Journal*, 9 November 1994.

17. "Prominent Baker Dies At Age 82," *The Courier-Journal*, 22 April 1965. The bakery has a framed copy of a full-page article from a 1927 *St. Matthews Booster* about its coming to St. Matthews.

18. "St. Matthews," *The Jeffersonian*," 15 March 1923. "Bethel Church," *The Jeffersonian*," 21 June 1923.

19. "Cornerstone At Bethel Placed," *The Courier-Journal*, 18 August 1924.

20. When this item of 18 June 1931 was reprinted fifty years later in the *Bethel Informant* on 24 June 1981, preparations were underway to make 800 gallons of turtle soup.

21. Zoning regulation variance request ZV 59-53U. Jefferson County Historic Preservation and Archives. "Bethel E.-R. Building Job Is Approved," *The Courier-Journal*, 25 June 1953.

22. "Baptists Will Dedicate New $250,000 Church," *The Courier-Journal*, 30 October 1949.

23. "St. Matthews Has Community Club," *The Courier-Journal*, 24 June 1924.

24. "St. Matthews will hold Community Festival on 'The Triangle' on August 6," *The Courier-Journal*, 26 July 1925. The article was positioned around a photograph of the organizing committee.

25. "St. Matthews Bidder For Courthouse," *The Louisville Herald*, 23 March 1926. "City Coming East," *The Jeffersonian*, 7 May 1925.

26. "Masons To Award Home Contracts," *The Courier-Journal*, 8 November 1924. Carl Kramer, *Louisville's Olmstedian Legacy* (Louisville, 1988), 20 and 52.

VI. PROHIBITION ENACTS CHANGE
PAGES 123-128

27. "8,000 Attend Dedication Here Of Masons' $2,000,000 Home," *The Courier-Journal*, 19 October 1927.

28. Martha Elson, "Masonic project revitalizes secluded Crescent Hill campus," *The Courier-Journal*, 24 September 1997.

29. Stanley Freville, "Polo Tournament Gets Under Way At Bowman Field This Afternoon," *Herald-Post*, 3 July 1926. The tournament included two field artillery squads and matches were played at Bowman Field and along Brownsboro Road.

30. "St. Matthews," *The Jeffersonian*, 18 March 1920.

31. Carrie Morrison, "'Betsey' is back," *The Voice-Tribune*, 19 August 1998.

32. Anna (also Annie) B. White married John Newton Simcoe. She died on 3 June 1935 at the age of 77.

33. "After growth, a new system," *The Voice*, 25 July 1974.

34. The Scripps-Howard chain purchased the newspaper in 1979, and two owners later, it briefly ceased publication before being purchased in 1987 by Southern Publishing and renamed *The New Voice*.

35. "City Coming East," *The Jeffersonian*, 7 May 1925.

36. "Fairlawn Lot Sale," *The Courier-Journal*, 18 April 1925.

37. "J. H. Wakefield, Louisville Developer for 50 Years, Dies," *The Courier-Journal*, 16 July 1969.

38. Catherine Holzheimer to J. C. Turner, 11 September 1926. Jefferson County Deed Book 1240, p. 94. Plat of three units recorded 13 October 1926, in Plat and Subdivision Book 6, p. 38. In the retrospective of St. Matthews published in *The Voice of St. Matthews* on 15 July 1954, the sale price was noted as "the astonishingly high sum of $3,000 an acre."

39. The deed was not made until 1925. Jefferson County Deed Book 1136, p. 191. Speed, *St. Matthews Makes Its Bow* (1938).

VI. PROHIBITION ENACTS CHANGE
PAGES 128-132

40. "Stratton O. Hammon 1904-1997," *The Voice-Tribune*, 29 October 1997. An overview, "The House(s) That Hammon Built," *Louisville* (February 1993): 20-25, leads with this house.

41. Joseph R. Jones, "Out of Sight, Out of Mind: Recovering the History of Cockfighting in Kentucky," *The Kentucky Review* 13 (Winter 1997): 3-48.

42. "Game Chicken Breeder Dead," *The Courier-Journal*, 15 December 1928.

43. The contiguous property owners petitioned Jefferson County Court to extend Breckenridge Lane on 15 October 1926.

44. "Formal Opening Of New Links Is Set For May 28," *The Louisville Times*, 16 May 1927. "Big Spring Golf Club, City's Newest, Is Formally Opened," *The Courier-Journal*, 18 September 1927.

45. Olmsted Brothers File No. 7834, Plan No. 5, 20 October 1927. Copy in Jefferson County Office of Historic Preservation and Archives.

46. "Excerpts from Major Street Plan Report," *Board of Trade Journal* 14 (October 1929): 21.

47. Richard Renneisen, "System of Superhighways Suggested for Postwar Louisville," *The Courier-Journal*, 27 August 1944.

48. Ed Edstrom, "City Offers New Route On Frankfort Avenue For Eastern Freeway," *The Courier-Journal*, 28 October 1947. "Water Company Calls Expressway Route Bad," *The Courier-Journal*, 17 August 1951.

49. Douglas Nunn, "Which Way?" *The Courier-Journal*, 6 April 1958.

50. David L. Junchen, *Encyclopedia of the American Theatre Organ* (Pasadena, 1985), 1: 284-286.

51. William Wallace Wiegleb died in 1969 at the age of 74. See obituary in *The Courier-Journal*, 19 February 1969.

52. Tommy Fitzgerald, *The Courier-Journal*, 24 and 25 June 1928.

53. "St. Matthews," *The Jeffersonian*," 22 March 1917.

VI. PROHIBITION ENACTS CHANGE
PAGES 132-137

54. *The Jeffersonian*, 27 September 1917, 7 March 1918, and 27 June 1918.

55. Dr. John N. Lewis purchased the 5-acre lot on Westport Road from Daniel Gilman in April 1838, only a month after Gilman had purchased it from Abraham Grimes. Charles K. Osborn recalled Grimes, a bachelor, being postmaster. Reminiscences of Charles K. Osborn, collected and recorded by Bonna Holzheimer. Beargrass-St. Matthews Historical Society.

56. "Joseph Oechsli," *The Courier-Journal*, 2 January 1936. Floyd Edwards, "Music...Family Style," *The Louisville Times*, 8 December 1961.

57. Carol Brandon Timmons, "Historic farmhouse stays undisturbed," *The Voice*, 5 June 1983.

58. *St. Matthews Booster*, 20 May 1926.

59. *Ibid.*

60. "St. Matthews To Get Plant," *The Courier-Journal*, 7 June 1930.

61. "Smoke Stack Beacon Will Warn Aviators," *Herald-Post*, 18 January 1931.

62. "Capitalist Gives Views On Business," *The Courier-Journal*, 1 January 1931.

63. Jack Moranz, "Louisville in Pen and Ink," *Herald-Post*, 5 August 1936.

64. "Lawrence B. Palmer-Ball Dies; Founded Asbestos Corporation," *The Courier-Journal*, 23 June 1961.

65. "New Mail Service At St. Matthews," *The Courier-Journal*, 23 August 1931.

66. Wilhelmine Franke, "Domestic Pageant In Old Kentucky: Ridgeway," *The Courier-Journal*, 2 June 1965.

67. "Mrs. Maude Cossar Dies Following 6-Month Illness," *The Herald-Post*, 24 November 1931. "Pneumonia Fatal To Aubrey Cossar; Rites Sunday," *The Herald-Post*, 26 December 1931.

68. Historic American Building Survey report prepared by F. Ray Leimkuehler, 6 December 1940.

69. "New Mail Service At St. Matthews," *The Courier-Journal*, 2 October 1931.

VI. PROHIBITION ENACTS CHANGE
PAGE 137

70. Helen Leopold, "Romantic Ridgeway," *The Louisville Times*, 27 March 1965. Joan Kay, "Living in a house with a past creates problems for the present," *The Courier-Journal*, 20 September 1978.

71. "Marvin F. Stich, 41, Dies," *The Courier-Journal*, 9 May 1946.

VII. BRING ON THE FLOOD: PAGES 139-143

1. "150 Petitioners Ask That St. Matthews Be Made Into City," *The Courier-Journal*, 31 October 1936.

2. "Small Area of St. Matthews Incorporated," *The Courier-Journal*, 5 December 1936.

3. "St. Matthews Residents Plan Public Debate On Annexation," *The Courier-Journal*, 6 June 1937.

4. "Suit Asks Annulment of St. Matthews Charter," *The Courier-Journal*, 20 June 1937.

5. "St. Matthews Residents to Vote On Incorporation," *The Courier-Journal*, 2 September 1937.

6. "Town of St. Matthews Votes For Dissolution of Charter," *The Courier-Journal*, 19 September 1937. "St. Matthews Charter Is Dissolved," *The Courier-Journal*, 4 December 1937.

7. *The City of Louisville and The County of Jefferson under a Republican Administration* (Louisville, 1919).

8. "Chandler Breaks Ground On Louisville's New Gateway," *The Courier-Journal*, 25 June 1937. Richard Renneisen, "Laying Kentucky's Finest Road," *The Courier-Journal*, 5 September 1937.

9. "Governor Chandler Speaks At Dedication of New Road," *The Courier-Journal*, 17 July 1938.

10. "After nine years, Mrs. Lewis departs," *The Voice of St. Matthews*, 9 July 1959. She died on 19 April 1975 at the age of 91, having taught music for 69 years. The school was sold to the Louisville Academy of Music.

VII. BRING ON THE FLOOD: PAGES 143-148

11. ZV 40-50U, Jefferson County Historic Preservation and Archives.

12. The old T. P. Taylor chain of drug stores, begun in 1879, was sold in 1929. In 1932, Horace Taylor and his brother, T. P. Taylor, Jr., bought back four of the stores and began to expand their holdings. "Horace Taylor, Official Of Drug Chain, Dies," *The Courier-Journal*, 26 March 1946. "Drugstores' President, T. P. Taylor, Jr., Is Dead," *The Courier-Journal*, 21 June 1953.

13. "Minding the stores," *The Courier-Journal*, 2 March 1988. "St. Matthews to Get Movie and 7 Stores," *The Courier-Journal*, 20 May 1939. "St. Matthews to Get 10 Stores and Theater," *The Courier-Journal*, 11 June 1939.

14. "Tonight Dedication Ceremony," *The Courier-Journal*, 21 December 1939.

15. Scott Hammen, "A movie-able feast...One man's dream awakens into theater for older films," *The Courier-Journal*, 16 June 1977.

16. Sheldon S. Shafer, "Theater shuts without warning," *The Courier-Journal*, 18 September 1998. Mark Shallcross, "Vogue closing just business; owners have great memories," *The Voice-Tribune*, 23 September 1998.

17. David Gerald Hogan, *Selling 'em by the Sack* (New York, 1997), 40 and 70-71.

18. "Our Man Stanley Finds Little Mansions," *The Commuter*, 9 February 1940.

19. Hogan, *Selling 'em by the Sack*, 52.

20. Interview of Alice O. Monohan, 3 October 1996.

21. "Work to Begin Friday On New Armory," *The Courier-Journal*, 21 November 1940. "St. Matthews Armory Completed," *The Courier-Journal*, 17 July 1942.

22. "500 German Prisoners Now Working At Ft. Knox," *The Courier-Journal*, 30 May 1944.

23. "St. Matthews to Dedicate Memorial to War Dead," *The Courier-Journal*, 3 November 1943. A photograph of the ceremony appeared in *The Courier-Journal*, 12 November 1943.

VII. BRING ON THE FLOOD: PAGES 148-151

24. "St. Matthews Awards Contract for Memorial," *The Courier-Journal*, 22 February 1946.

25. "St. Matthews-area resident, fountain caretaker dies at 76," *The New Voice*, 2 March 1988.

26. "First Night At Drive-In Theater Attracts 600 Automobile Loads," *The Courier-Journal*, 30 August 1941.

27. David Goetz, "The drive-in theater: At age 50, a has-been or still playing a part?" *The Courier-Journal*, 14 July 1983.

28. "St. Matthews Group Vetoes Incorporation," *The Courier-Journal*, 25 September 1941.

29. "St. Matthews Group Favors Incorporation," *The Courier-Journal*, 28 October 1941.

30. "300 Want St. Matthews To Be 'As Is,'" *The Courier-Journal*, 29 October 1941.

31. "Suburb Told Annexation Not Planned," *The Courier-Journal*, 7 November 1941.

32. John W. Kamper died on 2 February 1968 at the age of 85.

33. "St. Matthews Residents Get Incorporation Program; Leader Declares Louisville Plans Annexation," *The Courier-Journal*, 19 January 1942.

34. "Mayor Wyatt Terms Annexation Bill Unfair," *The Courier-Journal*, 27 January 1942.

35. "Group to Study Annexation," *The Courier-Journal*, 27 January 1942.

36. "Plan to Annex St. Matthews To City Denied," *The Courier-Journal*, 7 April 1943.

37. "St. Matthews Told Zoning Plans Are Fluid," *The Courier-Journal*, 11 April 1943.

38. "Fiscal Court Adopts Master Zoning Plan," *The Courier-Journal*, 11 May 1943.

39. "Wyatt Pledges Annexation Bill Changes," *The Courier-Journal*, 15 January 1944.

40. "97 Pct. Oppose Annexation, White Finds," *The Courier-Journal*, 22 March 1944.

VII. Bring On The Flood: pages 151-152

41. "Berg Favors Keeping St. Matthews Residential," *The Courier-Journal*, 6 December 1944.

42. "Move Started To Incorporate St. Matthews," *The Courier-Journal*, 4 April 1946.

43. George Burt, "St. Matthews Factions Argue But Neither Side Gains Ground," *The Courier-Journal*, 11 April 1946.

44. "St. Matthews' City Tax Rate Might Be High," *The Courier-Journal*, 12 April 1946.

45. Docket No. 9-34-44, Jefferson County Historic Preservation and Archives.

46. Robert Doty, "Council Passes Bills Taking Part Of St. Matthews," *The Courier-Journal*, 25 April 1946.

47. "Richlawn Files Petition For Incorporation," *The Courier-Journal*, 6 July 1946.

48. "Incorporation Law Held Invalid In St. Matthews Suit," *The Courier-Journal*, 7 September 1946.

49. "Appeals Court to Hear St. Matthews Status Fight," *The Courier-Journal*, 7 February 1947.

50. "Council Meets Today to Start Annexation of St. Matthews; Incorporation Act Ruled Void," *The Courier-Journal*, 17 May 1947.

51. "City Starts Action to Annex All of St. Matthews Area," *The Courier-Journal*, 18 May 1947.

52. "Judge Field Orders St. Matthews Annexed," *The Courier-Journal*, 25 November 1948.

53. "Louisville's Annexation Of St. Matthews Killed," *The Courier-Journal*, 21 January 1950.

54. "6th-Class City Of St. Matthews Is Incorporated," *The Courier-Journal*, 23 March 1950.

55. "City Purchases St. Matthews School Tract," *The Courier-Journal*, 1 October 1947.

56. An aerial photograph of the Mayme S. Waggener Junior High under construction appeared in *The Courier-Journal*, 15 May 1954.

VII. Bring On The Flood: pages 152-156

57. "Mrs. Waggener, Ex-Principal, Dies," *The Courier-Journal*, 3 January 1953.

58. Martha Elson, "As Chism's Hardware closes, cafe to open in St. Matthews," *The Courier-Journal*, 12 February 1997.

59. "Supermarket Hit By 3-Hour, $62,000 Blaze," *The Courier-Journal*, 6 May 1945.

60. "St. Matthews Grocery First In U. S. Conforming to A & P's Postwar Plan," *The Courier-Journal*, 12 May 1946.

61. "St. Matthews to Have New Shopping Center," *The Courier-Journal*, 11 December 1945. "Two City Stores Open St. Matthews Branches," *The Courier-Journal*, 3 December 1946.

62. Mary Hoagland, "Two veterans make a success of collecting St. Matthews garbage," *The Courier-Journal*, 6 October 1946.

63. Interview of Guy Redmon, 2 November 1996.

64. Jefferson County Plat and Subdivision Book 2, p.41, Jefferson County Deed Book 802, p. 571 and 950, p. 225. "Funeral to be Monday for G.W. Weaver, Sr., *The Courier-Journal*, 17 November 1956. "Raymond W. Davis," *The Courier-Journal*, 5 October 1987.

65. Mildred Lensing, "They Just Upped And Married," *The Courier-Journal*, 29 September 1946.

66. "St. Matthews Episcopalians Revive Church," *The Courier-Journal*, 2 September 1948.

67. Grady Clay, "Church-Building Has A Major Boom In Louisville and Throughout The U. S.," *The Courier-Journal*, 4 January 1953. "The Materials We Build With," *Louisville* 17 (March 1966): 30. Dana Bauer, "Fortieth anniversary prompts church to plant seed for future," *The Voice of St. Matthews*, 5 October 1988.

68. Jefferson County Historic Preservation and Archives files.

69. Jefferson County Historic Preservation and Archives files.

70. "Farm Bureau to Start Work On Headquarters," *The Courier-Journal*, 16 September 1947.

VII. Bring On The Flood: pages 156-159

71. "Farm Group Occupies New Building," *The Courier-Journal*, 14 November 1948.

72. "John B. Ratterman, Sr., 71, Dies," *The Courier-Journal*, 20 December 1949.

73. "Pioneer Undertaker." *The Courier-Journal*, 2 September 1894.

74. "Fourth Generation of Pearsons Marks Funeral Home Centennial," *The Courier-Journal*, 24 October 1948.

75. "Austin C. Pryor, Restauranteur 40 Years, Dies," *The Courier-Journal*, 6 July 1970.

76. "Gas Blast, 5 Blazes Keep Firemen Busy," *The Courier-Journal*, 13 December 1957.

77. Planning and Zoning Commission Case ZV 77-53U, Jefferson County Historic Preservation and Archives. "Restauranteur Buys St. Matthews Tract," *The Courier-Journal*, 19 April 1955. "Originator of restaurants, Robert L. Colglazier, dies," *The Courier-Journal*, 12 June 1977.

78. Grady Clay, "Expressways Are Going To Take A Bite Out of Existing Housing In Louisville," *The Courier-Journal*, 26 January 1951.

79. Richard Renneisen, "System of Superhighways Suggested for Postwar Louisville," *The Courier-Journal*, 27 August 1944.

80. "Zone Board Adds Belt Highways To County Plan," *The Courier-Journal*, 17 July 1946. "U. S. Gives Approval To Inner-Belt Highway," *The Courier-Journal*, 17 May 1947.

81. Ed Edstrom, "City Offers New Route On Frankfort Avenue For Eastern Freeway," *The Courier-Journal*, 28 October 1947.

82. "Water Company Calls Expressway Route Bad," *The Courier-Journal*, 17 August 1951.

83. Mike Brown, "20 Years to Get From Here to Here," *The Courier-Journal*, 5 August 1970.

VIII. On the Road to Retail: pages 161-165

1. "The Story of St. Matthews (Part II)," *The Voice of St. Matthews*, 22 July 1954.

2. Interview of R. W. "Buck" Marshall, 16 January 1998. Interview of Frank L. "Tubby" Barth, 20 January 1998. "Darrell Swope, Jr., president of Koster-Swope Buick, dies," *The Courier-Journal*, 13 June 1978. Fred Koster, chairman of car dealership, dies," *The Courier-Journal*, 25 April 1979.

3. "His Ledger Closed." *The Courier-Journal*, 9 November 1889. Although Bacon's obituary carefully noted that he opened his Louisville store in December 1846, the company celebrated its 150th anniversary in 1995. The native of Sunbury, Pennsylvania, was joined in business by four sons. He died in 1889 at the age of 78.

4. "Bacon's Plans Store In St. Matthews," *The Courier-Journal*, 31 October 1951. "Bacon's Manager Calls St. Matthews Louisville's No. 1 Suburban Market," *The Courier-Journal*, 4 November 1951.

5. See "Opening Tomorrow—10 A.M. The Newest," *The Courier-Journal*, 26 August 1953. A photograph of the crowd appeared in *The Courier-Journal*, 28 August 1953.

6. Judith Egerton, "Bacon's starts the party," *The Courier-Journal*, 25 March 1995. The Bacons chain was purchased by Dillard's in 1998, and the Shelbyville Road Home Store was put on the market. However, Dillard's decided to keep the stores open and change their familiar names. Sheldon S. Shafer, "All Bacons stores will remain open," *The Courier-Journal*, 11 February 1999.

7. "Motor Company Gets Garage Title In St. Matthews," *The Courier-Journal*, 2 April 1948.

8. "Thurston Cooke Dies Of Heart Attack at 57," *The Courier-Journal*, 6 September 1966.

9. Robert Hermann, "Successor Firm Named To Thurston Cooke Ford," *The Courier-Journal*, 27 July 1960.

VIII. On the Road to Retail: pages 165-167

10. When Lewis Washburne died he was living in Louisville on East Breckinridge Street. His headstone in Cave Hill Cemetery spelled his name Louis, and provided his birth and death dates as 29 September 1810-14 September 1893. His obituary, which appeared in *The Courier-Journal* on 15 September 1893, stated he had been a farmer in Jefferson County until twelve years before. For information about the Washburne residence in Warwick Villa, see JF402, Jefferson County Historic Preservation and Archives.

11. Interview of Carolyn Rudy Barth, 20 November 1998.

12. "Suit Filed by Sears Asks Zoning Change," *The Courier-Journal*, 26 November 1953. "Judge Rejects Sears' Appeal For New Store," *The Courier-Journal*, 13 March 1954. "Sears Takes Zoning Suit To High Court," *The Courier-Journal*, 10 August 1954. "Court Rules Site Sears Wants For Store Be Rezoned Commercial," *The Courier-Journal*, 17 December 1955.

13. "Sears Of St. Matthews Moving To New Store," *The Courier-Journal*, 27 September 1959. Carol Sutton, "New Sears Store Opens In St. Matthews Today," *The Courier-Journal*, 1 October 1959. Sheldon Shafer, "Metts group agrees to buy St. Matthews Sears store," *The Courier-Journal*, 30 March 1984.

14. "P. Frank Meisner," *The Courier-Journal*, 17 June 1956.

15. Louisa Barbara Bauer Meisner and husband Frank Meisner to Marshall Realty Company for $35,000, dated 4 September 1951. Jefferson County Deed Book 2792, p. 372.

16. Edward and Emma Johnson to R. H. and Flossie Marshall, 10 June 1928. Jefferson County Deed Book 1347, p. 55. Plat of Magnolia Subdivision was recorded in Jefferson County Plat and Subdivision Book 3, p. 52.

17. "Robert H. Marshall, 61, Manual Teacher, Dies," *The Courier-Journal*, 6 October 1943.

VIII. On the Road to Retail: pages 167-169

18. Interview of R. W. "Buck" Marshall, 16 January 1998.

19. "Zoners Are Still Undecided On Shopping-Center Plan," *The Courier-Journal*, 18 April 1952. Joe Oglesby, "1955 plans for shopping center chilled old-timers," *The Voice-Jeffersonian*, 9 April 1970.

20. Shopping Center Sought East of St. Matthews," *The Courier-Journal*, 22 May 1953.

21. Grady Clay, "Shopping Center Talk Booms Land Values," *The Courier-Journal*, 2 August 1953.

22. Grady Clay, *Close-Up: How to Read the American City* (New York, 1973), 87.

23. Larry R. Ford, *Cities and Buildings: Skyscrapers, Skid Rows, and Suburbs* (Baltimore, 1994), 226.

24. Grady Clay, "Future Shopping Area On Shelbyville Road Signs 5 Major Stores," *The Courier-Journal*, 21 March 1954.

25. Interview of Ralph Biernbaum, Lake Worth, Florida, 9 December 1996.

26. "Plans for Shelbyville Road Center Announced," *The Courier-Journal*, 23 May 1954. "23 Stores Extending Invitation to Opening," *The Courier-Journal*, 29 November 1955.

27. "Pioneer shopping center developer Joseph Charles Dahlem dies at 68," *The Courier-Journal*, 7 February 1973. Michael Quinlan, "Minding the stores," *The Courier-Journal*, 2 March 1988. John Bowman, "Dahlem develops shopping centers and friends," *Business First*, 9 July 1990.

28. Interview of Barbara Hewett Brown, 11 November 1997. Mrs. Brown died on 19 March 1999 at the age of 92.

29. Art Ehrenstrom, "The years in bookstore are recalled," *The Courier-Journal*, 28 December 1975.

VIII. On the Road to Retail: pages 169-172

30. Walt Reichert, "Bullish On Books," *Louisville* 46 (December 1991): 25-28. Sheldon Shafer, "Big Barnes & Noble bookstore going into new Plainview center," *The Courier-Journal*, 25 March 1995. David Goetz, "Hawley-Cooke opens book on third decade," *The Courier-Journal*, 7 June 1998.

31. Sheldon S. Shafer, "Shelbyville Road Plaza's plan to expand hits snag," *The Courier-Journal*, 29 November 1995. Sheldon S. Shafer, "Shelbyville Road Plaza may add space, restaurants," *The Courier-Journal*, 14 June 1996.

32. "Bank of Louisville To Open Branch on Shelbyville Road," *The Courier-Journal*, 29 June 1954. "Lincoln Bank To Open 2 New Branches Here," *The Courier-Journal*, 1 October 1954.

33. Sol Schulman, "Branch Bank To Open at St. Matthews Saturday," *The Courier-Journal*, 14 October 1954. "St. Matthews Branch Bank Opens Formally Tomorrow," *The Courier-Journal*, 11 March 1955.

34. "St. Matthews Zoning Body Is Sworn In With Advice To Practice 'Horse Sense,'" *The Courier-Journal*, 18 January 1951.

35. The full-page article by James Goble that appeared in *The Courier-Journal* on 21 January 1951 also contained an aerial photograph with the annexation boundaries superimposed.

36. A poll of the Peoples Committee of St. Matthews favored annexation by the city of Louisville over further annexation or incorporation by St. Matthews. "St. Matthews Annexation Favored 6 to 1," *The Courier-Journal*, 11 September 1953. "City of St. Matthews Annexes Business Area," *The Courier-Journal*, 15 October 1953.

37. The city of St. Matthews believed that 90 days from the adjournment of the legislature, when laws became effective, fell on June 19 instead of June 17. "St. Matthews To Become 4th-Class City Tomorrow," *The Courier-Journal*, 18 June 1954.

38. "St. Matthews Civic Plan Is Outlined," *The Courier-Journal*, 22 June 1954.

39. "Police Chief Sworn In At St. Matthews," *The Courier-Journal*, 14 July 1954.

VIII. On the Road to Retail: pages 173-175

40. "Former Head Of County's Police Dies," *The Courier-Journal*, 15 April 1957.

41. Joe Oglesby, "Police grow with the community," *The Voice-Jeffersonian*, 9 April 1970. *St. Matthews 1950-1995*, p. 3.

42. David W. Hacker, "St. Matthews Moves 1 Jump Ahead of Louisville," *The Louisville Times*, 18 June 1957.

43. Map of area annexed appeared in *The Voice of St. Matthews-Highlands*, 9 January 1964.

44. "St. Matthews Mayor Leaving September 30," *The Courier-Journal*, 19 September 1958. "James H. Noland, St. Matthews Pioneer And First Mayor, Dies," *The Courier-Journal*, 22 June 1960. Marilyn Frederick, "James Noland, sparkplug of a new city," *The Voice-Jeffersonian*, 9 April 1970.

45. Mildred Lensing, "Patrons for New Library Measured Up," *The Courier-Journal*, 5 October 1958.

46. Clarence E. Cason, "Live Towns Around Louisville," *The Louisville Herald*, 30 July 1922.

47. "New Branch Library Opened In St. Matthews," *The Courier-Journal*, 2 August 1938. "City Library to Close Branch At St. Matthews," *The Courier-Journal*, 30 July 1946.

48. "Mrs. Schumann checks out as head librarian," *The Voice-Jeffersonian*, 13 June 1968. "Libraries Dedicated at St. Matthews and Shively," *The Courier-Journal*, 6 April 1959.

49. Sheldon Shafer, "City councilman to become mayor of St. Matthews," *The Courier-Journal*, 25 September 1984. Judy Marrs, "St. Matthews adopts occupational tax," *The Courier-Journal*, 26 March 1986. A good overview of city government and the three mayors is contained in the commemorative booklet *St. Matthews, 1950-1995*.

50. Interview of Georgia Ellinger, 6 March 1997.

51. "Old Greathouse School Being Razed," *The Louisville Times*, 28 April 1960.

VIII. On the Road to Retail: pages 175-177

52. Carrie Morrison, "Thornbury's alumni planning a reunion," *The Voice-Tribune*, 16 September 1998.

53. Ben Z. Hershberg, "Toy-selling family's having more success, if less fun," *The Courier-Journal*, 16 December 1979.

54. "James G. Thornbury dies at age 75; founded toy-store chain in Louisville," *The Courier-Journal*, 22 January 1991.

55. Clarence E. Bauer died at the age of 83 on 24 December 1976. Motz Bauer died at the age of 93 on 17 April 1989.

56. Alexander Scott Bullitt and others to John Peay, 1 July 1814, Jefferson County Deed Book H, p. 435. John and Mildred Peay to Branham Arterburn, 11 January 1830, Jefferson County Deed Book CC, p. 490. Will of Branham Arterburn, 11 April 1831, Jefferson County Will Book 2, p. 433.

57. Thomas W. Bullitt, *My Life at Oxmoor* (Louisville, 1911), 7-8.

58. *The Courier-Journal*, 11 April 1878.

59. Elijah, John, Samuel, and Presley Arterburn, presumably brothers, were also listed in tax records after 1799. The spelling used in the returns for many years was Atterburn, then Arthurburn, and finally Arterburn.

60. Deed dated 24 June 1839, Jefferson County Deed Book 53, p. 553. In 1868, Rachel Arterburn made a division of property among her living sons, Harrison, Jordan, Tarlton, Norbourn, Wm. C., and Covington. Jefferson County Deed Book 136, p. 499.

61. "Slavery In Louisville," *The Louisville Times*, 23 September 1978.

62. "Succumbs To Typhoid," *The Courier-Journal*, 12 January 1901.

63. "W. Arterburn, Nursery Head, Dies In Ohio, *The Courier-Journal*, 10 August 1937.

64. "Jule B. Arterburn." *The Courier-Journal*, 4 August 1938.

65. Interview of C. L. Boden, Jr., 1 April 1998. His wife, Alice Arterburn Boden, is the granddaughter of Jule B. Arterburn.

VIII. ON THE ROAD TO RETAIL: PAGES 177-181

66. "Aged Citizen Dead," *The Courier-Journal*, 17 August 1901. "Mr. Covington Arterburn," *The Louisville Commercial*, 17 August 1901.

67. Darrell Sifford, "Memphis Thanks Helm Bruce For Museum After 35 Years," *The Courier-Journal*, 30 January 1966. "Ex-Alderman Helm Bruce Jr., Dies After Fall," *The Courier-Journal*, 10 November 1966.

68. Willard G. Rouse had retired from the firm but remained as vice chairman and was working on special projects when he died in 1971 at the age of 61. "Willard G. Rouse," *The New York Times*, 23 October 1971.

69. Sarah Lansdell, "Botanical Garden Atmosphere Planned For New Shopping Mall," *The Courier-Journal*, 9 July 1961. A rendering of the proposed mall was also published.

70. "8 Gold Spades Break Ground For The Mall," *The Courier-Journal*, 7 July 1961.

71. Grady Clay, "Builders Of Mall Here Plan Brand-New City In Maryland," *The Courier-Journal*, 24 November 1963.

72. Richard Zoglin, "The Urban Renewer, James W. Rouse: 1914-1996," *Time*, 22 April 1996.

73. Judith Egerton, "Rouse updating Louisville mall," *The Courier-Journal*, 20 July 1992. David Goetz, "Mall St. Matthews passes Oxmoor in popularity," *The Courier-Journal*, 22 January 1997.

74. "$750,000 Motor Lodge, Restaurant To Be Erected on Shelbyville Road," *The Courier-Journal*, 15 March 1959.

75. When Guy and Grace Jones purchased land from Herman Ochsner in July 1939 that had been part of the Louisville Nurseries, they already owned a contiguous lot. Guy Jones died in 1968 at the age of 58 (see *The Courier-Journal*, 11 February 1968).

76. "Landowner Holzheimer Dies At 84," *The Courier-Journal*, 7 March 1963.

77. Martha Elson, "Green space in St. Matthews may honor Holzheimer family," *The Courier-Journal*, 16 October 1996.

VIII. ON THE ROAD TO RETAIL: PAGES 182-185

78. The land was purchased from Herr by Kate Bahr in 1892 and sold to Mary Sibler in 1909. When the Siblers sold the property in 1914, the first mention was made of improvements and appurtenances; therefore the house is probably of 1910 vintage. Jefferson County Deed Books 389, p. 585; 700, p. 415; and 811, p. 457.

79. Interview of Norbourne H. "Skip" Thorpe, 6 March 1998.

80. Information supplied by Candace Perry, curator of the Kentucky Derby Museum.

81. "Murphy Rites To Be Monday," *Herald-Post*, 13 December 1929.

82. "Apartment Zoning Asked For Farm," *The Courier-Journal*, 11 June 1965.

83. "Clayton C. Moore," *The Courier-Journal*, 11 April 1985. Ken Shapero, "NTS plans shopping center, offices, homes on farm on Dutchmans Lane," *The Courier-Journal*, 21 October 1986.

84. Holly Holland, "St. Matthews farm being sold; buyer, plans are unclear," *The Courier-Journal*, 6 September 1986.

85. Simpson Lawson, "Lincoln Life Buys Tract For Home-Office Site," *The Courier-Journal*, 30 December 1961.

86. Anne Calvert, "High-Rises In The Potato Patch: the 'Uptown Down-towns,'" *Louisville* 26 (March 1975):35.

87. Interview of Norbourne H. Thorpe, 6 March 1998. John Meehan, "Suburb Yields Site To City," *The Courier-Journal*, 5 June 1962.

88. Simpson Lawson, "Lincoln Life Plans 'Gold Tower,'" *The Courier-Journal*, 3 August 1962.

89. Interview of Norbourne H. Thorpe, 6 March 1998.

90. Moyra Schroeder, "Lincoln Tower Excites Mrs. Wright," *The Louisville Times*, 16 March 1966.

91. Glenn Rutherford, "'Doily' building will be in the pink—sans pink," *The Louisville Times*, 4 December 1986. Glenn Rutherford, "Architect of 'doily' tower may raise the hue and cry with his choice of tint," *The Courier-Journal*, 18 May 1987.

VIII. ON THE ROAD TO RETAIL: PAGES 185-190

92. Grady Clay, "Lincoln Income's 'White Doily' Structure of Remarkable Merit," *The Courier-Journal*, 13 March 1966.

93. Even the Lincoln Tower's construction had been delayed by an FAA study. See 15-Story Building Delayed; F. A. A. Says It May Hinder Plans," *The Courier-Journal*, 11 October 1963.

94. "Expressway Connection for Major Highways Scheduled for Completion a Year from Now," *Louisville* 4 (December 1953): 6-9. For photographs and background see "Bob Hill, "You Can't Get There From Here: 40 Years On The Watterson," *The Louisville Times*, 16 September 1985.

95. "St. Matthews Firm Plans Building," *The Courier-Journal*, 4 January 1964.

96. Interview of Samuel G. Swope, 16 February 1998.

97. Louisville and Jefferson County Planning and Zoning Commission Application to Rezone #9-247-63, dated 29 October 1963.

98. Grady Clay, "Zone Plea Proposes Giant Development At Historic Oxmoor," *The Courier-Journal*, 3 November 1963.

99. Mac Griswold and Eleanor Weller, *The Golden Age of American Gardens* (New York, 1991), 196-197. Diane Heilenman, "Oxmoor: Simply Grand," *The Courier-Journal*, 19 October 1995.

100. Hoffman's widow, Virginia Kimball Hoffman, whom he married in 1927, still recalled the library when interviewed by Samuel W. Thomas in 1987. After Mrs. Hoffman died, her nephew, Lindley M. F. Hoffman, placed Burrall Hoffman's collection of plans, including those for Oxmoor, in the Centre Canadien d'Architecture, Montreal.

101. "Bullitt Estate Zone-Hearing Delay Asked," *The Courier-Journal*, 29 December 1963.

102. Lawrence Pryor, "Oxmoor Development Meets Zoning Rebuff," *The Courier-Journal*, 1 July 1966.

103. Al McCreary, "Huge Oxmoor Center to open this fall," *The Voice-Jeffersonian*, 9 April 1970.

VIII. ON THE ROAD TO RETAIL: PAGES 190-194

104. Charles Whitaker, "Shops 'n' crops," *The Louisville Times*, 2 August 1984.

105. Harry Toulmin, "An Account of the Stock, Produce, etc., of Colonel Bullet's Estate near the Falls of the Ohio, in Jefferson County," *The Western Country in 1793* (reprinted San Marino, 1948), 84-88.

106. Norbourn and Sallie C. Arterburn sold 89 acres to William Marshall Bullitt, 25 November 1931. Jefferson County Deed Book 1494, p. 2.

107. Sheldon Shafer, "Half of project behind Oxmoor recommended," The Courier-Journal, 21 December 1990.

108. Information contained in a letter from Mary Jean Kinsman to Frederick Sherman, 20 May 1982. Also see "Death of John I. Jacob," *The Courier-Journal*, 22 January 1873.

109. George William Beattie and Helen Pruitt Beattie, "Pioneer Linns of Kentucky," *The Filson Club History Quarterly* 20 (July 1946): 243. In February 1780, Linn was living, presumably in his station, on Dry Run of Beargrass Creek, now known as Weicher Creek (*ibid.*, 236).

110. "Dead And Alone," *The Courier-Journal*, 1 August 1892.

111. Samuel W. Thomas, *Churchill Downs: A Documentary History of America's Most Legendary Race Track* (Louisville, 1995), 33-34.

112. "Hurstbourne." *The Courier-Journal*, 8 September 1884.

113. Carl Kramer, *Louisville's Olmstedian Legacy* (Louisville, 1988), 56.

114. Lee Heiman, "52 Rooms, 9 Baths, 5 Peacocks," *The Courier-Journal* Magazine, 27 August 1950.

115. Ben Z. Hershberg, "In eastern Jefferson, long-developing drama has matured into a hit," *The Courier-Journal*, 4 March 1979. The article also profiles other developers.

116. "L. Leroy Highbaugh, Sr., Dies At 76," *The Courier-Journal*, 16 October 1965.

117. Simpson Lawson, "Hurstbourne To Become $100 Million Community," *The Courier-Journal*, 24 January 1965.

VIII. ON THE ROAD TO RETAIL: PAGES 194-198

118. Simpson Lawson, "Hurstbourne Planner O'Donnell Covers A Lot Of Ground—And Sea," *The Courier-Journal*, 24 January 1965.

119. George Yater, "L. L. Highbaugh Recreates 1793 Pioneer Home in Hurstbourne," *Louisville* 33 (September 1982): 32-35.

120. Al McCreary, "$50-million project starts May 1," *The Voice-Jeffersonian*, 9 April 1970.

121. Nina Walfoort, "Hurstbourne area thriving on 'edge,'" *The Courier-Journal*, 2 September 1997.

122. Samuel W. Thomas, *Changing Medicine, Constant Care: Kentucky Baptist Hospitals* (Louisville, 1990), 212-218.

123. "St. Matthews Shopping Center Site Rezoned," *The Courier-Journal*, 14 December 1966.

124. John Woodruff, "Largest Shop Unit Coming," *The Courier-Journal*, 19 August 1967.

125. "Plans for Shopping Center Dropped," *The Courier-Journal*, 12 November 1968.

126. Chris Waddle, "Sunday opening: Results are uneven," *The Courier-Journal*, 3 July 1972.

127. The deeds, dated 12 and 18 August 1868, were recorded Jefferson County Deed Book 139, pp. 329-332.

128. Jefferson County Deed Book 246, pp. 112-114.

129. "Liberty Bank, U. S. Trust Plan Merger," *The Courier-Journal*, 3 May 1955.

130. "Bethel Veech, Banker, Dies," *The Courier-Journal*, 9 May 1946.

131. "Funeral of J. Graham Brown, 87, 'Invisible Benefactor,' Is Tomorrow," *The Courier-Journal*, 31 March 1969.

132. "Sonia K. Uri dies; services tomorrow," *The Courier-Journal & Times*, 5 October 1975.

VIII. ON THE ROAD TO RETAIL: PAGES 199-203

133. The George Washington Party, organized in 1951, was named by B. W. Stevens. It was first challenged by the Community Party in 1955, then the Home Rule Party in 1957. See Joseph Oglesby, "Where government is done without a 'sugar bowl' or patronage," *The Voice-Jeffersonian*, 9 April 1970.

134. "St. Matthews Is Planning Own City Hall," *The Courier-Journal*, 31 December 1959. "$75,000 Brick Structure On 4-Acre Tract To House 500 Pupils, Be Opened In Fall," *The Courier-Journal*, 7 May 1939. "40 Pupils Enroll In First County Kindergarten," *The Courier-Journal*, 24 September 1940.

135. Martha Elson, "Brown Park work nearly done," *The Courier-Journal*, 25 April 1997.

136. Nina Walfoort, "Projects provide models for new neighborhood types," *The Courier-Journal*, 2 October 1997. Martha Elson, "Community center is new park project," *The Courier-Journal*, 4 November 1997.

137. Sketch of layout appeared in *The Courier-Journal*, 28 October 1949.

138. "Potato Festival to Open Wednesday At St. Matthews," *The Courier-Journal*, 29 June 1947.

139. "Bids For Drainage Work Opened," *The Jeffersonian*, 23 December 1915.

140. St. Matthews was the focus of problems with septic tanks in Martin E. Biemer's *Fifty years of service: A history of the first half-century of the Louisville and Jefferson County Metropolitan Sewer District* (Louisville, 1998), 10.

141. "Sewer Plan Wouldn't Use Beargrass," *The Courier-Journal*, 22 June 1948. "St. Matthews Sewer Work Starts Today," *The Courier-Journal*, 27 July 1948.

142. Martha Elson, "Residents seek relief from floods," *The Courier-Journal*, 2 April 1997.

INDEX

HENRY KAELIN BEING REASSURED BY HIS FATHER, AUGUST, ABOUT 1900. COURTESY OF PETER GUETIG.